How to Take a Drink From a Cactus:

Volume VIII of The Travels of Senator & Wendy V

- © 2019 by Wendy V. All rights reserved. No part of this publication may be reproduced or transmitted in any form or by any means, electronic or mechanical, including photocopy, recording, or any information storage and retrieval system, without the prior written consent of the author and/or publisher.

- Cover photography © 2019 by David Zuchowski
Cover design © 2019 by Wendy V.

ISBN: 978-0-99150-938-6

Other Titles by Wendy V

Travelogues:
How to Read a Compass in the Dark (2006)

How to Change a Flat on a Unicycle (2007)

How to Start a Fire Under the Sea (2009)

How to Eat a Pizza From a Can (2011)

How to Hitch a Ride With No Thumbs (2013)

How to Draw a Map of the Forest (2015)

How to Book a Flight for Last Year (2017)

Poetry:
Eventually, Finally (2007)

for Senator—

Elohim Shomri
26 May 2017

"The twin banks marched with wilderness as he remembered it-- the tangle of brier and cane impenetrable even to sight twenty feet away, the tall tremendous soaring of oak and gum and ash and hickory which had rung to no axe save the hunter's, had echoed to no machinery save the beat of old-time steam boats traversing it or to the snarling of launches like their own of people going into it to dwell for a week or two weeks because it was still wilderness."

~William Faulkner
Go Down, Moses

Table of Contents

Introduction	i
Sesquicelebration	1
Saving the Planet, One Nationally-Approved Nozzle at a Time	101
With Malice Toward None	133
The Eyes Have It, (or Vertical)	183
Lake Effect, (or Horizontal)	255
Derailed	283
Unconditional Surrender	305
Be It Ever So Humble	331
Afterword	359
Appendix A: Sesquicelebration Food Awards	361
Appendix B: Poem	363

Author's Note

Yep, still the same-- Senator, David, Daver, Davy Boy, etc.

Introduction

For years, people older than myself have cautioned me about the exponential passing of time. "Each year goes faster than the one before," is the common warning, sometimes issued from behind eyes that recall a glimmer of their own past while connecting to the present. When I first heard this, I took it as a silent mental challenge. What was it that made it feel this way to the majority of humans?

Perhaps it was simply mathematical. After all, each additional year that one lives renders all of his or her individual years as smaller pieces of the overall pie. Twelve months is half of the life of a two-year old. It is twenty percent of the life of a five-year old, or five percent of the life of a twenty-year old. Then when you are closer to my age, it is never-mind-what-percent.

On the other hand, maybe math has nothing to do with it. Maybe it is pure science. Since we are not characters who time travel in a novel, we have only ever lived in the present, and yet somehow everything we actually know is the past. The more we experience, the more *past* our mind is trying to reconcile. I suppose that could continually make it feel as though each year was passing quicker than the one before. (And if we want to throw English into our mix of subjects, I just broke a rule by ending a sentence with a preposition.) (I also just broke another one by starting a sentence with 'and', but I digress.)

For myself, I cannot say that each year passes faster than the previous year, but I can definitely admit that certain years in particular whiz by, leaving me spinning in a daze of wonder, appreciation, and exhaustion. Both Senator and I are having such a year at press time. One minute we were looking forward to our country's future, as we excitedly watched the inauguration of a new president who supported our values of faith, family, and freedom. The next minute we were just grateful that we were to have *any* future, but more on that later. Another season brought a new itinerary, exploring our 'Neighbour to the North' and seeing how many miles a vehicle could reasonably rack up in one month.

Now it is autumn, and I am pleased to be writing this with a blanket on my lap and a forthcoming cup of coffee. Still, I am mildly alarmed that there are less than twelve weeks left in the year. Although, to be fair, that will be the entire life, up to that point, of my niece, who is due to be born later this month. If you will excuse me, though, the timer just went off. My coffee is ready.

~Wendy V
October 2017

Chapter 1
Sesquicelebration: Early July 2017

I would be remiss if I did not point out a fact that should make you, Reader, very proud of me. Due to a variety of scheduling and budgeting factors, I grounded myself for an entire year. It was my longest stint without traveling in many years, and as Senator can tell you, I was feeling it. Staring down August, the following summer seemed as far away to me as it did for any school-aged child.

By September I was antsy, but my energy was soon channeled into another passion. For years Senator and I had debated the possibility of exercising our 2nd Amendment right to bear arms. Without going into all of the details, suffice it to say that in August we instantly reached a mutual family decision to take the plunge. After weeks of research and many conversations with trusted sources, we enrolled ourselves for a weekend date in a legal concealed carry course. In the span of a few hours, we knew we had made the right decision. In fact, we were both hooked, diverting our attention from travel pursuits for the time being.

Eventually though, a snowless January and half a year of staying put got the better of me. Since we had visited all fifty states and half of the Canadian provinces, I decided we might as well see the other five provinces. That was not the only reason to plan a Quebec/New Brunswick Prince Edward Island/Nova Scotia/Newfoundland tour. I had visited when I was sixteen and been enchanted by that facet of the rugged North Atlantic. On that trip, however, we had not made it to Newfoundland.* Now it was time to experience it with Senator.

I began to make out an agenda with the assumption that, like most places we visit, we probably would not have the chance to return. Predictably, the highlights centered around nature, history, and time away from people.† At some point in my planning, I made the delightful discovery that Canada was celebrating their sesquicentennial in 2017. *Congratulations, friends!* I then made the even more exciting discovery that, as part of the celebration, Canada's park system was waiving all fees to their national parks and historic sites. I looked at my notes, then back at the computer screen. That basically covered every aspect of our itinerary. *Many thanks, friends!*

I shared my findings with Senator. "The good news

---

* I can't imagine why. My parents were only covering all of the northeast United States, plus four provinces, while toting four kids in the family car for three weeks.

† I don't think I have ever hated cities and metro areas as much as I currently do. Perhaps I am just burned out on trips to Chicago, but a quick scan of national news on any given day tells me I am not likely to be changing my opinion any time soon.

is that we will save significant money on entrance fees to these parks," I began. "Although, just be warned, between being high tourist season and the free admission, there might be hoards of humans. We might have to put up with throngs of yuppie families try to check locations off their buckets lists."[*] He accepted my statement of disclosure, and we agreed to make the best of it, even if there were crowds.

As is my pattern, the vacation plans, once complete, were shelved for many months. After the usual amount of time, it was May. May started off well, with a school year wrapping up successfully and Senator's recording business humming along at a heightened active pace. Then the last week of the month took a turn. On Monday, I went to a routine medical check-up. As the office now had a new nurse practitioner, I decided to ask her opinion on a very minor issue I was having. The previous nurse practitioner, whom I had seen two years before, had assured me it was nothing. That agreed with my gut feeling, but I just wondered if maybe there was a tip the new nurse could give me. Not only did she not have any casual suggestions, but she informed me in no uncertain terms that the problem I had been comfortable living with was a big deal, definitely needed a biopsy, and never should have been treated lightly by the first nurse. *GONG!!!* Suddenly the ACME anvil from the cartoons dropped on my head. I would have to think about that one...

As I was mulling Monday's dilemma over in my mind, Thursday's appointment, an unrelated routine check-up, arrived. At least that would be a simple one. It also

---

[*] because your average hiker or nature lover does not use a term like 'bucket list'

had the advantage of being closer to home, and in a smaller town. I further took it as a good sign when I arrived early and was in and out before my scheduled appointment time.

Determining my next step, I tried to remain positive Friday morning, especially since I still had almost a week off between the spring semester and summer school. I decided that I would make another appointment with the doctor himself. I would explain that his own two nurse practitioners were 180° apart on their prognoses, and I would make him the deciding vote. Flipping the wall calendar to find an open date, I was about to grab the phone to call when it rang. The voice on the other end was calling with results from Thursday's routine check-up, and the phrase "questionable spots on the scan" was used. A follow-up appointment would be necessary. *Well, I'm just on a roll.* I put it out of my mind for the time being and focused on the night ahead. Senator and I had a recording session in Chicago, and we needed to get stuff together and leave early enough to fight Friday afternoon traffic.

As expected, the concert went smoothly. We even finished a solid hour earlier than usual. Looking forward to seeing our friends (who were in town from New York) the next morning, we called the work week done and began the drive home. About half an hour later, however, our night took a turn that made me forget all about the previous stresses of the week.

Senator was driving, and I was in the passenger seat, talking and watching the traffic, which in the Chicago suburbs is never light, no matter what time of year, day, or night you are in it. The next thing I knew, I couldn't see through the windshield. I realized the windshield was shattered from end to end and began to process it in slow motion. I thought we had hit a vehicle, and I turned to see if Senator was okay. As my view swept across the windshield, I saw a giant hole in the windshield, directly in front of him. The next fraction of a second was truly the worst moment of my life. As my view swept to where he was seated, I expected to see a horrific sight. Instead, thank God, I saw my boyfriend.

"Are you okay?! Are you okay?!" I yelled.

"I think so," he said, only slightly dazed. "Am I bleeding?" he added, starting to understand what was transpiring. As he asked, somehow his mind was present enough to pull the car safely to the side of the road, avoiding all of the nonstop traffic in multiple lanes. That, in itself, was a miracle.

"No," I answered firmly, as shocked as I was relieved. I then instructed him to turn off the car, remembering somewhere in the back of my mind that that is what you are supposed to remember to do after an accident.

My shaking hand started to dial 9-1-1 as I tried to further assess any injuries on either of us. To say that glass was everywhere is an understatement. Highway lights and headlights of cars zooming past illuminated the interior of our car, which had become its own warped fairyland of glittering glass dust. Surely we had to have some wounds that we were not aware of yet, perhaps due to shock. Senator opened his door to slowly get out. I scrutinized him as he took off his shirt, but the only thing we found were two swelled fingers and a few light scratches on his arms. I began to feel satisfied that, if we had originally failed to see any bleeding, we definitely would have noticed it by this time. As for myself, not only did I not have a scratch on me, but I was not even sore. I literally could not tell from a physical standpoint that anything had taken place.

As we waited by the side of the road for emergency services to arrive, I received my first revelation of what had actually happened. Again my brain was processing information in slow motion. *Hhmmm... I don't recall that piece of recording equipment. Gee... I hope we didn't accidentally pack something that belonged to the venue. Oh, I see. It's not a part of our gear at all, by golly. Why, in fact, I do not know what it is...* "Look!" I shouted over the traffic as I pointed to the driver side floor. There, situated contentedly on the left side of the floor mat was what looked like a barbell attached to a metal panel. I then realized that this bomb had come down through the windshield. Neither of us remember any impact or sound. There was just suddenly shattered glass and a large hole, squarely in front of where Senator's face had been. I showed Senator, and we were both in awe.

Emergency services soon arrived and confirmed that Senator was, indeed, fine. As they taped his fingers, I gave my statement to two state troopers who had responded to the 9-1-1 call. They looked in the car as I indicated our new acquisition, which I estimated to weigh about ten pounds. One of them identified it as a ratchet off of a flatbed truck, whatever that was.

Senator joined us and both officers repeated to him what they had been telling me: that we were "really lucky this was not a lot worse". We did not need convincing.

Already we were working out the physics in our mind, and there is no possible way that something that large and heavy, at that trajectory, could avoid doing major damage without divine intervention.* By its sheer location, it would have had to travel through his leg. There was no space around and nowhere it could have bounced. At the least, it should have shattered his left leg, and even that would have been after doing much worse to his upper half. In short, no one who saw the damage on the car could believe he was alive, let alone that he had walked away. As the repair shop tellingly put it, "So where was this car parked when this happened?"

"It wasn't!" I answered. "He was driving, sitting in that seat, twelve hours ago when it occurred!"

"What?! Oh, wow. That... I mean... that could have really... You could have... It could have been much worse!"

Oh yes. Believe me, we know.

After decompressing and trying to glean any meaning out of our experience, we did our best to return to normal life. In less than a week, I started summer school. "Boy do I have a story for you," I began to tell my coworker, who had served as my behind-the-scenes partner for the program I taught for the past decade.

"Yeah, I have something to tell you, too," she replied, "but you go first." I regaled her with my crazy tale, complete with visual aids. She, like others, was amazed that we were okay. I do not know if it made it easier or harder for her to break her news to me, but a few moments later I learned that she was quitting. I knew that it was the right move for her, and I was genuinely happy and excited

---

* Trust me; I got an A+ in Honors Physics!

on her behalf, but I was starting to get a little weary of so many unknown factors in my life.

Nevertheless, June marched on. The two follow-up doctor appointments, (which I had temporarily forgotten about,) turned out fine. Amid the other events, we had also been spending time in final visits with a dear aunt of Senator's, whom we lost at the end of the month. Even that, however, worked out peacefully and in proper timing. Exhausted though we were by the chaotic start of our summer, things gradually settled down. By the time we were ready to turn the page to July, we even had time to relax and have fun with my family.

*   *   *

"I'm very ready for this trip," I announced, eager to move on.

"Me, too," Senator replied, visibly glad to have a break from plenty of work sprinkled in among the drama. I could hardly believe we would have a whole month free from driving to Chicago, dealing with traffic, and navigating the negative climate some people had unnecessarily created in response to their political views. Enough! Time to hit the road. In fact, we must have been subconsciously ready too, since we stepped out the door, packed and ready, an hour and a half early.

The only thing missing was our guns, as Canada does not permit us to capably defend ourselves against troublemakers or rabid beavers. We had secured them in a private location near home before leaving, and I wondered if it would be strange to be without them for so long. As we cruised through Michigan, I joked with Senator about what not to say at the border, when the guards asked the requisite question of whether we were traveling with firearms.

"You mean like, I shouldn't scoff and say 'I wish!'" Senator suggested.

"Yes, that would be a good example of what not to say. You also probably shouldn't look sad, hang your head, and mope 'No'," I added.

"Or how about 'We got Trump now. Didn't we buy you guys or something?'"

"Another good example."

"What are we supposed to do if we're attacked like the people in Windsor were?" Senator asked, referencing a recent violent attack in Alberta. "Throw maple syrup at them?" Considering that I had had to surrender my pepper spray dispenser at the border the previous summer, that might be a good option. I assured him that we were not going to any big city or reputably bad area, and beyond that, we would rely on the effective combination of faith and common sense.

As it turned out, we would have plenty of time to practice our proper border responses, serious or otherwise. Though Port Huron is a busy entry point, and though eight lanes of traffic converged into three, everything still would have moved along smoothly, except that the digital signs were inaccurate and misleading. Since only the far right lane understood where to go, inefficiency reigned, and we got a grand view of two Great Lakes during an hour-and-fifteen-minute wait. We immediately decided to find an alternate crossing on the way home.

Anyway, we were in. It seemed fitting to honor Canada's 150th birthday with a brief overview of its history.

I had brought along a few pages of condensed background, so I read as Senator drove, enlightening both of us with struggles and events that often mirrored those of our own country. It was by no means an exhaustive source, and at times I thought it a little *too* dumbed down, but it served its purpose. I couldn't help laughing, though, when it actually said that in 1610 Henry Hudson discovered Hudson Bay. *Well, isn't that some coincidence.*

The rest of our day moved along, kilometer after kilometer under easy skies, along the southeast border of Ontario. Toronto was the only place our pace slowed, and we were glad that it would be the only large city we would have to pass directly through. Finally, about an hour later than expected, we arrived at our reserved hotel. We checked in and settled down for a short night before another long day in the car.

"I just need to check my email," said Senator.

"Okay, I'm going to hop in the shower and then go to sleep," I replied. Unfortunately, I stepped out of the shower not to a relaxing remainder of the night, but to an extremely disgruntled boyfriend. The email password was not working, and the email service was not cooperating. For me, this would be an inconvenience. For someone still navigating the challenges of self-employment, however, completely disappearing from clients for two weeks was a great detriment. Despite multiple efforts to remedy the situation, Senator was out of luck, and no one was getting quality sleep that night.

*   *   *

The next morning was drizzly and dismal. Not even the odd attempt at a formal breakfast by the average chain hotel lightened the mood. *Ah, crap.* Senator was still getting nowhere with his email communications, which meant he was 'in the cave' as they say, and not doing much communicating with me. By definition, the one thing a vacation is supposed to do is relieve the vacationer from work stress, but the email snag, along with no functioning phone-- no, we still had not upgraded to decent cell phones-- was raising blood pressures.[*]

French-only road signs were not helping Senator's mood, although I was secretly enjoying the immersion in a language that I usually did not get a chance to practice. While signs in Ontario had been bilingual, Quebec was having none of it. On the other hand, the few people we did encounter spoke English.[†] Maybe that's because they didn't want to suffer through any more of my French than necessary.

We continued through green, somewhat mountainous areas that reminded me of upstate New York or Pennsylvania. By mid-afternoon, we crossed into New Brunswick, reintroducing English and officially bringing us another time zone east into the Maritime Provinces. The

---

[*] Somehow, amid all of my planning, I had made the grave error of misunderstanding the coverage limits of our leashes. I thought the cell phones were supposed to be good in Canada, but as it turned out, they were only good for *calling* Canada from the United States. Furthermore, they were only good for calling Canada from select portions of the United States, rendering them virtually useless during much of our travel.

[†] Generally one can actually travel quite a distance without having to talk to strangers, thanks to pay-at-the-pump credit card machines. This convenience is negated, however, when the law of the land dictates full service.

next day we would see the ocean. In the meantime, however, we had to find something to eat. There had not been any viable options on the road, but at least we had the forethought to bring along a big batch of homemade pasta salad. While I had envisioned a lovely picnic spread, the reality was a delicate balancing act while driving. It was tasty, though.

With a little bit of time and a full stomach, Senator was relaxing a tad, but the work dilemma was hanging over both of us. I was glad when we checked into our quiet bed and breakfast and found we were the only ones there for the night. Once again, Senator made an attempt to retrieve his work messages. This was unsuccessful and actually worsened the matter. At some point in the process the email service decided he was an international intruder and shut him out completely. In addition to not knowing if people were trying to hire him, he had now most likely lost over 100 business contacts.

While it wasn't the worst thing that could happen to a person, it sure was not good news. I felt bad that I could offer absolutely no help, other than to change his contact information on his website and hope that if someone wanted him bad enough, they would be willing to do some searching. I knew he was very tempted to chuck the whole trip and go home to try to figure out a way to straighten out the mess, but to his credit and my sanity, he didn't. Instead, he scrolled through the channels, ignoring the French ones, until he found a comedy show for us. Maybe things would look better in the morning. At least we weren't attempting to camp anywhere.

* * *

Breakfast the next morning was excellently prepared, and our host was delightful, but Senator and I were both feeling sick. Neither of us had planned for his career to potentially end overnight, but I was determined to keep things in perspective. After all, it wasn't that long ago that we had survived what could have been a far greater catastrophe. There must be some solution; it was too stupid of a problem to hold him back. For the time being, though, there was nothing to do but plow ahead.

This particular journey was notable in that it was the first time that Senator and I took along a G.P.S. unit. Though this may surprise those who know how much we travel, it will be no shock to those who know our reluctance to involve any more technology than necessary in our lives. (See the last several pages.) I was not averse to including the new device, but after years of being the prime navigator in the household, I was not about to relinquish my title. I decided the most balanced approach was to bring my maps and notes and compare them with the magic route finder. After all, two heads were better than one, even if one of them was digital.

Our first real destination of the vacation was Fundy National Park, home of the world's highest tides. During the course of a day, a docked boat might float up forty or fifty feet, and then slowly drift down to the sand, where it will lean to one side or the other until the tide comes in again. This is caused by the bay's shape and depth-- a great marvel of nature. Another great marvel of nature is how we managed to end up on a muddy, deserted road.

From our bed and breakfast, my map showed a fairly straightforward route to Fundy National Park. It was not on the main highway, but it was the next-most-major road. It was the route I had worked out in February, and happily, the new G.P.S. agreed with it. The problem was that reality did not agree with either of them. It wasn't a case of majority rule; actuality was winning out. Naturally, it had also started to rain substantially, and naturally we found ourselves at a Y in the road that did not offer the hint of any sign. "There's no fork in the road on either map," I blurted out in frustration.

"Well there's a fork in *this* road!" replied Senator. Translation: *"My life was much simpler three days ago... when I had a job... and I wasn't wandering around the woods... in a foreign country... where even Wendy and a G.P.S. can't figure out where the @#$% we are... Isn't it enough that we conquered the States? Must we really take on Canada, too?*

Adding to the fun was the fact that all pavement had gradually morphed into gravel before fully transforming into mud. Both ways were a mess, and as we had a fifty-fifty shot, we randomly decided to turn left. Just then a pick-up truck coming down from the opposite direction stopped next to us. I was fairly certain it was the only Honda Fit he had seen anywhere near his homestead, or possibly in his lifetime. Inside was a friendly local, maybe in his late sixties, and what I guessed was his nephew or grandson. The driver rolled down his window with a smile. "Ya' lost? G.P.S. don't work right out here!" I wanted to explain that we weren't *those* people-- the kind with no plan, who just relied on their gadgets, but it would have been pointless. "Where ya' tryin' to get to?" I told him that our goal was Fundy National Park, wondering where else there even was to "get to". The man then proceeded to rattle off directions that, though a kind gesture, meant little to us in relation to where we were. I guess he was speaking Canadian.

We smiled, thanked him, and then decided to cut our losses. We agreed that the best move at that point would be to go back to our original location at the bed and breakfast and then take the longer way via the highway. At least we were sure of the way we had come. It would be longer than the supposedly direct route we were on, but in reality it would be shorter than more aimless wandering around and eventually running out of gas.

Back we went, and I was pleased that it actually was not as far as I thought it was. Once we were out of the woods (literally and figuratively), we easily found our way to the main highway and a gas station. It was even a self-serve station, so things were looking up. Having now mastered the more complicated process of using a Canadian gas pump credit card machine, I confidently began the first steps, as Senator went inside to use the bathroom.

So much for that. My credit card was not accepted. I heaved an audible sigh for no one's benefit but my own, as I marched inside to talk to the attendant. Stepping out of the bathroom, Senator saw me in line for the register. He asked me what the problem was, and I explained to him and the cashier, who was now available to help me. Thankfully, she pressed some secret buttons to fix the issue. I trotted back outside, wondering if we would have any relaxing days on this trip.

About an hour after I had hoped, we finally made it to Fundy National Park. All considered, the hassle of the nonexistent shortcut probably would not have seemed that bad if we weren't both concerned about Senator's business communication problem. Now we could see the ocean, though, and somehow that seemed hopeful to me. It was foggy and drizzly, but we needed to get out and hike for awhile.

Exiting the car, we grabbed the essentials for a half-hour trek along the Dickson Falls trail. Though humid, there were no mosquitoes. We had encountered this on other coastal hikes, so I am inclined to believe they do not like saltwater. Down along the waterfall we descended, passing families along the way. Considering that the national parks were not charging admission, there were not very many people.

The first walk did us good, and we were enjoying the fresh air, so we drove to another part of the park. A short walk from the parking lot gave us a view out over the foggy ocean. We found a stairway and descended to the rocky beach below. To our surprise, it was practically deserted.

Though we were not in the best place for viewing dramatic tidal shifts, nor did we have enough time to fully appreciate the difference, we could clearly see the high tide marks. Many interesting slimy strings and blobs also provided evidence of a very different shoreline. We continued walking along the water for a half mile or so. I could tell by Senator's distance and expression that he was brainstorming ways to sort out the email mess. I knew he could come up with something-- he always does-- but I knew he would not be settled until he did. We are alike in that way.*

The mist turned into a light rain as we made our way back to the car. Fundy National Park was not how I had pictured it. I suppose it would have been more spectacular if we had been there long enough to see a major tidal change. Maybe a more vibrant day with better visibility would have helped. The small visitor center further downplayed the park. Not having much in the way of interpretive displays, it gave the place the feel of a provincial beach more than a grand national park. Most likely the mild disappointment was due to our mood being as dampened as the shore.

That was okay; we were on to another new province together. On our way out of the park, we passed the dirt road that would have connected with the short cut that I had tried to take from the other end that morning. Silently we bypassed it, grateful to be heading toward the main highway, map and G.P.S. in solid agreement with reality. In about half an hour we were once again joining the TransCanada Highway.†

---

* If you really want to understand us, (though I'm not sure why you would feel this need,) read Dr. Kevin Leman's *Born to Win*, which explains the benefits and challenges of being a firstborn or functional firstborn. He also points out that the most difficult relationship combination is two of these people. Oops-- good thing we like a challenge!

† Though Senator had renamed the TransCanada Highway the "Purgatory Highway" during our travels in central Canada the previous year, (due to its stretches of drivers speeding up and slowing down at inopportune moments,) he had now apparently made his peace with the road. That was good, since a hefty chunk of each day would be spent on it. He will, however, be quick to point out that the shoulders are too small in some parts [*perhaps*], Toronto

New Brunswick was lovely, and the great forested parts reminded me of Maine, but I was excited to get back to the ocean, in waters more open than the narrow Bay of Fundy. I also wanted to see Prince Edward Island again. As a sixteen-year old, it had left the impression of a seaside village that had been swathed across with a paintbrush of perfectly-toned hues. There was red, but it was rusty-- not too bright. Green laid the groundwork, but it was not grassy or foresty or olivey; it was just appropriate. Gold flecks interrupted the landscape without becoming obtrusive or pretending to be Midwestern, and the entire crescent was surrounded by, well, Prince Edward Island Atlantic blue. Like many places I had returned to with Senator, I hoped that time had not altered it too much.

We soon approached the Confederate Bridge. Spanning eight miles, it is the only land-based method of reaching Prince Edward. Until the early 1990s, your car could only see the birth province of the Canadian Confederacy by taking the ferry.* As we approached the modern engineering marvel, it occurred to me that there would surely be a toll to cross it. "Oh, I bet they'll soak us for $15 or maybe even $20," I commented, smiling mildly in admission that they had us cornered.

"Well, whatever," replied Senator. When we reached the entrance to the bridge, I saw the sign listing the fees.

---

    traffic sucks [*agreed*], and drivers in Quebec are not to be trusted, simply based on their direct national and cultural ties to France [*sigh*].

* My dad wisely advises that no one take a ferry, ever, for any reason, whenever it can be avoided. As the most meticulous vehicle owner I know, I can easily visualize him cringing as people bang doors into the car next to them, unable to navigate the seven-inch aisles.

My eyes naturally scanned upward to the top of the list, ignoring the huge amounts below for larger vehicles.

"What?! You've got to be kidding! Our little passenger car had the grand sum of $46.50 written next to it. To be fair, it was in Canadian dollars, but a rough calculation still placed the pricey drive at about four and a half bucks per mile. Then another thought popped into my head. "Geez, I wonder if that's only one way!" Canadian or American, the thought of paying almost $100 to spend one day on an island almost made me reconsider seeing our eighth province together.

"Well, what can you do? We're here now," said Senator, still distracted by the email issue.

"Yeah, I know... but this better be as wonderful and romantic as Anne described!"*

We proceeded onto the bridge. No toll booth was in sight, so we settled in at a comfortable pace and enjoyed the gently mounting waves and the newly approaching scenery. As I had remembered, the rusty steep shoreline came into view. It was a funny sensation to be traveling over the tiny section of ocean in a car, but each mile served as another section of an open time-traveling tunnel that brought us closer to an island that had managed to maintain its timeless character. After a pleasant approach, we reached the other side.

"I guess we didn't have to pay coming across," remarked Senator.

"You're right, so at least we're not dropping a

---

* Anne Shirley, Lucy Maud Montgomery's spunky character in her 1908 classic set on her native Prince Edward Island *Anne of Green Gables* hundred bucks on this little tour. And actually, someone could beat the system if he moved from the mainland to the island and never left," I reasoned.

Once on the island, we drove toward our hotel on the north shore, crossing the center portion of Prince Edward. Small farms interrupted tasteful neighborhoods, and more colors were added to the anticipated palette. Neat, red, mounded rows lined potato farms, producing the province's signature vegetable. As a girl who believes the potato to be the most deliciously diverse food on Earth, I decided I might have to indulge during our brief stay.

I was also pleased to see how many old, wooden lobster traps were still in use. Sure there are newer, sleeker metal ones, but nothing says Northeast Atlantic tradition like those rustic crates bobbing on the sea. When I was sixteen, my dad actually brought one home for a souvenir. Something about the handcrafted wood and netting speaks to a traditional livelihood that has been in some families for many generations. It's a feeling even a vegetarian from the Midwest can appreciate.

Upon arriving at our hotel, which was more like a very low-key resort, we wondered if there had been a mistake. We turned the key and stepped into a fully-equipped suite, larger than some apartments I have been in. I knew we would have a little refrigerator and microwave, but I didn't expect a large living room area, full kitchen, and separate bedroom. Once again I learned how price is only one small factor of predicting quality when it comes to lodging.

More exciting than four pillows apiece, however, was what Senator accomplished. After wrestling with a somewhat slow internet connection, he learned, to neither of our surprises, that he was still blocked from his business correspondence. He then put into action the remedy that saved our vacation. Contacting our trusted friend and computer guru, Jason, Senator asked him if he could hack into the business email, bypassing the 'protective' measures that were threatening his career. As it turned out, the subversion was not necessary. The email service let Jason log in from back home. Simple-- maddeningly simple. Jason was then able to post a message letting clients know Senator was temporarily unavailable and would return correspondence when he was back in the States. This he even accomplished without a phone.

Instantly, the cloud was lifted. To this day I credit Jason with rescuing our trip, and possibly our relationship.[*] We could finally relax, and our collective sense of humor was back on full. We also realized we were very hungry. Fortunately, as Senator had been devising the master plan, I had been hiding out in the other room with the local phone book. Flipping through the restaurant section, I found the perfect café.

Capitalizing on the local star, Red Island Baked Potato featured all manner of robust Prince Edward Island potatoes. The menu listed appetizers, entrées, sides, and I think maybe even desserts, each with the same key ingredient. I was in spud heaven. After we each made our selections, Senator smiled across the small table at me. "See? Everything's fine," he announced, as casually as a guy on his third day of vacation should. After a

---

[*] Okay, I suppose that last statement is an exaggeration, but it sure helped us both have a lot more fun. Thanks again, Jason!

considerable wait-- no one was in a hurry, despite only two other parties in the room-- we were wolfing down mounds of starchy comfort.

We finished early enough, and the sun set late enough, that we had time for a drive to another part of the island. I had intended to stop by Port-la-Joye the next day before leaving Prince Edward, but going Tuesday evening would save time and possibly avoid more people. A little while later we found ourselves at the site of the first permanent European Settlement on the island. While the French had claimed it first, the British soon kicked them out and changed the namesake from Jean to Edward.

Regardless of who was in control, they all saw the same beauty. The curve of the shoreline offered a closer, more detailed view of the towering red cliffs. In the foreground, wildflowers carpeted the edges of the walking path that wrapped around and gently moved us toward the water. A golden sunset from the west bathed the evening in a quiet, contemplative glow. It looked so far off, yet this west was far more east than 'our' east. I drank it all in, as Senator fiddled around with the camera to set up the perfect shot. As is the drill, he then set the timer, ran toward me, pulled me in tight, and grinned, just in time to hear the faint *snap* of the shutter. There was no threat of anyone interrupting our photo; we were pleased to see no one else in any direction.

Back at our too-large suite, we rounded out an easy-going night by putting our feet up and channel surfing. Eventually Senator settled on a program. We decided to keep it light with a History Channel documentary about five Canadian World War II snipers. It wasn't that we had pictured that as the end our evening, but it was hard to resist the tales of these heroes, some of whom were giving interviews as men in their nineties. Riveted, we followed their story as they moved across the German-occupied Netherlands, de-Naziing one town at a time. Now those boys had some *real* stress.

    *   *   *

Wednesday morning we checked out of our accommodations, along with a bus full of senior citizens. They were mostly women and mostly on an Anne of Green Gables pilgrimage. Moving past the giddy ladies and a few patient and pleasant men, we grabbed a few nibbles from the continental breakfast station and found a table. We had a few more stops to squeeze in before leaving the island, so I gave Senator the rough itinerary, and we set out for our day.

We needed to gas up before going too far, so we pulled into a quiet corner station in a mainly residential area. "I can do it," offered Senator, as we both happily noted it was self-serve.

"No, I've got it," I said, now confident in my ability to master the Canadian gas pump process. *Okay, step 1.* Step 2 was not forthcoming, as I could not even find a slot in which to place my credit card. I felt like a fool as I searched the machine in vain.

Senator was watching, and he repeated his initial offer. "I can do it..." I shook my head, refusing his gesture in determination. I eventually had to admit defeat, though, so I walked into the building. No one else was there except the cashier, who asked if I needed help. I asked her if I needed to prepay inside, since I could not find a card slot.

She told me just to pump first, and then come in to pay. Then she added, with a grin, "From the States?"

"Yes, do we all ask?" She nodded in the affirmative, still smiling. At least I was not the only one of my fellow countrymen who was confounded by the machine. I was starting to think our neighbors to the north were making them all different on purpose.

As long as we were on Prince Edward Island, and might very well never return, I built a little time into the itinerary to visit Green Gables. Truth be told, though I had loved the books and the television series (the real one, as opposed to the crummy remake), I probably would not have bothered stopping at the Montgomery mecca if it were not free. The Canada 150 campaign of suspended admission fees lured me in, however, so we found ourselves on the trail of tour buses. We both hoped we would beat the crowds before we got sucked into a sea of retirees.

When we reached the parking lot, it was still relatively empty. "That's a good sign," Senator pointed out.

"Yes, and it's still pretty gray, so maybe the threat of rain will scare a few people away. After all, they say to allow a week on the island, so maybe the senior tourists will choose a different day."

"They say to allow a whole week here?" Senator looked lightly puzzled. I couldn't tell if it was because he was wondering what people could find to do to entertain themselves for a whole week, or why I had decided we could do it in a day.

We parked the car and walked through a barn with some interpretive displays. As expected, most of the visitors were women a generation or two older than me. A few sported straw hats with twin red yarn braids in homage to their favorite literary heroine. Children were also enjoying themselves, which hopefully meant that there might still be a few readers among the offspring of Millennials.

We then continued up to the farmhouse, which was designed after the one that inspired Lucy Maud Montgomery's Anne of Green Gables series. The white home did, indeed, have green gables. Inside, we toured the rooms in about ten minutes, glancing around at typical turn-of-the-century furniture and household goods. Since the items were not especially unique, and the home was more of a representation than an artifact, we switched our interest to the grounds.

In all directions the land sloped gently. It was primarily divided into lawn, forest, and vibrant perennial gardens. A few bumble bees buzzed lazily around, taking advantage of the buffet of colors in their prime spot, despite the growing numbers of tourists. We, of course, were drawn to the trail that opened into the 'Haunted Woods'. Fortunately, the iffy weather kept too many people from haunting our walk. For about a mile we looped around dense trees and shorter plants, enjoying the pine scent and the uncertain clouds before finding our way out again.

We had completed our Green Gables experience in about an hour, which was the perfect amount of time for two casual visitors who were not full-on Anne junkies. It was time to traverse the center of the island toward the national park. Along the way, occasional inlets wrapped around columns of large black dashes in the water. More wooden lobster traps floated in formation.

With the help of the tag-team map and G.P.S., we arrived at our destination, or so we were roughly sure. The left-hand turnoff certainly was not a major route. "Well, this road turns off, and it seems to be the only one that goes to the park..." I reasoned out loud. "I would think there would be a sign, though, since it is Prince Edward *National* Park..."

"Just tell me if you want me to turn here, because otherwise I have to go through the traffic light," explained Senator, as the invisible clock was ticking.

"Yeah, let's take it. From what we know, if it is the wrong road, we'll still end up at the Atlantic, so we can't be too disappointed." As it turned out, we had chosen the correct and only road that went to the park. Apparently it was not a major road because it did not need to be. Though it was July, and though it was free entry, only a few people were around. Primarily they were checking out the lighthouse.

We bypassed the lighthouse and drove to the end of the road. There we found a wide, deserted, dark red sand beach. The rain was holding off, and the sun was staying hidden, giving us ample time for a long beachfront walk. "I can't believe no one's here!" exclaimed Senator.

"Won't it be great if it's like this everywhere we go?" I asked enthusiastically. "I hope they're not all just waiting for us at the next park."

We spent almost an hour at the beach. Once in a while we came across fragments of crab remains or pieces of white driftwood that we kicked around lightly or threw back into the ocean. For a while, we sat on a dead log and just talked, satisfied in the fact that we had met our annual unofficial goal of needing a jacket in July. In the distance we could see more civilization in the form of houses, but we never saw any people until we were just about to leave.

Two women, their small children, a dog, and a stroller had somehow appeared on the sand. We had been further down the shoreline when they arrived, so we did not see them. It must have taken some determination on their part to get there, however, as the beach was a good ten feet below the bank. We had taken the stairs; who knows how they did it.

It was time to leave Prince Edward Island. Senator got in the driver's side, and we started back toward the Confederate Bridge, in direct defiance of our G.P.S.. She, (for we had already turned into people who personify an electronic device,) was quite exasperated with us for not driving toward the ferry dock, which technically was closer. This time we had to pay up, so I forked over a Canadian fifty and received the paltry change. As we started the eight-mile suspended journey across the sea, I twisted around for a last look at the Red Island. I was pleased to have brought Senator back to another place that I had loved as a teen, and even happier that it was still so pristine. Now we were on to Nova Scotia-- province number nine for us.

For the heck of it, I glanced down at the G.P.S. to see if she had accepted our rebellion and recalibrated the route to our next stop. Evidently one of three things had happened: 1.)she was very confused, 2.)she was boycotting us, or 3.)we had taken a very wrong turn. On the screen I could see the bridge, appropriately represented by a long golden line across the screen. The entire background was blue, which also made sense, given our position. The little purple car picture, however, which normally chugged along the gold line faithfully, was now planted firmly in the midst of the blue sea. *Hhmmm.* I showed Senator, who laughed. I believe my maps and I won that round over G.P.S.-girl.

In Nova Scotia we kicked up our speed to take advantage of the higher speed limits. Mile after mile we rolled along the hills northeastward. I was also taking advantage of the multicultural radio. A quick spin of the radio knob scanned through English, French, and even Gaelic channels. A few hours later, we were in Antigonish.*

During the planning phase of this trip, I had booked an array of accommodations. Some were hotels, some were inns, there were a few bed and breakfasts, and there was the 'micro boutique' in Antigonish. "What, pray tell, is a 'micro boutique'?" you may ask, perhaps envisioning a tiny store laden with fancy and overly-pricey items. It is, in fact, not a retail establishment at all, but rather an apartment building with studio units that look like they have been invaded by a hipster army of Ikea designers. Whatever. It got good reviews, the price was right, and the location was convenient to our route. We parked in the spacious back lot and got ready for a new experience.

The micro boutique experience is all about efficiency. One of the many touted benefits to we, the guests, is that the company sends a few confirmation emails prior to the

---

* I don't know why, but I had always thought this town was pronounced 'an-TIH-guh-nish'. Later, thanks to local radio, I learned that 'ANTI-go-nish' was more proper. Then again, it may be left up to personal preference.

vacation. Within these emails are policy details, useful tidbits, the room number, and the Codes. The Codes are magical numbers that give the guest access to the outside door as well as the individual room door. There is not a traditional front desk (efficiency!), but a kind and competent soul is promised to be on the property, should an issue arise, which, the guest is assured, it will not.

"Where do we go in?" asked Senator, openly not trusting the system.

"Well, this back door has a key pad, and I've got the code, so let's try it," I answered, trying to mask the fact that I also didn't trust the system. I carefully entered the four digits and ended with the asterisk as directed. Of course, nothing happened. More accurately, there was a distinct, whiny *you-ain't-gettin'-in-here* buzz.

Thankfully there was a front entrance, so we trekked around the building. Inside it looked like we had entered a small mall, with glass display windows for a few shops on either side. The name was starting to make some sense. As boasted, there was no front desk, but we did see an office space in another mod room in the back corner.

"Hello," I began, addressing the only person around. I went on to explain our dilemma with the magic, nonfunctioning codes. I hoped she would have some clue as to how to remedy the problem. When she quickly pulled up our reservation, I was encouraged.

"Oh, sorry about that," she explained. "Your codes were changed, but they didn't get the new ones out to you." *Hhmmm. I guess that would defeat the purpose of having a code then, would it not?* I thought to myself.

As she did not seem to be the person at fault, we

thanked her and took our new secret code back up the two flights of stairs. Cooking smells wafted around the hallways, making me wonder if people were taking advantage of the micro kitchens in the units, or just living there permanently. On our way to the room, we noticed the tiny but spotless laundry room. We planned to take advantage of the convenience later, in case we could not do so for the next several days. Finally we reached the room. Armed with the new and improved code, I tried again.

Attempt #1 was unsuccessful. "Here, let me try." Senator masterfully pushed all the same buttons, with the same disappointing result. Then we each tried it with various deliberate pauses between numbers. Still we were locked out.

When it became obvious that failure was the only result, we marched back down to the woman in the office. She could read our expressions before we said anything. "No luck?" she asked, somewhat timidly. Just in case we were missing some important step in the supposedly simple system, she accompanied us back to the third floor to try the lock herself. It was both satisfying and disheartening when she got exactly as far as we did.

Back downstairs we all trod. The woman was visibly baffled. For unclear reasons, she also had no one she could contact. Not knowing what to do, she searched through some papers and then checked a few emails. Now we could read *her* expression without any words. As expected, she was not the person who had issued the original or revised codes, ergo, she was not the person who could issue even newer and more improved codes. It appeared we were up a creek without a code.

Just then she got an idea. "Well, I do have this emergency code..." she offered as a last resort.

"Will it work each time?" I asked.

"Yes, it's the one the managers use to get into any room. It overrides all of the codes," she explained. So we were about to be trusted with the Master Code. I reasoned that it wasn't a problem that the managers knew it because 1.)managers are able to get into any room in an inn or hotel anyway, and 2.)based on our experience, no actual manager existed within the micro boutique realm. On the other hand, I thought it best not to point out the fact that we could now get into anyone else's room. We must have honest faces.

Inside the studio space, it was rather impressive how much they packed into a small area. There was a bed with just enough room to squeeze around it on the far side, but plenty of storage surrounding it. Two modern-looking chairs fit at a right angle around a small table and work space. Almost without leaving the chair, one could also utilize the kitchenette's coffee maker, mini (or micro?) fridge, and microwave. An overall feeling of mass-produced op art pervaded the décor. "I'm not a fan of the Hipster Boutique," announced Senator flatly, surveying our eighteen-hour home.

Then there was the bathroom. Having recently read a *National Geographic* article about the millions of people who still do their necessary business in the great outdoors-- no, I don't mean in an outhouse or latrine-- I am grateful for any clean, functioning bathroom. Ours was both, if micro. The only challenge was the Space Shower. I surveyed the Star Trek-like capsule. It seemed to be created for someone who was a foot taller than me and really into gadgets. There were enough dials and strangely placed shower heads for me to recognize that this was not a cheap device, but I could not appreciate its wonder if I could not figure out how to operate the darn thing. "Hey, Seeenatorrr..."

"Spider?" he asked, automatically.

"No, but thank you. Can you figure this thing out?" He did some minor investigative work, and soon I was reveling in a shower that would have made the Jetsons jealous.

The Hipster Boutique definitely had an odd vibe, but it was functional. It was also convenient to the main street. Dinner was a simple but hearty meal that required a pleasant walk about a block away, and we easily got back into our room using the powerful master code. Our night ended by making coffee from the bedside supply. On the suspended television, we were now glued to the latest installment of *American Sniper*. Senator sipped. "This isn't our coffee," he remarked in mock complaint, referencing our preferred brand from home.

"That's true, but at least we're not there," I responded, pointing to the television, which pictured a hell-hole in the desert where our soldiers were fighting jihadists. *God help them.*

*   *   *

Thursday morning we left the Hipster Boutique and crossed onto Cape Breton Island, North America's nod to all things Scottish. It was a mostly cloudy morning, which fit the scene nicely. Not as appropriate to the misty greenery was the abundance of construction. We had to stop and wait several times. While doing so, I kept noticing what looked like round, slatted, wooden crates, several feet square or rectangular. Most were placed near the road, at the end of people's property. I think they were probably some sort of antique or reference to local culture, but the more I studied them, the more it seemed like they were just elaborate covers for propane tanks or garbage cans.

In a couple of hours we were in the small and welcoming seaside town of Cheticamp, gateway to Cape Breton Highlands National Park. We made a quick pit stop in the visitor center to grab a park map, and I pulled out my preliminary trail notes for comparison. Because our time is always limited, and because I pack so much into each trip, I always do my hiking research ahead of time. Narrowing down a list of thirty potential trails to about eight saves time while on vacation and prevents backtracking. Of course, there usually seem to be some discrepancies when we actually get to parks. Here I must give proper recognition to Cape Breton Highlands. They win hands-down for the best consistency between their website information and their physical trail maps. All information was accurate, to scale, and depicted on the correct side of the road. *Tapadh leat!**

French was almost as prevalent as Gaelic, due to the strong Acadian heritage in the area. Signs along the main highway depicted the conjunction of Atlantic Canadian and European cultures. One sign in particular caught Senator's eye. "Hey! What's 'Prog Pond'?"

I laughed. I had also seen the colorful sign and open air collection of small wooden structures. Since Senator was driving, he had not had enough time to really read the

---

* thank you

name. "I think it actually says 'Frog Pond'," I explained. "but you shouldn't be too disappointed, because they are advertising coffee." He immediately pulled into the gravel lot.

While there were no epic rock compositions playing, there were living frogs singing in the pond behind the walk-up order window. We had not eaten, so we ordered a giant granola cookie to split and two black coffees. The sun had emerged from behind the clouds, setting us up for a great afternoon outdoors. There was just enough time to enjoy our pre-hike break at an outdoor café table, in view of the pond and several types of wildflowers.

Our first venture into the national park was on the Buttereau Trail. We climbed upward from the parking area and were soon rewarded with an open view to the varying blue sea and crashing waves. The picture was framed by bushes with twisted gray branches and bright red flowers. Random pines and a hardwood forest flanked the sides. As we turned back on the small detour we had taken to the view, we passed three other people who were hiking together.

Entering the quiet forest, we again found ourselves alone. That is, we were alone until we encountered the largest hare I have ever seen. As we approached, I expected him (or her, who knows?) to run, but the creature just stared at us for a moment, and then went back to chomping on a buffet of grasses and weeds. He or she was entirely too comfortable around humans for his or her own good, so I tried to scare the highland hare back into the woods. I even tried French, just in case, but nothing fazed him or her. Eventually we gave up and continued on our trail.

Further along the way, we saw the remains of a family homestead from almost a century ago. Maybe the giant hare had been a descendant of one of their rabbits. The family property also led to a beautiful view of a causeway that poked up just far enough to make a rustic road, when the water was not washing over it. The scenery was great, but I could not imagine the logistical hassle of living up there, especially in winter.

Our next stop was a bog trail. Though a bog is usually just a swamp with a better p.r. rep, this trail won points for its neatly looped boardwalk. As mosquitoes had not been an issue, it made the cut, remaining on the itinerary. There would be plenty of interesting plants, but the main draw was the guide pamphlet's promotion of it as a moose hot spot. From what I could see as we approached the first interpretive sign, it seemed reasonable to believe that the average eastern Canadian moose would find the region appealing. After all, there were plenty of fat aquatic lilies, an ample supply of fresh water, a lack of violent predators,* and an overall lovely terrain.

Walking along the trail, we looked around-- left, right, below, in the distance, right in front of us. In keeping with my near-perfect record of mooselessness, we saw not a one. Sensing our mild dismay, another bogger was excited to show us pictures of two large females that he and his wife had seen down the road earlier that morning. "Well," he explained, "you really can't see it well, here..." I glanced at his cell phone screen, observing only glare.

---

* I actually have no idea if moose have any natural enemies. After watching hours and hours of *Planet Earth*, however, I have come to believe that every creature has some other creature that's after it.

"Oh, yeah," I feigned.

"Here we go," he continued. "Here's another one," he said proudly.

"Oh, yeah," I repeated, since I saw the same glare I had seen the first time. We smiled and thanked him for his well-intentioned sharing. Maybe I should just start pretending that I have great photos from successful moose sightings. It would essentially be the same effect.

Yes, the moose were elusive again, but the trail was not a total loss. We did get to see some carnivorous plants. The fact that they were tucked among bouquets of delicate wildflowers somehow made them a bit more sinister. Come to think of it, can we be sure the plants didn't eat the moose? Someone from Parks Canada should probably look into that...

I was planning to take in a third trail, but I was starting to get antsy about time. We probably would have been okay, even with the construction that stopped us for a while on the only road through the park, but I was not taking any chances. For months I had been hatching a plan to finally see some whales. We had seen whales in the past, but only as specks on a distant horizon. This time would be the real deal-- supposedly guaranteed. We had a reserved cruise time and only one chance to make it happen, so I did not want anything to spoil our big date.

Our motel was located at the edge of the park entrance, and just about two miles up the road from the whale boat dock. We entered the motel office and waited our turn behind the only other person who was checking in. It was a good thing that we were allowing plenty of time, because the check-in process took three times as long as it should have. This was not because the owner (or his wife, who soon emerged from a rear kitchen) was incompetent; rather, he and she were too competent. They were excited to present us with a map, explicit directions in case we somehow lost our way along the only major road, and detailed reviews of many eateries, none of which we had asked about. We were also invited to the nightly fire, which was thoughtful, if irrelevant to our itinerary.

We brought the necessary gear into our room, setting sweatshirts near the door, in anticipation of a cool evening on the sea. "Do you have everything you need in the backpack?" I asked Senator.

"Yeah, the camera's ready. Got your reservation info?"

"Uh-huh. Give me a few minutes, and we can go."

Down the road a short drive we arrived at Captain Zodiac's booth. It did not look like anything major, but there was someone inside at the desk, and she did confirm my reservation and payment. At least I knew I had not been scammed. The woman instructed us to meet back there in a little over an hour. In the meantime, we could find something for dinner.

As readers of my travel series know, Senator and I are not particularly epicureans. While we love deep flavor, we do not seek out fancy meals or expensive restaurants. In fact, for our first two nights, dinner had consisted of scooping homemade pasta salad out of a large plastic container in the cooler into cups I had obtained from a hotel on the last trip.[*] We are generally happy with anything

---

[*] Should you ever decide to attempt this, I recommend bringing a very large scooping utensil, as opposed to dipping a third plastic

simple, as long as it is vegetarian. Usually on vacation this translates into veggie burgers, sub sandwiches, pasta, pizza, Mexican fare, or even freakishly large baked potatoes, as in the case of Prince Edward Island. I will go on record as stating that I do not recall it ever being an issue, even in Germany.

With this and our time limit in mind, we were pleased to find a small restaurant that advertised pizza and sandwiches. Inside Wabo's we were directed down the half-flight of stairs to choose our own seats, so we selected a table that overlooked the water. There were only two other parties in the place, so we had beat the rush. Before I was situated, Senator already had the menu open. "They have a cold veggie sub," he pointed out. "Comes with fries..."

"Sounds easy. Let's do that," I answered. Throw in two waters and we had a simple order, despite the fact that it took more than ten minutes for someone to come over to our table.

As we waited, I imagined what our cruise would be like. The evening was cooling off nicely, but the sun was still bright. It was not too windy, yet there were not many boaters out. Months ago I had narrowed down our potential tour to two companies. Dozens of them claim to convey humans to the realm of whales, and several guarantee sightings, but I was still skeptical of them for various reasons. The final contenders, I believed, were both valid and reputable. Their main difference lay in the type of boat they used. One housed twenty-five or thirty people inside a nice cabin, with windows on both sides. The other was a zodiac, with which I was unfamiliar. Far from being

---

cup into the potpourri like I did.

a vessel that rockets one through the constellations, a zodiac, I learned, is a cross between a small boat and an inflatable raft. You are correct, Reader, in picturing that the latter only holds a few people and leaves them exposed to the elements. Naturally, that's the one our two-member family had unanimously voted for.

My daydreaming was periodically interrupted by glances toward the kitchen. A few servers were casually chatting near a computer, and no one was in a hurry to do anything. "We have plenty of time," said Senator, reading my thoughts. Outside there were two more employees on the patio, attempting in vain to string up some lights. One dropped a bulb, which broke on the concrete. He seemed slightly surprised, but not overly concerned. I was starting to get annoyed. "Go ahead and check, then, since you'll be nervous until you do," instructed Senator. I excused myself and trotted out to our car to turn on the dash clock. He was right; we were still doing well time-wise, but the wait was getting ridiculous.

After waiting half an hour, a guy brought out our two plates. On them were scant subs and some thin fries. I could not for the life of me figure how placing some cold vegetables on bread and dropping a handful of pre-fab French fries could possibly take so long. Whatever. At least we could fill our stomachs and move on to our exciting evening.

I looked down at my supper. It was the worst sandwich I had ever seen. The bread was a partially stale white submarine bun. On it rested an embarrassed pink tomato slice, a piece or two of lettuce, half of a thin slice of cheese, and a smattering of raw mushrooms. A good sauce might have gone a long way in redeeming it, but this was the moment that I learned that the Maritime provinces love mayonnaise. The more the better, and the gloppier the better. This portion was both, obscuring anything salvageable. I moved on to the fries, which were cold. Senator picked a bit at his, and we were soon asking for our bill. It is one thing to get a crappy sandwich, although I don't know how anyone could screw it up. It is another thing to pay $30.00 for the treat. There was no time to wait for a manager, but I did answer honestly when the guy brought our bill and asked how everything was. I thought seeing most of what he brought still sitting on the plates would have answered his question, but he was as oblivious as the rest of the staff. I do not take wasting food lightly, but most of mine went into the trash.

As intended, we arrived back at the dock with plenty of time to spare. Fortunately there were a few sticks of string cheese and some canned peaches left in the cooler. Senator declined, so I ate them. Before long our lousy meal was forgotten as we were slipping into our life jackets and following Captain Wes and a family of four French-speakers out to the boat.

Because of water levels and lack of deck height, we had to maneuver our way down an eight-foot later to the boat. The smaller of the two boys was chattering away, and I was picking up enough French to know that he was as excited as I was. His 'Pa-pa' laughed and looked at us, humorously warning us. "I hope you folks weren't planning on a quiet evening!" No problem; it was refreshing to be around a child who was genuinely appreciative and full of wonder. He was neither bratty or attention-seeking. He just couldn't believe that, after all of his five years of life, he was finally going to see some whales up close. *I know just how you feel, Kid.*

The first thing one learns aboard a zodiac boat is that it moves along the water faster than expected. Our captain began by giving us some background information about the area and the current season as it related to wildlife. As he talked, we zipped away from the shore. The second thing one learns aboard a zodiac boat is that it moves extremely fast, barely touching the water, when the gas is kicked up. The captain repositioned us to better distribute the weight, and we were instantly zooming through the wind as we skimmed along the water's surface. I was glad to see the slightly surprised parents hanging on to their boys tightly. The younger one was squealing with delight. I think I may have been even louder.

Our first visitors were a gang of harbor porpoises. These good-natured creatures dove in synchronized waves, like they were drawing out a sound graph. Several times they came by to visit. A little further out, we saw a group of seals popping up and down like enthusiastic puppies. I was suddenly in a Disney cartoon, albeit one with French commentary.

Finally we reached our objective, spotting the celebrities about a hundred feet away. I resisted the urge to stand up in the boat, excited to see my first truly discernible wild whales. On cue, Senator readied the camera. As we were viewing one pod of pilot whales, another emerged in the distance. We also encountered a few minke whales.

Our captain continued to guide us toward the whales. I was so pleased that everything had worked out just as I had hoped. All six of us passengers were in awe. Senator alternated between trying to focus his video and making sure he was not missing out on the real experience of the moment.

It was then that I realized that we were not simply on a whale-watching tour; our tiny vessel was allowing us to get up close and personal with these creatures of the deep. Surpassing my expectations, we spent significant time just bobbing on the light waves, enjoying the company of multiple whales. All of them were far more casual about the situation than we were. At one point, their playful activity dropped off somewhat, and I assumed they had become bored with us and moved on. On the contrary, Captain Wes showed us that the bright sunset had actually sent a few of the whales under the shady cover of our boat.*

An hour or so later, we returned to the dock. Among the beautiful scenery, we had also seen a bald eagle, several birds with which we were unacquainted, and a white seal perched atop his favorite rock. The zodiac's small size also allowed us to worm our way into a sea cave, where we listened to the odd sound of waves crashing into the hollow. A waterfall snaking down the cliffs rounded out our view as we zipped back along the water's surface.

It would be hard to top the experience of seeing whales within a few feet of our boat. We were grateful and wind-whipped, which is a perfect combination for a great night's sleep. Just before climbing into bed, we opened the

---

*Did I ever think I would be sitting above a whale while it took a break from the sun? No, I did not. In fact, I do not believe the notion of a whale seeking shade would have occurred to me at any time during the rest of my life.

window of our motel. The air was cool and crisp-- a rare treat in July. We didn't even mind when, at 1:30 in the morning, it became apparent that we needed to close up. It gave us the opportunity to see the moonlight over the brook behind the motel.

*   *   *

Friday morning we were up early, which was good since we had lots to do. We still had not eaten substantially, so Senator needed something to fuel him. The only viable option was a buffet, so he bargained his way into a carry-out container. I generally have no appetite in the morning, and the dull, flavorless items in his styrofoam were not tempting me. As we made our way back into Cape Breton Highlands National Park, Senator noticed a sign for a local radio station. Appropriately, Acadian folk music became our audio backdrop as we climbed into the hills.

Our first hike of the morning was a solitary one. Stepping into the woods, we made our way along a stream, working backwards up a gradual incline toward McIntosh Falls. The forest was quiet except for the random squirrel. A mosquito or two buzzed around, but for the most part a decent breeze kept them away.

We then moved on to the Lone Shielding trail. I knew 'lone' and 'shielding', but I had no idea what the name meant when coupled. From what I could see, it was basically a very short walk through an old forest. According to the park's literature, the trees were, indeed, about 350 years old. The trail terminated at the also-strangely-named Scottish crofter's hut. As we learned, a 'crofter' was a tenant farmer, and one who lived in a glorified dirt hut at that. His home sported a thatched straw roof and an opening on one side that could be closed off by peat moss slabs during storms. Add that one to the list of careers that require much more fortitude than mine.

Leaving the west side of the park, we rounded the north coast by car. There the waves were a little wilder as we approached more open water. The sun was beaming, which is not typical for that part of Canada, and it highlighted the extended rock beaches below our curvy drive. Rounding the cliffs eventually brought us to the east side of the island, where the views possibly exceeded those of the west.

Halfway down the coast, we reached Green Cove. A short walk from the car led us to mounds of pinkish boulders. Flecks of sediment in the rock sparkled in the sun. As we climbed over the rocks and side-stepped the deep crevices, it struck me as one of the most dazzling shorelines I have ever seen. The ocean had also taken on a turquoise hue, topped with foam as waves crashed against a few rocks that had seceded from the shore. After posing for a photo, we found a perfect stone perch that fit us like a natural double recliner. I could have stayed there many more hours, which is saying a lot, as I very rarely enjoy sitting in the sun.

It was time to pay for our relaxing break with a real hike. The trail to Broad Mountain Cove was very steep, and it did not leave us encouraged by our abilities. The payoff was worth it, though. At the top, which sported a few signature Canadian red Adirondack chairs[*], one could

---

[*] As part of the big Canada 150 celebration, the park system placed these oversized chairs at strategic photographic locations, most of which required a significant walk or hike to reach. I think the idea

see several fresh water lakes, separated by a strip of land from the ocean. Evergreen treetops formed a pointy carpet, and again, the colors were rich. Though we were still panting a little bit, the air was noticeably different. I always wonder what it says about the air quality where we live, when I can literally feel the difference of cleaner air in my lungs. *Time to move.*

Our final trail at Cape Breton National Park led us to the Fresh Water Lookout. It was another steep trail, but it was short. There were no red chairs at the top, but there were two other couples, probably both in their 70s, who were discussing the geography of the region. "I know this is Nova Scotia," one man commented, "but for my money, Acadia National Park in Maine looks more like Scotland than Nova Scotia." *Really? Tell us more...* I eavesdropped. That settled it; I had just solidified my longtime goal of wanting to take Senator there. Maybe it would happen in 2018.

We were back on the Cape Breton Trail, heading south toward Baddeck. Whereas the other side of the island sported many signs in French, we were now strictly in Gaelic country, in search of its favorite son. As we exited onto the main street through town, we soon saw the attractive geometric features of the Alexander Graham Bell Historic Site. "Oh, that's right," I remembered. "This place has free admission this year, too!" After all, who doesn't

---

was that it unified and branded the park system, while introducing a fun audience-participation activity. I'm not sure how many visitors derived joy from sitting in the chairs or taking selfies to submit to the park's website, but I can guarantee that the workers who had the unfortunate task of lugging these clumsy pieces of tourist furniture around were not smiling.

love a bargain?

Though I had known about Bell's work with the deaf, and his imperative contribution to modern society with the invention of the telephone, I had no idea how far the man's drive and talents spread. The first display that caught my eye explained how he was able to help deaf people learn to form sounds and ultimately words. He began with a glove with letters stitched on various parts of the fingers. By placing the client's hand on his throat, the client could feel the vocal cord movement and associate it with a letter. The progress was unprecedented. At one point, even the family dog was a subject, learning to 'talk' several syllables.

Other displays highlighted Bell's work with flying machines. As a member of an early club obsessed with putting men into the air, he was constantly recalculating the mathematics and physics of sustainable flight. One result of his endeavors was a full-sized tetrahedron hydrofoil for the military. It was ready to go during World War I, but once the war ended, the orders stopped. His greater gift to the armed forces may have been his experiments devising ways to distill sea water for stranded sailors.

We meandered around the halls, taking in tales of Bell's long struggle to finally make transmittable sound a reality. Interestingly, once he achieved a major feat, he all but totally lost interest in it. He was always looking forward to the next pursuit. I would have particularly liked to explore more of his work involving solar-powered sound vibration. Perhaps Senator's studio could be powered by light!...

There was a little more driving to do for the day. We

needed to reach North Sydney, our last point before departing Nova Scotia by ferry. Once again we hopped on the highway, turning our route east to cross Boularderie Island. Thick trees and shimmering water seemed to always be in view. This was not the kind of Friday afternoon commute we knew at home.

By dinner time we had arrived at our bed and breakfast. It had good reviews, but I had mainly chosen it for its convenient location within view of the ferry to Newfoundland. While it was easy to find the ferry, it was not as easy to see which end of the home was the front. What seemed to be the entrance was not, so we pulled around the back street, which looked like more of a front door.

Sitting on the porch was an older gentleman, whom I assumed was another guest. We smiled and nodded a hello, and knocked on the front (or back) door. The Mayor, (as Senator later dubbed him,) sat rocking on the front (or back) porch as we stepped up. No one answered, so we let ourselves inside, which is customary in such places. "Well, *that* certainly wasn't the owner," I surmised, indicating the man on the porch. "Hello?..." I called out. We continued right on through the house until we reached the (front or back) porch on the other end.

"Are you sure we're not actually just trespassing in someone else's house?" inquired Senator, wisely. Now that he mentioned it, the thought had crossed my mind.

Just as doubt was setting in, we found a note next to a house phone that said to call the host. Thankfully, we were in the right place after all. The owner had been working up in her attic. A few minutes later she joined us, apologizing for her dust and work attire. As she checked us in, she told us that we could park on the other (front? back?) side. She then double-checked our dietary preferences and showed us to a room that sported a 1980s take on something that fell between Victoriana and bordello. It was, nonetheless, clean and comfortable.

We unpacked our things and got ready to go back out again. We had no real plans, but we needed to eat and do laundry, in anticipation of much hiking and a lack of clothes-washing options where we were going in Newfoundland. Being the planner I am, I had the names and addresses of six different laundromats in the vicinity. I had also been amassing a nice stock of Loonies and Toonies.*

On our way out the (front? back?) door, we again encountered the man whom we had now determined was neither the owner nor another guest. As we passed him, we did a quick dip of the head and wave in acknowledgment. He elaborated further on the current situation, staring up discontentedly, not exactly at us and not exactly into space. "Nobody pocks back they-uh," he began. "I dunno why. Everybody comes hee-uh."

"Okay," I responded.

"Have a nice night," Senator added.

"Who was that guy, anyway," I asked Senator, once we were out of earshot. "A neighbor who just hangs out on her porch?"

"Maybe... I'm just calling him 'The Mayor'." That

---

* Canadian one- and two- dollar coins, respectively. Personally, I would have spelled it "Twonie", but the Canadians seem okay with the animation-like name.

was probably the most accurate name he could have bestowed on the gentleman.

Now, Reader, let's take some time for a quick trivia game: what do five out of six of the items listed on my page of laundromats have in common? Take your time... Yes, that is correct; they do not exist. As I mentioned, I had done my homework, locating various options in both North Sydney (where we were) and Sydney (about twenty minutes away). Being no optimist, I had no delusions that the first two or three would pan out, but I did not expect to score so badly. We found #1 ("Brad's") easily enough, but Brad certainly had no laundromat attached to his establishment, whatever else he did have attached.

While stopping for gas, we also learned about a secret laundromat, just a few blocks away. That one, despite its lack of internet presence, did indeed exist, but it closed at 6:00pm. Visions of being kicked out with our clothes still soapy and dripping put the kibosh on that. North Sydney options depleted, we headed back onto the highway.

The entire area was located on the coast, so we did not mind the drive. The G.P.S. was also taking some of the hassle out of the excursion. It easily led us to laundromats #2-#5, all of which either appeared to be apartment flats or completely abandoned buildings in dumpy parts of town. "There's *got* to be some viable laundromat. It looks like an area that would have a laundromat. I would think there would be one somewhere along these main roads. There's everything else," I said, noticing the variety of fast food joints, car dealers, retailers, banks, liquor stores, and other such places.

Fortunately, #6 was both where it said it was and

open. Naturally, it was the furthest away from our room, clocking in at a cool thirty-five minute commute. It, too, was in a dumpy building, but the machines were clean and they functioned. As part of my master plan, I had also measured out laundry detergent in squirt bottles, secured within resealable bags. As anticipated, one was leaking, so we decided to use it first, carefully balancing it with our sack of dirty clothes and our bag of coins. What I had not anticipated-- there's always one factor, or it wouldn't be vacation-- was that the machines only took quarters.

"Quarters?!" I said, dismayed. "Just washing each load is going to be more than a buck apiece anyway. Who still uses quarters?"

"People who opened their laundromats when you could do a load of clothes for a quarter," replied Senator logically. He had me there. As I shoved my supply of Loonies and Toonies into my pocket, we scrounged around for quarters, somehow finding enough for both loads. With the load swishing around, we left in pursuit of some food.

A few blocks up the street we had seen a pizza place. Being nowhere near Chicago, we did not have any great expectations for a marvelous pizza, but we would be content with passable. Besides, the place reminded us of a little pizzeria that used to be about a mile from where Senator grew up. Both had their charms, I thought, as I waited in the car. Senator went inside, ordered, and reported the twenty minute wait time when he returned.

We drove back to the laundromat, ready for the mass transition from the washers to the dryers. This, of course, also involved negotiating a change deal with the employees next door, who ran a convenience store. To their credit, they were cooperative, if most likely pot-heads. Now we had at least enough quarters to get the dryers going a respectable amount of time, which is some feat, considering they were each twenty-five cents per five minutes.

It was pizza time, so we drove back down the street for six blocks. We were very hungry by this point, and bringing the steaming box into the car made us ravenous. Paying in cash had also gained a few more necessary quarters, so things were progressing. We decided to drive back to the laundromat, so we could add dryer time mid-dinner. Thankfully, we had the trusty emergency picnic kit along for the ride. Balancing the box on top of the console, we devoured triangles of mediocre pizza, while keeping an eye on the questionable homeless guy who was wandering around the lot.

We successfully finished supper and found a garbage can nearby for the trash. The front seat of the pizza-scented car had now been cleared to fold laundry. Why not use the tables inside the laundromat, you ask? That would be because 1.)there were no tables, 2.)there were flies, 3.)even if there had been tables and not flies, I would not have put our clean laundry on them, and 4.)we didn't want to hang out near the guys we had to bother a second time to make change for the dryers.*

With our bellies and suitcase full, we made the drive back to our room in North Sydney. I still do not know if we were parked in the front or the back of the house, but at least The Mayor was not waiting for us on the porch. We entered the house, climbed the stairs to the 80s bordello,

---

* To be fair, one of the quarters should have been donated by them anyway, as the first dryer we engaged did not work properly.

and started to unwind for the night. Politely, a mosquito waited patiently until the lights were out and we were ready for bed before striking. I wonder if The Mayor got a good show when all the lights came on, and two undressed warriors stalked their buzzing attacker. *Smack!*

*   *   *

The next morning we got ready and met our fellow guests around the breakfast table. Despite my vegetarian diet request, we each found a sizable hunk of Polish sausage on our plate. Maybe our host assumed Senator's last name overrode my instruction on the reservation confirmation. I felt bad wasting food, but we left the meat untouched.

As we ate, we listened to the conversation around us. There is really only one reason people come to North Sydney, and that is to leave North Sydney. In other words, the ferry is the biggest game in town, and naturally, it is easy to glean information about Newfoundland. In fact, I believe it was the first time I had ever met anyone who had been to Newfoundland. All of my research had been conducted via written material or internet research, and based on my unofficial survey, the average person in our circle of acquaintances was not even convinced there was such a place as Newfoundland. We had been to every other state and province though, and there was no way we were missing out on this mysterious and wonderful island. Thus, we absorbed what we could.

Every bed and breakfast is different, but those that use the communal breakfast format (never preferred) as a rule always have a table master. While this is not a formal position, I believe it must be encoded in some international bylaws, because I have never seen a group of strangers breakfasting together without a self-appointed leader. In this case, John enlightened us with tales of his multiple trips over to the island for business. Coincidentally, he also happened to be an expert hiker, and he was more than happy to regale us with trail advice. In reality, I appreciated it, because I could read between the lines and filter out the b.s. enough to confirm that I had chosen some of the best trails to make the most of Gros Morne National Park. He also told a tale of one ferry trip he took that was delayed due to a small onboard fire. I was neither encouraged nor scared off by this.

Filled with no sausage, but a little bit of baloney, we were on our way. You know me well enough by now, Reader, to know that I insisted we leave early... even though there was no traffic... and it was a weekend morning... and we could see the Marine Atlantic ferry terminal from the front (or back?) of the inn. In five minutes we were there. The woman at the first booth asked if we had reservations. "Yes-- for all three of us." Senator looked at me quizzically. "Me, him, and our car, " I gestured. Senator nodded in new understanding.

"Okay," she said. "You're a little bit early, but you'll just pull up into lane seven. Once boarding begins, you'll just follow the line in front of you. The deck hands will guide you."

The process was smooth, simple, and as advertised. Senator and I parked in the appropriate line, unbuckled our seat belts, reclined our seats, and sat back to enjoy the forced relaxation. It was sunny, dry, and in the low 70s. Add in an ocean view, and the ability to get out and walk around whenever we wanted, and it made for a very pleasant wait. This, indeed, was important, as multiple announcements progressively pushed back our time of departure. "Good thing we left early," joked Senator.

At one point I noticed some black smoke pouring out above the ship. I could not see it fully, but I assumed it was coming from a smoke stack. Still, John's story passed through my mind. Another bilingual announcement was made. At least I was getting French practice in. I had not needed the English version all morning to know that we were not going anywhere fast.

When it was all said and done, we were three-and-a-half hours late, but it was an entirely different experience than waiting for a delayed flight. For one, you have the comfort and privacy of your own vehicle and all of your belongings at hand.[*] Snacks are free, if you bring your cooler, as opposed to the overpriced crap in airport terminals. People are also more relaxed. They chat and smile as they wander up and down the lanes, noting each other's license plates or pets.[†] All things considered, I think I would take a delayed ferry over an on-time flight.

Finally we boarded. Around we spiraled, landing on a middle deck among the nine. Coming from the Midwest, I think of ferries as small boats that shuttle a few dozen cars

---

[*] If you are fortunate enough to be driving a recreational vehicle, you also have your very own bathroom!

[†] In my own meanderings around the forty or so cars around us, I learned that we were the only Yanks, except for a few New York license plates. I suppose there may have been more Americans who were driving Nova Scotia rental cars, but based on observation, I think they were almost all Canadians, which also could have accounted for the more laid-back wait.

across small shortcuts on the Great Lakes. This is not the case when one traverses the sea between Nova Scotia and Newfoundland. There are two options. We took the shorter line, which was only a six or seven hour passage, as opposed to sixteen hours. Rather than a few dozen cars, the ship (for it is a full-sized vessel) holds hundreds of vehicles, including several semi trailers. Most impressive of all, my Dad will be pleased to learn that the parking spots have ample space around them. The entire boarding procedure is an operation more akin to that of a cruise ship than a water taxi.

Once aboard, we got our bearings and found our reserved seats. It probably was not necessary to reserve specific comfortable seats, but it was nice to have an indoor base where we could park ourselves and read or play Farkel when we were not roaming the ship or up on the observation deck. We watched as the northern tip of Cape Breton Island gradually faded to a dark figure, and then moved out of view completely. Now it was just us and the Atlantic, though if we squinted, we could see a fuzzy rock silhouetted in the distance ahead. I was slightly disappointed not to see more marine wildlife, but it was exciting to be at sea nonetheless.* As I have pondered many times before, I can not imagine how people have had the guts to cross the entire Atlantic for centuries. These people are my ancestors, and they were tougher than I am. If it had been up to me, we would all still be struggling around various European countries.

We were about four hours into the voyage, and the

---

* unless you count the dead whale carcass that forced us to lightly modify our course fruit cups and sunflower seeds we had nibbled earlier had expired. As part of the one-day cruise experience, we thought we would splurge and have dinner in the boat's restaurant. After all, options would be limited when we pulled into port around 9:00pm. Alas, this did not pan out. Without warning, the ship's kitchen closed halfway through the trip. Despite the fact that we had left hours later than anticipated, the restaurant staff evidently kept their hours religiously, even if that meant turning away three hours' worth of hungry customers. "Looks like potato chips from the vending machine..." said Senator as he read the restaurant's 'CLOSED' sign. Nearby, a group of senior citizen ladies were quite upset. We were not as upset, but we were as hungry, and he wasn't kidding about the potato chips.

"Good thing I still have this bag of Loonies and Toonies," I offered. Eight Canadian dollars later, we had consumed enough potatoes, salt, and grease to tide us over for a few more hours, complimented by the ubiquitous Canadian coffee brand Van Houtte.[*]

Back in our seats, we awaited the last leg of our arrival into port. Ahead we could see the rugged green-topped rock cliffs and mounds forming the coastline. A light fog permeated one side, but we could still see the colorful, boxy homes that dotted the shore in seemingly random patterns. Reds, blues, yellows, greens, and other

---

[*] Most carry-out coffee is mediocre. Van Houtte's is just bad, yet it was the only kind of java available for much of our trip. They must have massive coast-to-coast contracts. "More Van Suck coffee here," became Senator's familiar pronouncement upon returning from many a gas station or coffee shop.

hues were finished in white trim. All appeared neatly kept, and none were ostentatious. In other places, thousands of miles away, waterfront property like this would have only supported mansions. Here, the land, the sea, and the life belonged to the people. This was Newfie country.

We disembarked via a maze of chaotic instructions and more waiting. At least I had had the forethought to book a room in the same town as the ferry landing. Otherwise we would have had a two-and-a-half hour drive to the next town of any size. That's two-and-a-half hours, mostly in the dark, likely dodging the moose, whose concentrated numbers in Newfoundland were famous. *No thanks*. We were pleased to again be less than a mile away from where we were staying. In fact, the ship was the biggest object in view out of our bedroom window.

By the time we checked in and settled our gear, it was 10:00pm. Fortunately and surprisingly, there was a pizza place open just two blocks down the road. Even better, their self-reported claim to fame was a seasoned crust. We chose pesto, and sat at a table while we waited. The dining room was almost empty, but we had plans for another impromptu car picnic, parked in view of the choppy black sea.

Soon the box arrived, and we took it out to the car. The adjacent parking lot provided dinner with a view, and I again employed the emergency picnic kit while Senator bent the box lid around, forming a dashboard platter. The first thing we noticed was that there was no pesto anywhere on said pizza. Whatever; there was also no meat, so we were still in the running. The second thing we noticed was that the sauce, which was ample compared to the scant cheese, was more of a watered-down ketchupy stew than tomato sauce. Absent were the beloved garlic and oregano flavors we Chicagoans love. Then it dawned on us. We were not just far from Chicago; we were far from the mainland. Though there are farms in Newfoundland, they are not prominent, and one does not see gangs of grazing dairy cattle or miles of tomato vines. Thankful for a meal nonetheless, we filled ourselves. Back at the room we pulled the shade to block out the ferry's lights, took hot showers, set the alarm, and promptly collapsed-- until the ship's blaring horn almost scared the Van Suck out of us at 1:00am. "Good night... again."

*   *   *

Sunday morning I awoke at 5:30am. For those of you keeping score at home, that's 3:00am Chicago time. This is not who I am, but a combination of Senator's congested snoring and a subconscious excitement that I had actually reached Newfoundland pushed me out of bed. It was a misty, overcast day, which looked beautiful against the coast, but I was hoping the weather would cooperate enough to get some hiking in.

We got ready and gathered our things, shuffling past a few other guests in the kitchen on our way out to the car. We figured we would pack our gear and then go back in for a bite while checking out. Oddly, our host was nowhere to be seen. Another couple explained that it was self-serve, but looking in the refrigerator yielded no viable options. Grabbing a quick cup of coffee was not possible either, as the pot was empty. We were not about to waste time making coffee or waiting around for an absent owner, so we set the room key on the counter and left. We would see her in a few days anyway, as I had booked the same place for our last night before leaving on the ferry.

Fortunately, there was a Subway (and plenty of Van Suck coffee) right up the road to fuel us as we began the three hour drive north. A mostly empty highway that is situated between the Long Range Mountains and the ocean is a supremely enjoyable drive, especially when the prospect of seeing moose looms. At least, I assume there were moose in the area. Actually the digital construction sign warned us to "Watch for Mouse", so perhaps I should have been on the lookout for giant rodents.[*]

Local radio had now become our tradition, and we learned a few things during our northward journey on The Rock.[†] First of all, fishing is everything in Newfoundland. Geographically this makes sense, and we had assumed as much. Historically and politically, we would later learn just how crucial this was. As the fishing reports continued, we also learned a few acceptable ways in which to pronounce Newfoundland, none of which Americans use. I had been informed by reliable sources prior to our trip that we should not say "NEW-fund-lund", as I had always heard it pronounced. Actual pronunciation, however, varied. It seemed that "NEW-FOUND-LAND", "new-FUND-lind", and "new-found-LAND" were all acceptable in appropriate context, with the last one used most often. We also detected a unique accent that I could attempt to describe as an Irish-Canadian-Elvish hybrid.

The whole route was a scenic wonder. Glimpses of the ocean showed deep blue and white caps spilling in at

---

[*] or perhaps some Rats Of Unusual Size?
[†] nickname for Newfoundland

predictable intervals. The mountains to the east were a solid dark brown spine that gradually grew in altitude while remaining low enough to make reaching peaks believable. Some of the foreground was forested with birch and maple, but most was meadow. When I say meadow, I do not just mean lush, uncut grasses; the ground was continuously carpeted with a rainbow bouquet. I have never seen such thick, vibrant wildflowers. The prairie certainly had nothing on this. At least a dozen shapes and colors were present. I thought perhaps this was just an especially fertile area, but everywhere we went on the island over the next several days was the same. I was continually in awe of God's palette.

In spite of the warnings, we saw no mouse or moose or mice or meese. For at least fifteen minutes of the drive, we were between continuous rows of metal fencing on both sides of the highway. Apparently there was wildlife that frolicked in the vicinity, but it was hiding from us. Same old story. On the other hand, maybe it was all part of an elaborate hoax. If so, the locals had certainly spent plenty to carry it out.

By late morning we found ourselves at Gros Morne National Park, scenic jewel of Newfoundland. To warm up and delve into the scene, we took the first trail we came to. Southeast Brook Falls was a short, easy walk to a mild waterfall that slipped gently over broad rocks. It was pleasant, but we were eager to get to more interesting trails. Before doing so, however, we sprayed up in self-defense; there had been a disappointing amount of buzzing that was too close for comfort.

On toward the Mattie Mitchell trail we drove.

Basically, we were working our way from the southern outskirts up to the main part of the park. We parked the car, noting we were the only ones who had bothered to pull off the road there. Usually that meant the trail was decidedly lame or spectacularly isolated. In this case, it was neither; it was just too short for most people to bother with. We were not getting back to Gros Morne anytime soon, so we took a few minutes to educate ourselves. The path was overgrown, but we easily marched along it until we found the interpretive sign. Mattie Mitchell, we learned, was somewhat of a local legend. This trapper and hunter knew the region's rocks, meadows, and forests inside and out, and served many a client as a guide. Soldiers found his services invaluable while on leave and looking for some adventure. No doubt he helped them locate the nearest Tim Horton's.[*]

    Down the road from the Mitchell trail was the visitor center. The timing was convenient as we were ready for a pit stop, and I was interested in learning more about the region's history and geology. Neither of these events occurred, however, due to a power outage, the blame for which Senator placed squarely on the shoulders of Canada's leftist prime minister. The park rangers stood behind the desk apologetically, offering maps and faking guesses as to when the power would be back on.

    As long as we were ahead of schedule, we decided to

---

[*] Tim Horton's restaurants are everywhere in Canada. I would fully expect to find them above the Arctic Circle. I do not know who Tim Horton is, but based on how many times we saw his name plastered across signs and advertisements, I assume he must be Emperor of Canada by now.

check out the man-made highlight of Gros Morne National Park-- Lobster Cove Head Lighthouse. Perfectly situated atop a rocky crag, on a point that broke the shoreline into two distinct curves, sat Lobster Cove Head Lighthouse. It was carpeted with a dense field of wildflowers, making it as poignant and picturesque as the lighthouses that make it onto wall calendars. In fact, it was great enough to be July, (which everyone knows is the best lighthouse photo month).

We wandered the grounds, surveying as much of the 360° as we could. I noticed two more of the trademark oversized red chairs on the embankment. As I craned my neck to see the light, Senator discovered a narrow path that led down to the beach. When we followed it, we could see the town in which we would be staying across the small harbor. Everywhere there was rock, ranging from chunky boulders to flat, angled slats that would have made perfect stepping stone pavers.

As we reached the top again, Senator noticed a sign written in chalk, inviting the public to a talk at the lighthouse. Looking toward the lighthouse, we saw a group of about a dozen visitors intently listening to a friendly and enthusiastic redhead. Intrigued, we slid our way into the back row to see what she had to say. As with other similar talks, she discussed the history of the lighthouse and details of family life when one's dad is a light tender. Lobster Cove Head lighthouse ran along in the manner she described until the Coast Guard took it over in the 1970s. Ever diligent, when the last keeper left the light and moved to a house in town across the harbor, he was known to critique the job the Coast Guard was doing, maintaining that he had been much better at it. He may have been accurate, since no horn was currently blowing, despite a heavy wall of fog swirling in from the sea.

Moreso than the facts about the lighthouse, I was paying attention to the woman's dialect. She was certainly educated, but she used what we would immediately notice as a lot of bad grammar. This was our first encounter with Newfie-speak. One key element is that verb singulars and plurals are usually reversed. Examples would include, "They has come from a great distance," and "When she have taken the ferry..." The spoken pitch is usually higher as well, like an animated Irisher telling a merry tale at a pub. Red hair, distinctly round faces, and a mischievous squint complete the delivery.

Since there was plenty of daylight left, we chose to drive the forty-five minutes around the coast to a more remote area of the park. When we were listening to fellow guests at the inn where we stayed before crossing to Newfoundland, the one trail that we were told we *must* take was the Tablelands trail. I had planned to do this anyway, drawn by reviews and its unique geological content. When I described it to Senator, he gave the enthusiastic thumbs up.

The Tablelands look like a desert that got lost. The terrain is composed of brownish crumbly rock, and not much else. There are no plants, giving it a sort of moonscape. Like the desert, a wild, dry wind whips through, strongly pushing against he or she who traverses it. Unlike the desert, on the opposite horizon the mountains are verdant, fully of life, including-- they assure us-- moose. It fools the senses, especially since the breeze is very cool and refreshing. The odd combination occurs because the Tablelands are not a traditional desert, as in the American Southwest. Rather, they are a section of Earth's mantle that has been pushed up through the surface to form a plateau. This meant that we had walked on the newest land on Earth in Hawaii, the oldest land on Earth in Montana, and the deepest land on Earth in Newfoundland. I felt proud that all three were on my home continent, though I could hardly take credit for any of them.

Though the trail was only two miles in, on fairly level ground, the wind continued to increase the workout. When we reached the end, there was a small waterfall, creating a stream that cut through the middle of the nothingness. The water source must have come from snow on the mountain peaks; we could see one last shadowed field of white holding out, though it was mid-summer. Plenty of people had taken the trail along with us, and a geology class or some young scientists were using a variety of electronic gear to track wind and rock data.

Though I called it the "end of the trail", there was really not much to distinguish it as a termination point, save for a boardwalk platform that dead-ended. Beyond the end, a kid continued to explore. He was about eight or nine, still in view of parents, and no one had attempted to stop him, so we did the same, grabbing another photo. Senator looked enraptured, spreading his arms out to feel the full force of the dry breeze. I paused a minute to take in the moon, which looked big as it was situated between two peaks.

It was time to drive to the little town of Rocky Harbour to find our room. We were looking forward to actually staying two nights in a row at the same place, since it was the only time during this highly nomadic trip that that would happen. While the views were gorgeous, it was important to keep one's eyes on the road. No, the moose were not showing their long faces; there was a significant section of the national park where the middle stripe had worn off the road. This was tricky considering there were two opposing lanes.

We checked in to a very homey, quiet room. The stop was brief, though, because we were in need of some dinner. Senator had long since burned off his light breakfast, and the fruit I ate that morning had also expired. Without many options, Earl's looked as good as anywhere else, and they had a line, which we took as a positive omen. It looked like there would be a wait for a table, but we were alongside the ocean on a beautiful night, so it would not be like waiting on a street in a city.

"Yeah, looks like they're taking names for a wait list," said Senator, overhearing a family give their name to a girl behind a counter.

"That's no big deal, but we should probably decide between us, before we go up there, how long we're willing to wait," I responded, as if we had a Plan B.

"Good idea," agreed Senator. "How about twenty minutes?"

"Yeah, that's just what I was thinking."

In unison, we approached the hostess. "Hi, can you tell me about how long the wait for a table is?" asked Senator.

"About thirty minutes," she answered.

"Okay, we'll take it," he said, as we both nodded,

laughing internally at the unspoken unanimous decision to scrap our maximum wait.

Earl's was known and revered for its excellent mooseburgers and seafood, neither of which would work for us. Pizza #3 it was. Between the laundromat fiasco and the late ferry arrival, we were becoming quite adept at scouting out pizza as a last resort. Because we were ravenous after the forty-minute wait for our table, I also ordered some onion rings to munch on until the pizza came.

If we did not realize it before, we were soon assured that no one was getting out of Earl's quickly. Twenty minutes into our wait, a bus boy came over to inform us that the kitchen was out of onion rings. *Oh boy*, I thought. *This is going to be awhile.* "Could we get an order of fried mushrooms instead?" I blurted out, remembering that they were also on the menu, which now seemed like a short story I had read long ago. He nodded pleasantly and trotted back to the kitchen.

As we waited, Senator unwrapped a new cd he had purchased in the adjacent gift shop during the first phase of our wait. It had been a difficult decision; there was an entire wall devoted to local folk singers performing such regional hits as "Moose Hunt" and "Thank God We're Surrounded by Water". Though we laughed at it, it was also another clue to the tight, interdependent nature of the island. Could a local, live folk scene of jigs and ballads be supported in such a small population at home? We doubted it.

Our thoughts turned to food as our server brought out what looked like a soup cup. I wondered if we were about to accidentally get some clam chowder. As she set down the cup, she announced that our mushrooms were ready. We both looked into the cup, and then at each other. We might have looked at our server, but she was already happily serving another table, who had probably been there since yesterday. Actually, there was not really anything we could have asked her without feeling stupid. After all, I had ordered "fried mushrooms", and the feeble, brown, slimy pieces in the bowl were indeed mushrooms that had been fried. "I guess they don't bread 'em here," observed Senator, "or use whole mushrooms."

"Live and learn..."

When our pizza arrived, we judged it as decent, if oddly oval. At least we knew it had not come from a grocery store freezer. It sure beat the stew-sauce they were using on Pizza #2 in Port-aux-Basques. We devoured it, probably raising curiosity in onlookers who wondered how anyone could pass up the province's best mooseburgers.

Our server came back a while later to check in on the vegetarians. Since we had her attention, I thought I'd get a little more education, and perhaps some dessert. During our trip, we had seen and heard several references to partridge berries and bakeapples, two fruits that were native to the area and treasured among Newfoundlanders. Remembering our pleasure the previous summer at discovering how delicious huckleberries were, I asked her for a description.

She frowned in thought, looking as though I had truly stumped her, or perhaps that she could not believe someone had lived to my ripe old age without having sampled either. "How would I describe them?" she started, truly puzzled.

"Yeah-ss,[*] what would you compare them to? Are they sweet? Or more tart?..."

"Well," she began again, "partridge berries just have their own taste-- a little like a cranberry, but not really..." *So much for partridge berries.* She continued, "...And bakeapples are..." I was waiting for her to describe something like a bite of homemade apple pie that grew on a bush. "...just bakeapples. You can't describe the taste."

Thank you for enlightening us. It was now after 9:00pm. "Oh, before you go, can we please have our bill?" I asked, deciding that dessert would be too complicated and probably take too long.

"Just tell her you were at Table 8," she instructed, with a light wave of her hand to indicate the girl over at the register.

I remembered the girl; she was the one who had started our adventure at Earl's by luring us in with her deceptive talk of a thirty-minute wait. We did as we were told, but the girl held two different bills in her hands, each for Table 8. Recognizing our order, I pointed to the one that was ours, mentally noting that it was about half as much as the other Table 8 bill. "Okay," she said with a shrug, not bothering to investigate my claim, and processed my payment. I guess a lot of people are more trusting than I

---

[*] I attempted a correction to "Yes", trying to repent of my Midwestern slang. While in Newfoundland, I also realized other aspects of our dialect that did not translate. For instance, when a server or retail worker asks me if I need anything, I tend to respond by saying brightly, "I'm good!" That does not answer their question, and the askers must think me vain to be enthusiastically complimenting myself.

am.

Everything in the town more or less hugged the two-mile curve around the harbor. Our inn sat in the middle of the curve, so we stopped in a junk shop on the way back to our room. As we wandered through it, local music played, charming the residents and ensnaring the tourists. I am happy to report that the genre of sea shanty is alive and well, as evidenced by one that caught our ears. "JACK is every inch a saiiiii-lor; FIVE and twenty years a whaaaaa-ler..."

Throughout the region, each town somehow supported several of what I dubbed the 'three-pronged-businesses'. A small establishment would advertise that they were a café, with lodging. Inside were a handful of tables. Upstairs one could find two or three rooms, most likely fully booked during summer. In another section of the same building, the owners would run a gift or craft shop. Sometimes these sold quality, locally sewn clothing, but more often they typically contained items with Newfie sayings or moose jokes. The microbrewery craze has also found its way to Newfoundland. One can purchase overpriced beer that claims to be made with 20,000-year old iceberg water, offering some silver lining to hipsters alarmed by global warming.

Speaking of water, back at our room I noticed that the tap water had a slight golden tint to it. Senator had already drunk a glass and declared it delicious. I chose to finish some leftover bottled water, just in case. Since our internet search yielded no stories of contaminated water in the area, I assume he probably ingested some local minerals. At least, that's what I am going with.

The only thing left to do was to scroll through the channels until we were tired enough to doze off. Our sleep was more screwed up than it had ever been on a vacation, but we kept making the most of each day. Just as we were considering calling it a night, all of the channels underwent a bizarre change. Anything on the picture that was white or light turned to blue. Suddenly all Caucasians were Smurfs, which naturally led me to wonder: would we have even noticed, had we been watching a performance of Blue Man Group?

*   *   *

Monday morning required two snooze alarms to get going, but any more were out of the question. We had a big day ahead that included another boat ride. This time we were not in search of sea life; we had reservations to cruise around the park's most scenic area. Since late winter I had been anticipating our boat ride on the Western Brook Pond.[*]

A few doors down from our inn was the Treasure Box. Like so many other places, it claimed to be a café in addition to its other offerings. We pulled into the gravel lot and tried to inconspicuously peer inside to see if it looked promising. Before we could assess it, the round-faced smiling owner put out his cigarette and welcomed us to come in with him.

The three of us walked in together, and he instructed us to help ourselves to coffee and sit anywhere. The colorful dining area had four tables and plenty of charm. We found menus at our chosen seats and took a minute to browse. "Hey, they have partridge berry pancakes!" I exclaimed. "I know what I'm having," I announced, eager

---
[*] In Newfoundland, all lakes are called ponds, regardless of size.

to try the new, supposedly indescribable fruit.*

The owner came over to take our order, pleased at my enthusiasm, and happy to chat with anyone who wandered in. Through our conversation, he immediately detected that we were foreigners, and like others we encountered, he was tickled that we had traveled so far to visit Newfoundland. Coincidentally, he had also spent some time working just two hours south of where we live. I did not expect to hear that; he seemed like someone who never would have had any interest in leaving the island.

He interrupted himself at one point to welcome a couple who had come in and were eyeing the muffins in the bakery case. "Here fer muffins 'n' coffee?" he asked them, not really waiting for an answer before getting back to whatever bits of wisdom he was offering us. A moment later he was darting to the kitchen to bring out someone's order. After he served them, his attention turned back to the couple waiting by the bakery case. "Oh, so you were serious aboot da' muffins, eh?" They grinned, knowing that he would have come to assist them sooner or later. This guy was truly a character and local star-- even if it was in a tiny town.

The morning started off foggy, but it mostly burned off during our half-hour drive to the trailhead for our boat ride. We saw no moose on our commute, even though time of day and conditions were ideal. Reaching the parking lot, we saw on the notice board that our tour was running on schedule, so we grabbed our gear and started along the

---

* While my pancakes were small, they were delicious. For the record, I would describe a partridge berry as a sweeter version of a cranberry.

forty-five minute walk to the boat ramp. It took us through pine forests, along masses of wildflowers, and on a boardwalk over a large bog, where we at least saw moose tracks, but still no moose. Finally we could see the cliffs of Western Brook Pond emerge, like a painted backdrop in a movie. Though Western Brook Pond is known as a fjord, it cannot technically be called one, since it is fresh water. True fjords are inlets from the sea, and therefore salty.

It continued to get sunnier as we approached. When we reached the boat launch complex, I got in line to confirm our reservation. With tickets in hand, we secured our place near the front of the line, determined to get a seat on the open top deck. As we waited, we talked with a couple from Ontario. They asked us about Chicago, and we promptly told them to avoid it if at all possible. We asked them about where they had been, and what they had done in Gros Morne. Their activities included dinner at a very slow (but good) restaurant. We all had a good laugh when we realized they had been at Earl's' the night before, too.

On the upper level of the boat, two extremely friendly Newfoundlanders were ready to assist us to our seats and start the narration. It was clear that they loved their job and were proud to show off their region. The boat bobbed slightly as more passengers shifted the weight while finding their seats. One of the guides wobbled. "Jingles!"[*] he exclaimed. "I has to get me sea legs!" We have now been to all fifty states and all ten provinces, and Senator and I agree that as a group, no one is happier than the people of Newfoundland. It probably comes from

---

[*] We heard this expression a few times while in Newfoundland. The best translation to American English is "Gee!"

having a short summer.

The boat ride was about an hour from the dock to the far end of the narrow body of water. The temperature was in the low 70s, but the sun was unbelievably hot as it shone down on us from a near-cloudless sky. I used the sweater I had brought for shade instead of warmth. As we floated along, 2,000-foot cliffs formed walls on either side of our watery hall. Most had very green tops and jagged sides, reminding me of pictures of Scandinavia. Long, thin waterfalls poured down some of the rocks, and a few pockets of snow remained. Still, the sun was relentless.

The most dramatic view in the park was near the end of our outbound ride. We sat back and enjoyed the scenic panorama, and then turned the boat around to begin our ride back. Suddenly we underwent the most extreme climate shift we had ever experienced. In the same location, just spun around 180°, a very cool wind now rushed at us. The temperature instantly dropped about fifteen degrees. That, combined with the quickly vanishing sun, had everyone bringing out jackets, or wishing they had thought to pack them. I resisted putting mine on until I was literally shivering, and I loved it.

Just ten or twelve minutes later, the fog had not only rolled in, but it had completely enveloped us. All visibility was gone, so it was fortunate that we had already witnessed all of the grand scenery. It was solid gray in all directions. We could have been 100 miles out into the northern Atlantic. The crew must have been reading my mind; they cranked the speakers to play some local sea shanties. We perked up when we heard our new favorite, Jack the Sailor. The whole scene could not have been better if it had been staged.

Due to the change in weather, the tour after ours was canceled. I was so glad I had chosen the time slot I did. As we walked back along the trail toward the parking lot, we saw many disappointed and some annoyed people marching their way back out. They had apparently not read the cancellation sign at the beginning of the trail, or had arrived before the cancellation was decided. We thought it best not to discuss what a wonderful time we had until we were alone in the car.

We continued to walk back, noting the ever-present lack of moose. Then I smelled something awful. "Moose droppings?" asked Senator.

"No, this is something different. I smelled it on the way in. It's kind of like that gross sour smell from a dish rag that's been left damp too long. I think it's actually from some plants, or maybe a chemical reaction from something decaying in the marsh."

Near the parking lot, we stopped at a bathroom. I do not include this detail for personal reasons, Reader. I only add it to note that Newfoundland, though magical in many ways, loses big points for restroom accessibility. The flusher in this particular bathroom was not working, and you can imagine the resulting issues. The day before, we had encountered another bathroom that was out of order, and yet another one that was closed. Senator half-jokingly blamed Trudeau. I concurred.

Since we were already at the north end of the park, we drove to the trailhead for Steve's Trail. I do not know who Steve was or is, but he had a determined collection of flies who continued to buzz us until we doused ourselves in a cocktail of natural and deetful bug spray.* Not having the convenient anatomy of a male, I still needed a bathroom. We found an outhouse by the parking lot, but the door did not close all the way. As Senator stood guard, I peed with a view of the trail, which fortunately had no one walking it at the moment.

The trail took us down to some pines and through an open, sloping meadow. On the way, we met a worker using a weed whacker, because not enough people had come through. The path culminated in a secluded fisherman's cove. It appeared to be a well-kept secret, perhaps due to the good fishing. We were still baffled as to why more people were not taking advantage of the Canada 150 celebration. We weren't complaining.

After leaving Steve's Trail, our stomachs spoke up to remind us that we were hungry. We had walked five miles, and it had been about seven hours since we last ate. It was time to look for fuel, for us and the car. We drove south out of the park back to Rocky Harbour, the booming metropolis of a few hundred people.

Café #1 was no longer in existence, but they must have decided that since the "LODGING" and "GIFT SHOP" portions were still valid, there was no need to destroy a perfectly good sign. Two out of three ain't bad. Café #2 offered a single vegetarian option-- a cold cheese and pear sandwich. I tried to picture it, but it sounded too

---

* Oh yes, there was a time when we strictly adhered to all natural bug repellents. Miles of hiking and many seasons outdoors have convinced us that such remedies only work against organic bugs, the hippies of the insect world, who are usually too lazy or too vegetarian to bite anyway.

unappealingly weird for the expensive price they listed.

The next strategy was to drive down to Rocky Harbour's sister town, Norris Point. We did not mind; it gave us an excuse to bum around some more of the beautiful coastal inlets. Unfortunately, two more cafés were crossed off the list. One offered mozzarella sticks as the only meatless dish, but we reasoned that a plate of fried junk food probably was not the best choice. Then there was the fourth place, which was a simple pub with a very nice view, but the kitchen was closed on Mondays. It also goes without saying that no Subway or fast food chain had made it to the region, which was not a bad thing-- just a hungry thing.

Lack of food notwithstanding, the trip to Norris Point was not in vain. Throughout the drive, we saw the strangest fog I have ever seen. There was not just a single morning burn-off like at home. Instead, there was extremely bright sun the entire day, with regular cycles of thick fog and clear skies.

We also came across an abandoned amusement park. This overgrown, derelict gem was too good to pass up, so we pulled the car into a random spot in the meadow and got out. The door to the game room was locked, and by the looks of it, had been so for years. The highlight of the property was a dry water (now dust) slide that landed ghostly occupants in a thick field of wildflowers. There we sat for several minutes, picturing what it must have been like in its heyday, and wondering why it had closed.

It was midafternoon. We had been having fun, but we did not want to waste anymore time, so we decided to head back to the Treasure Box, where we had eaten that morning. They did have a veggie wrap, so that would work. On thing we learned was that, due to the physical geography of the island, vegetables were not abundant, and therefore, more expensive than meat. Our wraps were small, but that gave me an excuse to try the other mystery fruit. I ordered a mini bakeapple tart, and waited to be introduced to a new taste sensation.

A short time after finishing my wrap, my tiny tart arrived. The fruit looked like a yellow raspberry, and I was about to dig in. I first inhaled the scent. Then I sniffed my fork. Then I sniffed myself, confused. "I know that smell... and it's not good," I told Senator. My brain processed further, and I put it together. I recognized the smell from the morning. When I had thought it reeked like damp dish rags, I had been smelling bakeapples on the bog trail. The tart was subsequently wasted, leaving me feeling guilty again.

The last trail that we planned to tackle at Gros Morne National Park was the Berry Hill Trail. I had hoped to find wild berries (except for bakeapples), and consequently, the type of wildlife that hunts for berries. Up we climbed, spiraling the large hill and taking advantage of the great views in all directions. Forest and lush ferns covered all sides. As for the animal life, our total count stood at one squirrel, two toads, and a mouse. Maybe there was something to that warning about watching for "mouse" after all.[*]

There were just a few hours of recreational time left

---

[*] According to multiple sources, Newfoundland has more moose per square mile than anywhere else on Earth. That means they had to work extra hard to avoid us, which they all successfully did.

at Gros Morne, so it was an easy decision to spend them at the lighthouse. No one was around as we walked down the wooden stairs to the beach. The fog was rolling in quickly once more. This time it looked like it was in for the night. Together we watched silently as it swallowed Rocky Harbour, like an amorphous creature in a low budget horror film. If it was such a movie, we would have been the teenagers who never had a chance. We couldn't help but notice that the light was still off, and the fog horn never did sound. Never should have let the old keeper go...

The late lunch was holding us enough to make dinner unnecessary, but it sounded like a good night to try some dessert. It was only in the mid-60s, but it felt much warmer, rendering it a perfect scene for a partridge berry sundae. "That's not the dish rag one, right?" confirmed Senator.

"No, that's the burgundy sort-of-cranberry one," I assured him. We took our sundaes across the road to park by the harbor. As we ate, we watched two men pulling a rowboat in with a rope They were parked along the "Drive at your own risk" pier road jutting across the water for a few hundred feet. Soon a truck pulled up behind them, and another man got out. Then another parked behind him, and two teenage boys got out. We craned our necks to see if there was a problem. Were they stuck or stalled? Did they need help? No, it was just locals stopping to chat and shoot the breeze, not worrying that they were all parked on a single-car width road.

It was only a mile or so back to our room, and we were glad not to have to drive far. It did not take us long to get cleaned up and ready for bed. I knew we would fall asleep quickly, but I put the t.v. on for a few minutes anyway. Who knows when we'll get the chance to see blue people again?

*   *   *

Tuesday morning was a rough start. We had both had a very bad night sleep-wise. Various factors led to interrupted breathing on Senator's part. That led to me waking up to make sure he wasn't suffocating, which in turn led to me waking him up to try to reposition him. It was a vicious cycle that led to a grand total of about four hours of nonconsecutive sleep. *Oh well, on with the day.*

We had originally planned to drive up the peninsula to Port-aux-Choix, but there really was not time. Plus, there was nothing there that we had not already witnessed scenery-wise. If we wanted to truly do it properly, we would need a full week. If we ever get back to Newfoundland, we will go to L'Anse aux Meadows (an original Viking settlement) and then cut over to see some icebergs. In the meantime, we would have to settle for a provincial park instead. It was just twenty miles out of our way back to the Port-aux-Basques ferry, so it would fit in easily.

The morning had some fog, but it was moving out quickly. Unlike Monday, it did not show signs of returning. It was sunny and already heating up. It was not the weather people generally picture when they think of the North Atlantic. The warm, dry breezes again reminded us of the desert in spring.

On our way to the provincial park, we stopped at a truck stop for a late breakfast. The food was bland, but there was always vinegar present as the go-to condiment on restaurant tables. Donair* sauce was also a staple, though for the life of me I can't think why. Yet, the good citizens of the Maritime provinces love the stuff. I think if they had been with the Israelites when the manna rained down, there would have been at least a few Newfies who looked around and asked with a grin, "Yah, but wuln't it be better if God have spread some donair on 't? Jingles, that'd be great!"† In keeping with another local tradition, the women's bathroom was, of course, closed for cleaning.

The last half of the drive to Squires Memorial Provincial Park was on a gravel road. Though this is never ideal, what else did we have to do? There was nothing else on the agenda for the day. As the mercury climbed to over 90°F, the tires kicked up a long, trailing dust cloud. Our car now looked like Charlie Brown's friend, Pig Pen, as we rolled along the countryside.

Soon we arrived at Squires Memorial Provincial Park.‡ Though we attempted to be good U.S. ambassadors by paying our entrance fee, there was no one at the booth, and no box in which to leave cash. From what we could see, there were only a few cars in the entire park, so we found the trailhead to the waterfall and got out. The sun was still hot, but there was immediate relief along the shaded path through the forest.

The short walk ended at the bottom of a wooden staircase. Stepping off of the stairs led us onto wide,

---

* disgusting white gloppy, dairy or mayonnaisy concoction with sugar and vinegar
† We have, since our adventure in Newfoundland, fondly named our G.P.S. unit 'Jingles'. We have referred to her by that name ever since.
‡ named for a beneficial but later disgraced politician

rounded rocks, which dropped off into relatively shallow rapids. Spanning the river was a wide waterfall of about ten feet. As the sun hit the riotous water, it looked like cola-- dark brown but clear, with foaming bubbles where the cascade struck the rocks below. Senator scoped the area for a good spot to take a picture. While he was concentrating on foregrounds and backgrounds, I was just watching the water.

Then I saw one. SPLASH! I think I did, anyway. I watched the same place for a few more seconds. Then another black streak slapped into the rushing water. I had seen nature programs about salmon swimming upstream to spawn, but until you have personally witnessed them jumping, flopping, flinging, and hurling themselves against the current, you cannot imagine how wildly hilarious it is.

When I saw clearly what was going on, I yelled in surprise and delight. Senator looked up, halfway expecting to find me in the river. Then I pointed to a few hot spots and directed him to watch closely. Mesmerized by the fish, we watched for almost half an hour. Many were airborne, and some reached unthinkable heights for animals that are not supposed to be out of water. As we got ready to leave, three people were descending the stairway toward us. I was pleased to be able to show them the salmon. They seemed grateful, unless they had seen it a hundred times before, and were just humoring me.

We left the provincial park and made our way back to the main highway. Heading south, we stopped for gas and a cup of coffee. The wind continued to dust the road and our car. All three of us needed showers. As Senator went in to pay, I tried to clean off some of the dust from the back window, but most of the vehicle was still some shade of brown or tan.

Upon reaching Port-aux-Basques, we drove around to scope out some dinner options. We are not picky, but looking for any basic vegetarian meal was getting to be a hassle. Frankly, I was missing my own home cooking, if that's not too vain to admit. It was the one factor beckoning me homeward.

For the second time in just a few days, we checked into the same bed and breakfast. When I say "checked in", it was more like we let ourselves in through the unlocked door. I saw an older gentleman come walking into the kitchen, so I quickly defended our invasion. "Hello, we have a reservation..." I began.

"Good for you!" was his snappy but smiling response. Then I understood. "So do we!" He was not an owner, but another guest. Soon his wife joined him, explaining that they, too, had let themselves in. They had spoken to the owner on the phone, and she said she would be along soon, but that was more than an hour ago.

Since, to our great annoyance, our cell phones did not work on foreign soil, we used the owner's own house phone to call her. Senator spoke with her briefly. "What did she say?" I asked.

He shrugged. "She said she'd be here later. Then I asked her if we should just take the same room we had last time."

"What did she say to that?"

"'Sure.' She didn't really seem to care." That fit with her being nowhere in the vicinity when we had tried to check out a few days earlier. I was curious as to whether she had even bothered to charge our credit card. Hopefully not.

I had not made any specific plans for the evening, partly because I did not know how late we would be arriving, and partly because our only other activity in Newfoundland was to take the ferry out of port. We had to at least eat, though, especially considering the lack of edible options on the boat. With very low expectations at this point, we wandered into the other pizza place in town, hoping that it did not use soup for sauce or top every dinner with a plop of donair. Amazingly, we stumbled upon an excellent restaurant. The crust wasn't too thin, there was actual pizza sauce spread on top, and the veggies and cheese tasted like, well, veggies and cheese. It was even round. Jingles! I can safely declare it the best Canadian-prepared meal we have eaten. Knowing that it might be our last decent meal for a while, however, we also splurged on a box of maple cream cookies for the next day's crossing back to Nova Scotia.

As we were about to pull into the parking space at our bed and (not really) breakfast, we saw some activity in the town park, just down the street. Several vendors were set up in a row of colorful booths along the water's edge. A little further from the water was a large performance space, complete with stage and dance floor, created to look like the deck of a boat. As luck and the average Newfie would have it, a band was churning out folk favorites including, you guessed it, Jack the Sailor. By now we could sing along with the multigenerational crowd of natives, even if our looks completely stood out. As we enjoyed the impromptu concert, one friendly kid repeatedly came up to us to say hi and show us his dance moves, which were a cross between hopping, rolling, and twisting. Somehow it all worked out, giving us a perfect ending to our Newfoundland experience. Even now it seems kind of like a dream.

Back at our room we cleaned up and sat down to relax. Through reading material and piecing together themes from the lyrics of our new cd, Senator had become very interested in the history of Newfoundland, and particularly how the cod industry both made and broke them, especially when the government got involved. Ever resourceful, he had found a documentary to watch on our computer, but we both fell asleep almost instantly. We never did see our bed and breakfast host. I'm sure glad we didn't waste our evening waiting around for her.

*   *   *

No, we never did see our host, even as we prepared to leave Wednesday morning. I put a note and my contact information with the key on the counter, and left it at that.[*] Likewise, we knew better than to expect any reasonable breakfast, so we drove through our reliable Subway on the way to the ferry. Senator got an egg sandwich and some hash browns, and I grabbed a muffin.

It was a foggy morning, making the green on top of the jagged rocks even deeper. Those rocks would have been merciless on a day like today, if a ship met them in the wrong way. In the meantime, we were preparing to board our own boat. Fortunately, both it and we were running on time. The staff was well-organized, too, unlike that of the first ferry we took. It was shaping up to be a better

---

[*] Upon reviewing bills later, I saw that she did charge us the correct amount (darn!), but we never heard a word from her.

crossing.

Part of the tighter system meant receiving our boarding passes and being asked to pull in to the next line, where they would instruct us where to park. Senator was eating his hash browns and almost drove right past the next checkpoint, forgetting the extra step. This may have been strike one against us. As he stopped the car abruptly, the woman at the booth asked us if we had any plants on board. "No," answered Senator, swallowing another bite.

Then she asked if we had any potatoes aboard. I was about to tell her we did not, but Senator thought for a second and then replied, "Just these," indicating his hash browns. *Never would have thought of that.*

"You can finish those," she said, not really knowing whether or not to take him seriously. She laughed as she motioned us onward to the next station, where a security guard came to examine car. After looking at the front and back of the vehicle, he questioned the license plate. "Where's that from," he asked, pointing. *Uh-oh, strike two.* He had every right to inquire. One of the many disgraces of our home state is the tell-tale corroded and rusty metal bumps that adorn many of our plates. When we told him they were Illinois plates, he had no further questions, which, ironically, spoke volumes.

We must have been at least partially on the suspicious list, however, because the next step was opening the cooler to check for any contraband vegetation. Without explanation, we were then told to pull around to get sprayed off. "Hey, free car wash!" I said with a shrug. Though no plants or potatoes were on board (not counting those in Senator's stomach), our car had collected enough dirt to qualify as its own plant, necessitating a wash. After the impromptu car shower, we learned that a dangerous fungus or bacteria had been destroying potato crops. Newfoundland authorities were taking measures to contain it, which explained why spuds were more expensive there.

The ferry was still running on time. At the exact scheduled moment, the boat pulled away from the dock. The fog was thick, and we quickly lost sight of the rocky shore. White sky and gray-green water surrounded us. At regular intervals the fog horn reminded us we were still on a moving vessel, but otherwise, we were adrift in three dimensions. It was cold, damp, and windy-- everything a summer ferry crossing should be. Though it later turned sunny, it was still pleasant. We read, walked, talked, and played a few rounds of Farkel. When it came time to disembark, the process was easy, calm, and efficient, leading us to wonder why the boat coming over had been so different.

After we drove off the boat, we headed for Louisbourg, Nova Scotia. By 7:15pm we had checked into our hotel. It was the best room on the trip. We were right on the ocean, with a second story view of a lighthouse to the left and a view of the skyline of Fortress Louisbourg to the right. In the middle of the panorama the fog debated whether to roll in or stay put.

It was tempting to linger in the spacious suite, but it was time for the nightly ritual of hunting for dinner. We dropped our gear off and scoured the internet and local ads for somewhere to eat. Yet again, we determined that pizza was our best bet. Plus, if we took it to go, we could take advantage of the room's table by the patio doors, giving us the best seat in town. In fifteen minutes, we popped out the door and onto the main street through town.

To no one's (including you, Reader) surprise, the first plan did not work out, as the pizza place closed by 7:30pm. Two other restaurants in town closed by 8:00pm. We looked at the clock; that would not be enough time. The only other eatery served strictly seafood. It was now 8:15pm, and we were well into another low-calorie day.

Our last hope was a convenience store in the last block before we reached our hotel. "Oh happy day! They're open until the outrageous hour of 9:00pm!" I exclaimed, sarcastically and hungrily. Senator parked the car, and we descended upon the place like a couple of agents on a raid. There were only three aisles, and they were almost half empty. That did not slow us down, though. Without words we split up to divide and conquer. The cashier probably thought we were there to rob the place, but we just wanted food, and we were willing to pay the inflated rates that non-seafood commanded. In mere moments Senator scooped up the only cheese pizza in the freezer case, along with extra cheese to doctor it up. I was working the scant produce section, taking possession of the only green thing I could find-- a pepper that was definitely on its last good day. Anticipating a further lack of fruit and veggie availability the next day, we grabbed two semi-ripe bananas and added them to the pile before paying. "And thank you for staying open past 8:00pm!" I yelled to the cashier over my shoulder as we left.

Our suite had a kitchenette, complete with a stove, but there was no pan on which to place the pizza. Determined to make it work, we rooted through the drawers and cabinets to see what else we could come up with. "We could use this dish if we microwave the pizza..." I suggested. "...And here's a cutting board and knife..." In the end, our ingredients and improvisation skills combined to create a deliciously hearty pizza.

The rest of the evening was spent relishing the ocean breeze and the sunset. Just when it got dark enough to suit a romantic North Atlantic seaside mood, however, a bright security light at edge of balcony was triggered and came on automatically. It shined around the patio doors and ruined our dusky view, turning it into an annoying fluorescent wash out. We slept with the patio door open, but we pulled the curtain closed across it. Not to be cheated, at 5:00am, as soon as I subconsciously sensed that the beastly light had shut off, I got up to reopen the curtain to take advantage of a few more hours or fresh air.* The view, however, I slept through.

*   *   *

Our room by the sea included the option of purchasing two eggs and toast for breakfast for ten dollars. One could get some bacon, but no veggies were in the vicinity. Senator took them up on it, since he doesn't do well if he skips eating in the morning. I passed, wondering if I could make it until we were at least back in New

---

* The room was comfortable and had great potential, but they did not think things out intelligently in the curtain and view department. In addition to the poor balcony light planning, there was no curtain on the front door. The window only led to a stairwell, but at the right angle, one could also see up into the second floor bathroom. This did not occur to me until I was drying off after my shower, with the bathroom door open. The only thing that would have enhanced the situation was if the lighthouse beacon reached into our suite as well.

Brunswick. The waitress was surprised; it was a radical move for someone to refuse paying four times as much as a basic, bland breakfast was worth. I did not care, though, we were just a very short drive from Fortress Louisbourg, North America's largest reconstruction project.

Because breakfast was over in little more than a few bites, we arrived at Fortress Louisbourg early, providing us a great parking space and time to walk the area surrounding the visitor center. For a while we followed a sidewalk, then departed the path to cross an enclosed glen that would have been perfect for a picnic lunch. Beyond the misty glen, we crossed a road and found ourselves at the coast. We did not make it all the way to the beach, however. We were distracted by a small but stately nineteenth century graveyard. In the center of the rounded, chalky colored tablets, a life-sized crucifix rose up from the fog in silent solemnity.

The fort itself required a short bus ride, so we got in line and took one of the first shuttles to the side gate. From our vantage point, we could see that the land was almost entirely surrounded by water, and the fortress was encircled by high walls. Wildflowers grew over most of the embankments, defying the winds that seemed to come from multiple directions. Though saltwater was within view, a few fresh water ponds dotted the area. Each one was claimed by a loon who watched the new arrivals intently. As the sentry greeted us, we passed through the gate that served as our time machine. The bulk of our day would be spent in the 1700s.

Fortress Louisbourg is comprised of about thirty reproduction buildings, each of which recreates an important structure that was necessary to the daily functions of a military fort. In particular, Fortress Louisbourg stood as a stronghold in New France, giving the respective crown a point of protection, authority, and economic gain. At least, it did so until the British took it over. That seemed to be a common theme in the Maritimes.

Our first stop of the morning was the blacksmith's shop. While the morning was still cool, his fire was blazing and ready to forge. Already his long leather apron bore the marks of soot from the ironware he had been working on. We watched for a few moments, and then wandered next door.

Here was another kind of fire. The heat was lower and the products more delicate. Rows of handmade loaves rose on the flat oven surface, waiting their turn to be brought out by the large wooden paddle. Better still, since this was 'living history', the bakers were selling their wares. O happy day! I dug through my sack for a few dollars to purchase a dense, steaming loaf of the "poor soldiers' bread". In other words, we were feasting on a delicious hunk of wheat and rye blend, while those who paid a little more had to make do with the less tasty white bread. It was also probably the healthiest food we had eaten on the trip, aside from the pasta salad and fruit I had brought from home.

Making our way around the same side of the fortress, we spent ample time in the soldiers' hall. The attractive stone and red trimmed building was about a block long, with an arched passageway in the center, leading to the parade grounds. Inside, my favorite part was the ornate chapel, which outshone many modern churches.

It certainly would have been a welcome sanctuary from the rigors of military life, as well as the simple, cramped living quarters. Sleeping in shifts, sixteen men (or boys, often) shared a room about the size of an average hotel suite. Personal possessions were few, and personal privacy was nonexistent.

Outside the same immense building, it was time to watch the firearm demonstration. I was a little skeptical at first, because the costumed soldier was a young woman. As a fan of firearms myself, this is not a sexist comment; I just prefer my historical depictions to be as accurate as possible. Once she began, however, it was easy to overlook her erroneous gender in light of the wealth of information she shared. We watched as the entire process of firing a smooth-barreled period rifle was explained and performed in detail. Our soldier also expounded on all of the many things that could go wrong with the event, not including running out of time before the British approached.

After the rifle demonstration, we crossed through the passageway to the courtyard. The small parade area was sufficient for the necessary drills to prepare the soldiers. We looked on with others as the procession entered, accompanied by drums and fifes. Once in place, commands were shouted and men snapped the appropriate movements in response. The display culminated in the firing of a few cannons on the rampart walls.

After leaving the soldiers' hall, we started to explore the other half of the fortress, beginning with a farm. For any establishment to be self-sufficient, producing food was essential. What the ocean did not yield, the farm supplied. The master of the farm was not the top brass, or even the king. This yard was run by a tom turkey who flapped wildly at us, flaring his authority in no uncertain terms. I think he thought he was a rooster, but I imagined he would learn his true identity at the end of the high tourist season, which conveniently concluded right before Canadian Thanksgiving.

We continued to wander through several buildings and storehouses. In one room, a man and woman were binding books, patiently showing children how they stitched each volume. At the inn, another man entertained visitors with a hurdy-gurdy, which, like bagpipes, always lures me into its droney trance. Perhaps the best-appointed building was that of the sea merchant. Soft, cushioned chairs, a giant wardrobe, and ample curtains around the beds brought all of the creature comforts that the eighteenth century had to offer right to the middle of the military base.

The fortress was not short on innovation, either. In one kitchen, we saw a smartly designed clockwork-like mechanism used to automatically turn a spit over an open fire. In another kitchen, we saw olive oil jars hung from pegs. Their unique, conic shape allowed sediment to settle at the bottom, keeping the oil clear and pure. At the sea merchant's home, I asked about a peg board with twine. I had never seen one like it. The interpreter educated us, explaining that it was used by counting knots to track nautical miles.

Not all inventions were tangible. When it came to punishing offenders for their wrongdoing, residents of Louisbourg had taken public humiliation to an art form. In such a small community, and considering there was a good chance the alleged offender was bunking with the alleged victim, it was an effective motivator for morality. Just as importantly, the spectacle of a publicly taunted bad boy in stocks at the main crossroads offered an entertaining diversion, breaking up the monotony of life at a military fortress.

Not every event at the the crossroads involved petty crime. Senator and I decided to take up the crier on his invitation to watch the children's fairy tale skit. Not generally into kids' performances, I think we surprised ourselves when we found ourselves seated on a log bench, near the front of the action. It actually was quite funny, and the French narration was simple enough that I could understand all of it. It wasn't every day I could practice my French while watching eighteenth century children's theatre.

The last building we visited was a fisherman's house. It was set apart from the rest of the buildings, near the side gate we had entered when we first arrived. The reenactor inside gave us a brief tour of the two-room cottage, again emphasizing the importance of cod to the fortress' and region's economy. It was plentiful and profitable in the teeming coastal waters. Coupled with the high demand from Catholic France, and the ability to keep a dried cod for up to three years, it was a perfect recipe for beneficial trade.*

Senator continued to be fascinated by the history of the cod fishing industry, particularly in Newfoundland. The more he researched, the more he understood that the act of fishing was integrated with so much more than just a

---

* just add water; the original convenience food

paycheck. It was culture, tradition, adventure, social bond, and a deep connection with ancestors who had endured more than their fair share of difficulties. Towns and families triumphed when cod triumphed. That is why it was so devastating about thirty years ago when the Canadian government's interference ravaged Newfoundland's fishing industry. The excuse for limiting catches to fifteen fish per day was that the waters were overfished, but somehow many giant corporations seemed to get around the rules. Livelihoods were lost overnight, replaced with insulting $10,000 CA annual compensation payout. Even with the welfare check, the average fishing family only averages about $25,000 CA per year. For a proud and tough people who thrive on hard work and survival, forced idleness has been soul-crushing. As Senator observed, it is especially confounding when one considers how much money the government blows on endowments for the arts, bankrolling crappy bands on the the public's dime.

    It was late afternoon, and we had explored every corner of Louisbourg. Since we had plenty of summer daylight and we were still energetic, we decided to start the drive homeward. Once we were in the car, we did not want to stop for dinner, and we knew better than to think there might be any good options anyway, so we decided to eat local. Within the hour, we were pulling through a drive-through to hand a fistful of cash to Tim Horton (or one of his associates) in exchange for a mundane brown bag. "How's your sandwich?" asked Senator.

    "Well..." I chewed, swallowed hard, and wiped my lips. "I think, I'd have to say that," I began, "despite the new low at which we have set the culinary bar on this trip, that was the absolute worst grilled cheese sandwich I have ever had. And yours?..."

"Same," replied Senator flatly. "It just makes me want to drive home faster."

Several hours later, in western Nova Scotia, we stopped at a Holiday Inn. We had not made a reservation, so it was mildly overpriced. That was still preferable to driving too late and wandering through moose country in search of lodging. The price also included breakfast, which would save valuable time in the morning. I already had a feeling that we were going to drive further than I had planned the next day.

As most nights on the road end, this one concluded with just enough television to drop off before the first show finished. Before nodding out, I did pick up a few useful tips from an Alaskan survivalist. I now know that, if feeling run down while in the northern woods, I can tap the nutrient-rich sap of birch trees.[*] Then, if I have a few more hours of leisure time on my hands, I can boil down the bark to create a pitch to use as a bug repellent. *Now there's one method Senator hasn't tried yet for mosquitoes.*

*   *   *

We were still about twenty-five hours from home, but we had a full three days in which to tackle it. Though we did not discuss it, I think we both knew we would not take that long if we could help it. As there were no planned stops to see anything exciting on the way home, we were just ready for our own bed, our own bath, and definitely our own cooking. I do not mean to offend our dear neighbors to the north, but if one is not a seafood eater, the

---

[*] Pancakes, anyone?

Maritimes are no culinary paradise.

Before leaving our hotel, we claimed a table and grabbed a few items from the breakfast buffet. "Hey, I recognize them," said Senator, indicating two couples a few tables over. I looked over, surprised, wondering who he could possibly know in the middle of Nova Scotia. "They were on our ferry boat back from Newfoundland the other day."

I looked again, thinking back. *Yep, he was right.* "That's impressive!"

"The fact that we ran into them again?"

"That, but moreso that you noticed it."

"Oh, I pay attention," said Senator, narrowing his eyes and nodding his head slowly in a feign smugness.

We finished our breakfast and left our hotel. Senator had programmed our home address into the G.P.S.. Immediately Jingles directed us to take the only obvious road homeward. "I'm turning this thing off until we get lost," I decided.

"Okay, but what happens if we end up driving in the ocean again?" asked Senator, referencing Jingles' erroneous interpretation of us driving over the Confederation Bridge.

"Then we'll get even better gas mileage," I shot back, burying 'her' in the backpack.

Just before we said good-bye to Nova Scotia, we spotted a bald eagle flying a short distance from the highway. Senator and I never lose our fascination for eagles, but we did notice that those on the East Coast were a little smaller than those at home or in central Canada. About an hour later, we saw another one, this time in New Brunswick. It was as though our feathered ambassador was bidding us safe travels as we left Canada, nearing the Maine border.

As we approached the border, we encountered a little drizzle. It only lasted fifteen minutes. It reminded me how blessed we had been with easy driving weather. Out of the 7,000 miles we eventually logged during the trip, only an hour and a half of it took place in the rain. That's at least as impressive as running into people from a ferry ride hundreds of miles away.

Unfortunately, though the rain was brief, the temperature continued to climb. An hour into Maine it had reached the low 90s. We had experienced this before in Maine, but it still surprised me that it could get so hot there. The moose were having none of it as well; their record for non-appearance was intact. Traffic, however, was thickening quickly. Thankfully, most of it was on the northbound side.

We continued down I-95, through the tiny southeast corner of New Hampshire that technically allows it to claim status as a seaside state. Then we merged into the throngs of Bostonians escaping to western Massachusetts. It was Friday evening and everyone was on the move, coming or going somewhere. I have a feeling we were the only ones going to Illinois, though.

At an almost reasonable hour, we stopped and got a room for the night. There was just enough time to eat, rest a bit, and watch yet another World War II documentary that we only seem to see in hotels. Two sides were arguing about Hitler's death. One offered proof that Hitler, like many other Nazis, escaped Berlin in the last days of the Third Reich. Ah, but the opposing expert brought in a forensic dentist who said that Russian-held dental fragments exactly matched the dictator's dental records. Furthermore, a portion of the deceased's skull showed the bullet exit wound, as well as glass in the mouth, suggesting that he took a cyanide capsule. At least we would have plenty to discuss on the way home.

*   *   *

Saturday morning we packed up the few items we had taken into the hotel and started out westward on the Massachusetts Turnpike. Generally when traveling on the toll roads, drivers have the option of slowing down and going through the toll booths or speeding right on through the EZ Pass lane, where spy cameras read their devices and charge the drivers' accounts automatically. We, not having need of an EZ Pass at home, opt for the old-fashioned, people-monitored lanes.* In Massachusetts, however, we encountered an unfamiliar sign. It proudly announced the state's "Electronic Tolling" and informed us that we would be billed by mail, compliments of their license plate-reading machines. "Well," I said, "Apparently we can expect a bill for a few bucks. That, of course, is assuming they can read our mostly-corroded, barely decipherable license plate, whose state name is positioned conveniently so it sits halfway covered by the license plate surround."

"Hhmmm..." pondered Senator.

"Either that, or they arrest us at the state line," I theorized.†

---

*   I like to believe we are keeping people in jobs, particularly when I pay in mass quantities of pennies, nickels, and dimes.

†   As of writing this book, we have never heard any more about our debt to the great state of Massachusetts. As we are slated to travel

We drove on, crossing into New York. At one point traffic slowed to a crawl. As we inched our way past the emergency crew, it became apparent that we had happened upon a recent accident. I looked around for a vehicle but saw none. Perhaps it was in the ditch along the road? Nope. "Hey, look!" I said, louder than necessary. About one and a half stories up, in a tree, was a car. It had run up with enough force to bow the trunk over. I wondered what in the world had led to that turn (no pun intended) of events, as I thought a silent prayer.

Passing the accident, we cruised on across the state, taking advantage of the unspoken rule to speed. Then came the familiar little slice of Pennsylvania-- this year without a blizzard. Ohio, on the other hand, offered plenty of time for conversation, or, in our case, an impromptu verbal award ceremony. The theme of the awards revolved around food we had consumed during the trip. Because I know the suspense is killing you, a list of the winners has been provided in Appendix A.

It was probably not long after the awards ceremony that I realized we were going all the way home that night. There would be no more stops. As long as we were awake enough, that was fine by me. Saving a night's hotel bill would also help, as we were cutting things very close on the budget.

Only another six hours lay between us and our cozy, comfortable abode. Western Ohio was boring, as was most of Indiana, until a crop duster came into view. Up he swept, over he swooped, and down he dove. Each time he flew

---

through the state again next summer, we will find out just how serious electronic tolling is taken.

out of our line of sight, I was sure he would crash. It was unnerving and a little dizzying to watch him. Fortunately he did not release any chemicals on us. That would not have been a pleasant homecoming.

Neither was the Illinois traffic. At 10:30 at night, every lane on I-80/90 was solid, going either direction. People were driving like idiots, and several times Senator was forced to swerve or hit the brakes to prevent an accident. "Ya' know what I think?" I asked Senator, once things had eased up.

"No, what?"

"I think that we owe it to ourselves to never drive on this stretch of highway again. If we only pass through this way on vacation, then there is no reason we can't take a little longer and avoid it. We deserve it," I proclaimed.

"Sounds like a good plan to me," Senator agreed. At 11:30pm, we pulled into the alley behind our house. We had been on the road for fourteen days-- our longest trip to date. With the exception of a two-night stand in Rocky Harbour, we had driven to a new location each day. Now we were home, at least for a few days.

Chapter 2
Saving the Planet, One Nationally-Approved Nozzle at a Time: Late July 2017

I recently told Senator that once I am retired, we will never again travel in the high tourist season. Until then, July is go time. In this case, I had allowed all of two days at home between trips. Thanks to Senator's determination to get us home in a final long driving marathon by Saturday night, we had stretched that to three days at home. Sunday, Monday, and Tuesday we managed to fill with catching up on house work, booking business dates, unpacking, and repacking. Oh yes-- I also cooked, a lot.

For the second time, we were heading up to my parents' cabin in Ontario. We had had a great time the year before, taking full advantage of the cooler temperatures, the remote location, and the utter relaxation by the lake. The first year, partly to alleviate some of the meal planning, and partly because I like to cook, I had brought along several dinners for the four of us to share. It worked so well that we unanimously decided to make it a tradition.

Thus, the event began. Pots, pans, and casserole dishes were employed to cook and assemble dishes. The cutting board saw a rainbow of solid vegetables chopped, diced, sliced, and moved on to their higher purpose. Pieces of the food processor bore the remnants of blocks of cheese that had been shredded to enhance the appropriate dishes-- (minus a spoonful or two-- cook's privilege). In the end, the large, medium, and small coolers were all stuffed. I couldn't wait until we were.

*   *   *

Wednesday morning we left the state again, heading west for less than half an hour before turning due north. I was more relaxed during this drive than I had been the year before. Most of the unknown factors had been conquered. Senator loved the cabin and the lake as much as I did. He had fit in well and was also completely comfortable spending several days staying with my parents.* Add in the fact that his back was feeling good, (as opposed to the pain he had incurred by throwing it out just before we left for Ontario the first time,) and we were set for a great week.

We continued on, driving under partly cloudy skies, pleased to lose more traffic with every hour we traveled. In Minnesota we stopped at a Subway to grab some quick dinner. Though we have successfully navigated the art of

---

* He had assured me multiple times that this would be the case, but as the 'link', I was still apprehensive until I knew everyone was enjoying themselves.

consuming the abundantly stuffed concoctions while in the car, it is not always the best plan. Inside we went, placing our orders before selecting one of the four stark tables on which to eat our supper.

As we waited for the construction of our sandwiches, one of the employees noticed our license plate through the full-length glass windows. "Musician?" he asked, automatically directing his question at Senator. In turn, Senator politely gave a vague nod, not really wanting to discuss his life story, but appreciating the man's friendliness nonetheless. Our new pal was pleased to announce that Senator reminded him of his cousin, Wolfgang, who was also a musician. We all smiled, and I watched as the man loaded peppers and pickles onto the already heaping mound of veggies.

"Yep, you're just like him," the man remarked, tickled by whatever similarities he perceived. "Me, though... I'm not a musician. I just like music, and I like guitars." He folded the top of the bun over, smashing it effectively to hold in the goods. He paused, gestured with the paring knife for effect, and continued. "Once I got a guitar out of the dump-- the dump! I just wanted to put it on my wall. Then I found out it was worth $900.00!" The knife came down, expertly slicing the sandwich in half. He looked up again, anticipating our reaction.

"Wow, that's great!" we both responded. Then Senator's practical side took over. "Now what you need to do is put that one on eBay, and use some of the money to buy a new guitar for your wall. Pocket the rest."

The man thought for a minute. "Yeah, that's a pretty good idea. Maybe I will..." I liked the guy. It didn't hurt that he made a delicious veggie sandwich, too.

One change we made from the previous year's trip was to cross the border the first night, instead of waiting until the next day. We figured it would save time in the morning, maximizing our stay at Birch Harbour. As I drove up to the checkpoint, Senator handed me our driver's licenses and passports. No one else was in line, so a border patrol agent leaned out of his booth and began the usual line of questioning about how long we would be in Canada, what we were bringing, how much money we had, and if we were smuggling alcohol, tobacco, or firearms. Then he threw in a new one that I had never heard while crossing an international border. "How are you two related?" he asked.

He took me a little off guard, and I had to think for a second. *It will probably complicate things if I say that he's my Essential Other.* "Boyfriend-girlfriend," I answered.

The man looked for a second, deciding if he liked my answer. Then he followed it up. "Has *he* ever been to Canada before?" Though he pointed at Senator, he distinctly addressed his question to me.

Again, I had to think a second before I spoke. My initial reaction ran along the lines of *why don't you ask him yourself? Or better yet, just look at his passport that you are holding!* Somehow the fact that Senator had just been in the country four days earlier did not seem like it would work in our favor. Instead, I opted for a simple, "Yes." The border agent seemed satisfied with that answer. He returned our passports, thanked us, and wished us a happy holiday.

I would love to know why he asked me (and only

me) those questions. I could understand asking about how we were related if one of us looked like a minor, but that is not possible anymore, even on a good day. The second question was even more strange. I am still baffled as to what they were looking for. Maybe they pull stuff out of a random bank of questions, just to keep visitors on their toes. Maybe they amuse each other by seeing who can come up with the weirdest questions. Maybe they post videos of us looking stupid. Maybe they make money off of those videos.

It was early evening when we reached the hotel. Senator was tired from a marathon of studio work he had squeezed into the few days since the last trip. As a result, he fell asleep early, leaving me to the mercy of Canadian cable. As the remnants of sunset eked through the slit in the curtains, I found myself absorbed in a nature show. The subject, bears, seemed like an appropriate introduction to the great, remote North that we were eagerly anticipating entering the next day. I was enlightened to learn, via the magic of underwater cameras, that sometimes bears fish for salmon by shuffling their feet along stream bottoms and kicking the fish up to the surface. From there, they can clobber them with their massive paws and feast away. Thinking back to the jumping salmon in Newfoundland, it almost made me want to try it. Perhaps I will one day.

*   *   *

Thursday morning Senator was quiet. I wasn't completely sure he was enjoying himself, but I think it was more a matter relating to his (yet again) self-imposed limitation of caffeine. Gradually he perked up (no pun intended), and we stepped out into the clear, bright day. It took a little squiggling around construction impediments to get back onto the highway, but we were soon on our way out of town.

There's no need to specify which town, as there is really only one of any size. Once one leaves the Fort Frances city limits, it's on to ribbons of road meandering between lakes, forests, and meadows. If lucky, one might see some wildlife, up to and including: hawks, eagles, deer, bears, raccoons, groundhogs, moose, or some of the fastest-driving Canadians in the country.[*] Also if lucky, one will not have to use one's cellular phone, which one found out only weeks before is completely nonfunctioning outside of the United States. Thankfully, we had the foresight to fill up the tank, check the oil and tires, and say a prayer for safety, so we did not have any issues in the two-hour stretch of wilderness.[†]

Sooner than we had expected, we arrived at Birch Harbour. Aside from my parents' yelled greetings from the cabin, it was very quiet. Quiet, and still. Strangely, the constant wind that normally sweeps up the hill from the lake was absent. For once, the towels drying on the clothes line were actually hanging vertically.

The other thing we could not help but notice was the large boat shelter in the yard near the road. "Well, I guess they finally got their boat," I said, stating the obvious. I was

---

[*] Generally Americans outpace Canadians behind the wheel, but Highway 502 is an exception. I attribute it to the many curves and small, rolling hills that are best navigated by locals, assuming one does not want to end up in one of the thousands of lakes or ponds. On the other hand, it could just be American fishermen and hunters with rented Ontario trucks.

[†] Yes, I know. Next trip we will *really* get a decent phone. I promise.

trying to remember what the weather forecast had said and wondering if we would be able to get out for a ride or two during the next few days. As Senator and I exited the car and began to grab an armload of gear, my dad reached us.

"How you guys doing?" he asked, with a big smile.

"We're great. How about you guys?* I see you've got the boat, or at least the boat shelter," I returned.

"Hello!" interjected my mom, invisible from somewhere beyond the kitchen window curtain.

"We're good... now," answered my dad. I cocked my head, quizzically. "Wait until we tell you the saga of the boat." *Oh good-- a teaser.*

The three of us hauled clothes, a bag of necessaries, and a few coolers' worth of food into the house. As instructed, my mom had left me just enough space in their refrigerator. As we unpacked and found a home for each item, my mom caught up with us, asking about our drive up and giving us a few tidbits about the local scene. She also added a precautionary note. "Just so you know, once or twice we saw a little garter snake hanging out on the stone steps by the kitchen door."

The image of a serpentine enemy lying in wait to attack my ankles or trigger a cardiopulmonary event immediately caught my attention. "You mean the steps I just came down?" I asked, straightening up in heightened alert.

"Yes," she admitted, "but we haven't seen him in about a week or more," she added. Her attempts to alleviate any fears I had were only mildly effective.

---

* Is calling any group of people 'guys' a Midwest thing, or just slang that I will forever use?

"So basically that means he's due to come back any time?" I interpreted. My dad grinned again, rolling his eyes at our shared propensity for occasional pessimism.

"I think he's gone for good," said my mom. Then she changed the subject. "This all looks great!" she commented, surveying the different dishes.

"As you know, it's all vegetarian, so I hope that's okay," I said.

"Oh, no problem!" said my mom, always gracious and appreciative of someone else volunteering to cook. "We don't always eat meat at dinner," she explained.

From the other room, I heard Senator's voice. I was unaware that he had been listening to us. "Well, you won't tonight, either!" he commented. Here I have to pause, Reader, and express my gratitude for a family that is real and easy-going. Yes, we each have our quirks, but ultimately I was taught to have a sense of humor and recognize a blessed and peaceful moment when I see it. I don't ever want to lose that, especially when surrounded by such natural beauty.

Once we were satisfactorily situated on the porch, my dad began the tale of the grand coordinated effort to acquire a boat. For years my parents had been dreaming and talking and planning about one day owning a boat. When retirement finally came, it seemed like the plan could reach reality. In 2016 they took the plunge, mapping out a strategy to put a boat into a lake that had no access from their property, and which happened to be in a foreign country. They were up for the challenge. As two detail-oriented individuals, my parents had each stage ready to roll together seamlessly.

As plans go, however, they had to depend on others, and as others go, however, dependability could not be assumed. There were issues with the gravel delivery, a supply order that was erroneously canceled for no apparent reason, confusion at the border (despite plenty of preparatory communication), and myriad other hassles. Any of them could have sunk[*] the project of less determined folks, but my parents persevered. In the end, it paid off. The boat was in the water, and my brother had arranged his vacation to help my dad build the shelter. Before he and his family left the week before, they had had just enough time for a maiden voyage. Presently there were only two hours clocked on the vessel.

My dad concluded his story with an invitation. "So... if you guys feel like it... want to go out for a ride?" Of course we did. After hearing all of that, though, we felt guilty just swooping in for the fun part.

"Yes, we'd love to," we answered enthusiastically.

"But please let us know if we can assist with anything." Senator had finished my thought.

"I may do that," my dad said. "I'm still learning the ropes myself."

In half an hour we were on the water. In between watching the eagles and loons and enjoying the scenery of the rocky, forested islands, we all improved our navigation skills. My dad continued his education and familiarization with the many digital gadgets meant to guide and protect. Due to some mobility issues, my mom opted to stay at the cabin while we were out, but she was eager to hear about the trip when we came back.

---

[*] literally and figuratively

It was a good time to start thinking about dinner, so I got out the casserole I had brought. As I popped it into the oven, my mom started putting together a salad. We chatted about the local geography and other aspects of the Canadian terrain, continuously working around each other in the small kitchen. "I can't wait to hear about your last trip," my mom said, knowing that I would fully indulge her in details, stories, and visual aids. "Oh, and I have one more update for you," she added. "Yeah, we think we might have had a little visitor last night." She hesitated.

"What's that?" I asked, my mind flashing to the snake.

"Last night, when we were asleep, we were woken up by a scratching sound..."* I listened closer. "When your dad went to investigate-- it seemed to be coming from your room-- he figured it was a mouse, but he couldn't find anything." The plot thickens. "No food had been disturbed, and we did not find any other 'evidence'," she continued, using an understood euphemism for crap. "So, it is possible there's a mouse in the wall, but we're not sure," she concluded. While the kid in me would have thrilled at the prospect of an impromptu rodent friend, I just hoped nothing would chew through our clothes. Even if we did encounter an occasional critter, we could not complain; for ten months a year, no humans invade their sanctuary here. It is really more of a wonder that it had never happened before.

On that note, it was time for supper. We sat down to the familiar table with views of the lake and the trees. I

---

*Unless it leads to a great urban legend, that's never an opening that ends well.

noticed that there still wasn't much of a breeze on the side yard hill, which was extremely rare. It was warmer than usual, too. I think the temperature topped 80°F. As we learned, it was predicted to get even hotter while we were there. Taking a proactive approach, I declared that I was hoping for snow. "No," I amended, "I'm *planning* on a blizzard."

Senator nodded in agreement, and my dad blessed the food. Just as he finished, my mom put in a good word for me. "And please let Wendy get her blizzard," was the simple addendum. I love that she did that, and I love more that she said it completely seriously. It reminded me of her mother, my Grandma Klimek. When I was about five, inspired by multiple Gloria Vanderbilt jeans commercials, I made the momentous decision to change my name to Gloria. Grandma Klimek was the sole person to recognize my new identity. Without the hint of a grin, she referred to me as Gloria until I notified her of my rescission of the moniker.

After dinner we found our silently assumed spots on the porch. My parents are some of the few people who are actually interested in others' vacation details, so the evening's entertainment was settled. I started in on the stories, and Senator filled in details that I forgot. My dad asked questions, and for the record, was skeptical about my claim that a car ferry actually had enough room to walk around one's parked vehicle. My mom soaked up every minute of it, simultaneously finger-tracing our route on her giant Rand McNally map and making mental notes in case of a possible trip of her own to Newfoundland someday. She only paused for the occasional *SNAP!* of the mosquito-zapping racket.*

The travel stories morphed into other memories of crazy experiences on the road. When the sun got tired of listening to us, it set, comfortably sinking into stage left as the stars emerged from the other entrance. We all sat quietly for a while, probably each dozing in the dark. An hour or so later, a dense, delicious, gooey spice cake was foisted on us amid no objections. Eventually, it was time to turn in.

Senator and I went through our routine, said our good-nights, and went to bed. I was just about asleep when Senator spoke up. "Do you hear it?" he asked.

"Hear what?" I mumbled. I sort of did, though, maybe.

"There's scratching. I think we found our mouse." Now I was up. I snapped on the light and moved our suitcases. "I think it's in the drawers," said Senator.

We thought we had it narrowed down to two drawers. I was all set to go in and scoop out the invader. By this time, my dad was in our room, and my mom was in the adjacent hallway, asking if we could see anything. Strangely, though, we could not find any critter. We removed drawers and knocked the walls of the closet above, but nothing showed itself. My parents felt bad, but there was nothing for any of us to do but go to sleep. Hopefully we would not wake up to chewed up clothes, but we were not overly worried about it.

*   *   *

Friday morning was heating up quickly. I could feel the warmth through the curtains as I reluctantly opened my

---
*   Every home should have one.

eyes. It wasn't early, but it wasn't quite late enough, either. As I stumbled around the bed to the other side, I focused my gaze on our suitcase, which sat atop the drawers. Despite the mysterious scratching the night before, there was no sign of any gnawing or rodent damage. Maybe we had all hallucinated it. Something in the spice cake, perhaps?

It was the start of our first full day at the cabin, and though it was hotter than desired, we intended to make full use of the lake, starting with the canoe. Before setting out for our upper-body workout, we attempted our version of a healthy breakfast, travel-style. While planning the food for the trip, we hit on the great idea of making smoothies to start each day. Along with the investment of a new blender for the occasion, we had brought a bag of frozen blueberries and a bag of naked, frozen bananas. If you are wondering how frozen fruit held up in a cooler that was transported a day and a half in a car, through three states and one province, the answer is: not very well. With some effort, I managed to chisel off a hunk of brown, semi-icy banana blob and drop it into the blender. To that I added a juicy handful of cold, partially deflated blueberries. The end result was still tasty, but there were lessons to be learned for next time.

True to form, Senator had finally relaxed enough to let himself actually be on vacation. Unlike the previous trip, this one had absolutely no expectation of the ability to communicate with the business world, so there was no disappointment to be had on that front. In fact, he was anxious to zip on his life vest and grab a paddle. Leaving the land and a mosquito or two behind, we launched out into the lake.

Our first year at Birch Harbour we had taken the canoe out twice, venturing further the second time. In the 2017 inaugural run, we easily rounded two islands, placing us further out than we had gone either time. I took it as a positive sign, even if we were getting pretty sweated up. As always, every direction yielded a new view of island boulders, mostly carpeted with pine and some birch trees. They were all similar, yet each had distinct characteristics. One was totally claimed by eagles, attested to by their intense stares as we circled it.

"Are you ready to head back?" asked Senator.

"I suppose so," I answered. "How long do you think we were gone?"

"I don't know. Maybe an hour and a half?"

"Someday we'll buy a cheap watch and remember to bring it," I said, knowing that the likelihood of that would be somewhere in the neighborhood of me getting my snow storm.[*]

My parents were glad to see us when we returned. Judging by the shadows (and the clock on the wall), we had been gone about an hour and forty-five minutes. We took off our life jackets and hoisted the canoe upside-down onto its rack, careful to balance it between the proper beams. The weather was downright hot, and it took a little while for us to dry off. It was still far better than at home, though. There it would have taken all day to dry off, due to the miserable humidity.

When one's time at the lake is limited, the best thing

---

[*] No, our sad little cell phones could not be relied upon for even this minor task.

to follow up time in a boat, is more time in a boat. The first one required muscles; the second one only required lounging. My dad had been preparing the pontoon for yet another mini-voyage, and he invited us to come along. This time my mom was able to join us, completing the foursome and leaving us free to roam until our stomachs called us back.

By now we were experienced deck hands, so Senator and I manned/womaned our stations, pulling up bumpers and tying necessary ropes into masses that we pretended were legitimate sailors' knots. My mom watched, asking questions and garnering her own education of the boat that she could hardly believe was a reality. The captain carefully eased out of the little harbor and onto the open water, regularly monitoring our depth and the G.P.S., which traced our route like a sophisticated Etch-a-Sketch.

Before I knew it, we had lazed away a few hours. The most energy we had expended had been in chasing a few persistent flies away. I suppose we also got a little exercise shifting in our seats to take advantage of the canopy's shade. Even so, I had also managed to recline myself into a mild sunburn on part of my legs. "See!" pointed out Senator. "And you were getting on *me* about not using enough sunscreen." *Touché.*

The hot afternoon made a cold sandwich dinner sound easy and appealing. Plus, eating lighter left enough room to later enjoy more of my mom's 'lead cake'.[*] "I hope it cools off somewhat tomorrow," mused Senator, assuming

---

[*] Her terminology, not mine. Though we laughed about how dense the cake was, it was actually a compliment, due to the amount of goodness she had packed into her masterpiece.

his position among us on the beloved porch.

"I hope so, too," said my mom, dishing out dessert.

"I think this was supposed to be the hottest day of the whole summer," my dad added as he accepted his portion of the lead delight.

"I'm still holding out for my blizzard," I declared firmly.

We passed the rest of the night watching the moon arch over the water and catching up on more visiting. When bedtime came, we never did hear our scratching friend. I thought maybe we had scared him off. Senator hypothesized that it was actually a bug he had heard making a strangely similar noise in the trees that afternoon. At any rate, we were soon asleep.

*   *   *

Once again we woke up to uncharacteristic warmth for that part of Ontario. As we each cycled through our morning routine casually, my dad checked the radio forecast. Unfortunately, all sources predicted a hot and humid day. Senator cringed at the thought of humidity. That was exactly what we were trying to escape.

"We might have to install the window air conditioner," said my dad, reluctant to close up the cabin from the fresh air. It seemed such a shame to shut out nature.

"Well, there is a pretty strong wind, so maybe things won't get that hot," replied my mom, optimistically.

"Yeah, but this is definitely going to be an impediment to my snow," I acknowledged, as I started to hack off hunks of frozen banana mush. My parents set out some fruit and cereal, and Senator and I made our smoothies. After breakfast, we lingered, listening to a devotional reading from the Gospel. As always, I was encouraged by the 'food'. The prospect of a snowy weekend in July was doubtful, but my faith was supported in other ways.

After breakfast Senator and I set off for canoe ride #2. As soon as we were on the water, we could feel the pull of the wind, so we hugged the shoreline to keep a tighter course. I thought it might not be as fun, but it unexpectedly allowed us to see features of the land we had not noticed before. Each cabin had its own distinct color and personality-- red and playful, by the water's edge; brown and understated, further up toward the road; bluish-gray and dilapidated, rotting in melancholy stubbornness. Likewise, each inlet was uniquely shaped. The constant changes helped us get to know the feel of the canoe more intricately, and we experimented with different paddling techniques.[*]

There was no denying we were hot again, but the threatened humidity was not materializing. For this, we were truly grateful. By the time we got back to the cabin, the wind had picked up even more, perhaps staving off any dampness. It was definitely staving off bugs, so it was the perfect time to enjoy the swing on the hillside. Soon it felt like we were almost flying as straight-out as the flag and the towels on the clothesline. I think the breeze might have been trying to make up for lost time, since it had been so still the day before.

My parents joined us, and we rocked and swung and talked. Occasionally old stories would emerge about our

---

[*] all of which I will have certainly forgotten by the time we return

visits with Papa and Grandma when the cabin had been theirs. As I recall, a few dumb tales from our various jobs were also retold, usually culminating with a recognition of the lack of common sense among the leadership in most industries. In between, three of us pointed out interesting birds, while my dad kept his eyes trained on the water, scanning the surface for any hint that the waves were calming down. Eventually, the wind had dropped off to his satisfaction.

"Anyone want to try a boat ride?" he offered. Without hesitation we all eagerly accepted. "Now, if it changes, we might have to come back sooner than expected..." was his disclaimer. We all understood. Heck, I didn't care if we went out for ten minutes and turned around. Any time on the lake was a bonus compared to a day at home, and no one was going to insist on foolish risks, if it came to that.

Once again, Senator and I took our positions for shove-off, pretending we had been doing it all of our lives. My dad steered us in a new direction this time. We wound our way back into a part of the lake with which I was unfamiliar. On one quiet island, we saw a doe and her fawn coming down to the water's edge for a drink. They were mildly startled when they saw us, but not enough to give up their cool refreshment.

A few islands later, we saw some evidence of human activity. There was a handmade wooden sign, but we were at the wrong angle to read it. We guessed that it probably said something along the lines of "Go away! This means you!" Or maybe, "I'd turn back if I were you..."

After at least an hour, we did turn back, but not

because of the sign. It was evening, and everyone was getting hungry. We also had big entertainment plans for the night, involving, you guessed it, history and nature. Homeward we puttered, watching what seemed like mainland break up into a maze of islands as we approached. I could find my way around some of it, but sooner or later, I would end up lost in the endless rock-tree horizons.

It was still quite warm when we got back. I hated to start the oven, but the consistent breeze was blowing through the cabin like a reliable fan. Anyway, duty called. It was pizza night, and in the deep woods, one does not simply pick up the phone and call the nearest pizza joint. I suppose one could, but it would probably be located at least thirty miles away, and that's not counting any moose detours that might interrupt the delivery. No, no one was making any "thirty minutes or less" guarantees out here. We made our own.

Bellies full of pizza and a comfortable drop in the temperature set the stage for the big event. Before leaving home, Senator, enthralled with the history of the Newfoundlanders and their plight against centuries of odds, had made a dvd of a three-part documentary called *Vanished in the Mist*. Before dozing off in our respective chairs, our lively foursome learned about the early Viking roots of the land, and the later complicated relationship between English, French, and Basque fisherman. The fishing was hot, and the drama was even hotter.

*   *   *

Sunday morning started out a little differently. Unfortunately, the weather was not the difference. Not only was it just as hot as the previous few days; it was hotter. In fact, the weather man on the t.v. was excited to report that it was very possible that the day would break heat records. This was not boding well for my plans to play in the snow that afternoon. I sat at the breakfast table and looked at the hill out the window. It only had to drop another sixty degrees (less in Celsius) to get a good sled run going...

Our plans were different, though. For the past many years during their stays at Birch Harbour, my parents have attended Sunday church services at a little church in the nearby 'town'. I could not even tell you what denomination it was, but the general policy of the congregation was that everybody was welcome, and nobody was formal. It seemed like a safe bet. We accepted my parents' invitation to join them for some international worship and asked about the expected time of departure. "We usually leave about 10:30," said my dad. That suited us well-- enough time to get ready and spare time to watch the waterfowl before shoving off.

At the appointed time, we each found our spots in my parents' vehicle, and my dad chauffeured us to church. It was steaming up quickly, so I made a mental note that I might need to enlist the prayers of the entire congregation if I was to see even mild flurries. On second thought, perhaps they had more pressing business with the Almighty. I quietly decided to relinquish my climatic wants to the hand of Providence, come hail or high water.

We arrived at church and spilled out of the four doors of the vehicle. Immediately friendly faces were greeting my parents with smiles and small talk. Of course, they were excited to meet the new guests, as well. We shook hands all around as my parents introduced us, and then repeated the process several more times as we entered the foyer of the building.

As advertised, everyone was casual. I believe the pastor was in shorts. Four generations of church members fluttered around socially as they found their usual pews. As it turned out, we were prominently up front in the second row. I had hoped to remain more obscure, but row two is where the four Yankees landed. Many people were excited about the "beautiful day", and a few slyly grinned about certain people's absence possibly being related to it. Hot summer is a novelty there. *Trust me, Kids; it gets old really fast*, I thought.

Before getting to the morning's sermon, we sang songs and a few announcements were read. Then one of the leaders opened up the floor for any prayer requests or praise reports. This, as far as I can tell, is a Protestant phenomenon. If you did not grow up with it, it might catch you off guard. While our Catholic and Orthodox brethren[*] regularly pray for one another's needs, the Protestants find this incomplete without recognizing the Lord's blessings in each other's lives. We are a celebratory people, as evidenced by countless casserole recipes that I am convinced were invented for the sole purpose of church basement fellowships. If I wasn't a guest and did not hate being in the spotlight, I would have shared our story of surviving a ten-pound chunk of metal being hurled through our car window while driving at a high rate of speed. It was okay, though; there was no lack of praise reports. Several people

---

* and 'sistern'?

joyfully lined up to make brief statements of thanksgiving. The last sweet lady concluded with, "And we are thankful that Jim and Mary's kids are here today!" We straightened up in our seats, and I'm sure I turned a little red. See what I mean? They can catch you off guard.

After church we went back to the cabin. There was plenty of time for a canoe trip, so we strapped on our life jackets and grabbed our oars and officially approved Canadian boat safety kit. With a single motion, we flipped our familiar red friend right-side-up and launched her into the water. We were off for our third canoe ride in as many days-- not bad. It was our sweatiest, but as my mom pointed out, "If you get tired of paddling, you can always just tow it back across the ice." (She was not yet aware that I had made my peace with the weather, accepting that there would not likely be a snow storm.)

Of course, a distinct benefit of remaining significantly above freezing was that we could also go out for another ride on the pontoon. Just before we left, my mom spotted a bald eagle in the tree near the porch. We estimated it to be a teenager-- not quite in adulthood. As we each stepped down the stone stairway to the dock, its eyes were trained on us, breaking away only occasionally to check the status of possible prey on the water.

It was interesting how much more confident and experienced my dad seemed, compared to just a few days before. He was a natural. I think the boat liked him, too. It may have been skeptical about us, though. We only worked with it for a few minutes at the beginning of each voyage. Then our job consisted of lounging.

On this trip, we meandered back through more

channels with which I was unfamiliar. While we surveyed the usual rocks, trees, and a few fellow boaters, one scene caught our eyes. In the distance, we saw a loon. This is common on Eagle Lake, but this moment was special. On top of this loon's back was a fuzzy little loonling.[*] I had seen pictures of this, but I had never seen it in person. Though we were still plenty far from the pair, the mother, (who normally would have dipped beneath the surface by this point,) let out her alarmed yell at regular intervals, constantly turning her body to square off with us, in case we should start toward them. We left them alone, grateful for the unusual sight. When we were almost completely out of her view, she finally stopped her distress call.

Our captain returned us to the cabin, where we noticed that the teen eagle had departed. The fishing must have been too irresistible. We were hungry, too. Though the weather was still hot, cheesy mostaccioli was too tempting to skip, so we fired up the oven just long enough to melt the mozzarella. A light breeze and a fresh, cold salad kept it all tolerable.

After dinner we settled in for Part Two of *Vanished in the Mist*. To be honest, it was difficult to watch. The poor Newfoundlanders suffered through untold tragedies, often exacerbated by severe winter conditions. Watching raw footage of brave sealers jumping among the ice floes raised my blood pressure. I can't imagine how anyone survived more than one hunting season. Yet, their stamina continued, impacting their optimism right into the current generation.

The night sky was quickly filling in as we moved to

---
* probably not the scientific name for a baby loon

the porch. In the dark northern woods, overlooking a lake, even a half moon can be bright. Once again we watched it scoot across the sky, uninterested in our conversations as it moved westward. It had finally cooled off. In another hour or two, we would even require a blanket. In the meantime, all we required was some lead cake.

* * *

Sunday had just missed setting heat records, and Monday was starting out almost as warm. Before the main heat of the day set in, Senator and I wanted to get out for one final canoe ride. We sat down with my parents for a quick breakfast, and then got ready to go. For the sake of convenience, I had kept our bag of toiletries on the bathroom floor, within reach of the shower. Just as I returned my comb to its proper nook in the bag, a black spider ran out from behind the bag. I screamed and temporarily froze, trying to assess my next move. I knew I would need to strike quickly and effectively, so I grabbed the bag in my left hand while smacking down a slipper with my right hand.

Tragically, my plan went awry. The elusive arachnid seized his opportunity to flee to the sanctuary beneath the bed. Oh, no! A mouse in the room would have been fine; this was another matter entirely. I swiped a broom under the bed several times, carefully watching all sides for the fugitive to coming running out. By this time, Senator had also supplied me with a flashlight, which I used like a prison search light. Somehow, despite my best efforts (and Senator's, for he had a vested interest in locating the source of my anxiety), we never found the spider. I managed to convince myself that he wanted nothing to do with us, but it was not easy. There was a lot of bag shaking going on every time I needed to get into the backpack or suitcase. I prefer to think that the mouse was really a rodent-angel who took care of the spider on my behalf. *Hey, whatever works.*

Out on the water we could really feel the wind. It had been steadily picking up all morning. Our original plan to stick close to the shoreline failed when the angle of the wind kept spinning us sideways. We gave up and turned directly into the wind, which had the effect of allowing us to skim over the mounting ripples with the breeze in our face. It was a big improvement. It was also probably debatable as to whether we should have gone in the first place, but we were glad we did. Our last canoe expedition for at least a year was a satisfying success.

When we reached the shoreline, we brought the canoe out of the water and flipped it. This time we portaged it all the way up to the garage, where it would be housed until someone else might want to use it.[*] Once it was properly secured, Senator, my dad, and I marched back down to the boat dock for the next project. It was time for the first re-fueling of the boat.

In theory, this should be a simple process. Anticipating that it would not be, my wise father had humbly enlisted Senator's assistance. I volunteered my services as well. In preparation of the event, my dad had done his homework and purchased several containers that were officially approved by the Canadian government.

---

[*] Results of an informal family survey suggest that the other siblings and their mates tend to prefer the kayaks. They like the speed; we like working in the same vessel.

Each one had its very own eco-friendly spout from which to pour fuel. My dad has also taken the small fleet of containers to the gas (or petrol) station and carefully filled them.

"Are you sure you don't mind helping?" my dad asked one more time for confirmation.

"No, no problem! Let's go do it," answered Senator. I tagged along, wondering what my dad knew that we did not. Something told him that this was not a one-man operation. Maybe it was because of the wind.

In fact, the wind was not helping matters, but we prevailed. Despite the bouncy waves, we maneuvered the boat to the opposite side of the dock, in order to have the gas tank on the correct side. Then we replaced the bumpers into the necessary positions and retied the boat to the other posts. Senator and I then steadied the boat. So far, so good.

That should have been the tricky part, but it was nothing compared to the final phase. My dad screwed the nozzles into the container holes and attempted to begin pouring. First nothing came out. Then there was a drizzle. It chugged-chugged a bit more, necessitating frequent repositioning of the awkward, full container. It became clear that it was a two-person job just holding the container, so Senator helped support it.

The real issue was the environmentally-friendly nozzle. Created to save fuel, it had a completely stupid design, which lacked any venting. Trying to pour gas from it was akin to shaking a ketchup bottle before it got flowing. To say that it was inefficient is an understatement. To keep a long story from being longer, I'll conclude by saying that at least a pint of gas ended up in the lake, more was on our hands, and we inhaled far more fumes than we would have, had the leftists not been so damned opposed to common sense. Strangling regulation scores again!

After the gassing up fiasco, I joined my mom on the porch to relax for a while. Well, that is only half true. I kicked up my feet, but I had work to do. It was time to catch up on my book notes, since it was the longest I had gone without updating notes while on vacation. (Here, Reader, you can mentally fill in all the details that I have probably forgotten.) Once that was finished, I continued my responsibilities by writing my assigned entry in the Birch Harbour guest book.

Just as I finished, Senator came in. "Oh, good. It's your turn," I announced, passing him the book. He groaned mildly, but he accepted his duty without argument. My mom smiled, but did not say anything. Last year the matter had been settled, and Senator had come away with the knowledge that there was no getting out of it.

The wind continued to pick up, rendering any further boat rides impossible. As it did a few days before, the swing on the yard's hill beckoned, inviting us to visit in between pushing the hair back out of our eyes. After an hour or so, I left the others to start preparing dinner. Inside, with all of the windows open, the strong breeze was even more concentrated, rushing through the cabin and sending overhead lanterns swaying. Between the perceived motion and the view of the water below, it gave the illusion of being in a ship's cabin at sea. It was yet another magical aspect of Birch Harbour.

As we ate dinner, we could see the sky shifting to a darker shade. My mom flipped on the t.v. to check the weather forecast. As we learned, the breeze was blowing around more than just lanterns. A fast-moving thunderstorm was headed our way. This would require a full battening down of the hatches.

As soon as we finished our dinner, the regular windows were closed. In the process, we noticed a few fisherman who were determined to stay on the lake, despite the lightening in the distance. To make matters worse, one of them was standing up. It seems there are always people who refuse to believe that they are vulnerable to nature's forces.

Next we worked together to lower storm panels into place to protect the porch from a deluge. Years before, my dad had custom-built each one to fit the windows, no two of which were alike. Multiple bolts were slid into place, and we were shut in. It was surprising how dark and quiet the home was without the lake side exposed. I love a good storm, but I was eager for it to pass, just to alleviate the slightly claustrophobic feeling.

Almost as soon as we had settled in to our strange fortress, the rain let up. Soon afterward, the thunder moved off to the distance as well. When a safe amount of time had passed, we repeated the window process, in reverse. When the last dark brown panel was lifted, the sunset beamed all the way across the porch. Trees and eaves continued to drip, but the evening was calm. The temperature was cooling off nicely too, as though it had been waiting to shake off the abnormal heat wave.

As nature returned to its regularly scheduled program, we sat down to the conclusion of *Vanished in the Mist*. Part Three placed Newfoundland in the position of having to choose between self-dominion under England[*] or confederating with Canada. In the 1940s Canada won, but it is debatable if Newfoundland did. Since then, their characteristic out-ports have been disappearing, and big government intervention has devastated much of the cod industry and the local economy. Perhaps one day there will be a Part Four, allowing the islanders to reclaim more of their heritage.

* * *

Tuesday morning was beautiful... just in time to leave. We packed most of our stuff and sat down for a final breakfast with my parents. My dad led one more devotion and concluded by extending an invitation to stay another day. Though it had been wonderful, and every aspect of the visit tempted us to linger, work called. Senator had recordings lined up, and I needed to shift my brain back to the school mode.

It was hard to say good-bye. My parents thanked us for coming, as though we had done *them* a favor. Reluctantly, we walked up the yard to where the car was parked. It was loaded; there were no more excuses to hang around longer. As my parents stepped up near the car, it was a flashback to a generation ago, when my grandparents would stand in the same place, in the same pose, often with misty eyes as our crew pulled out. Time can be downright cruel.

Despite hating to say good-bye, the drive was relatively easy. We did not have any minimum of how far we needed to go, so there was no pressure in that area. When we felt like stopping, we found ourselves a little

---

[*] a somewhat odd hybrid of independence and colonial status

north of Eau Claire, Wisconsin. We had gone a respectable distance, so we checked into a hotel in a quiet corner of town.

Inside our room, we unpacked a few essentials and then left again to gas up and find a sandwich. Less than a mile from our hotel was a Subway, which was good enough for us. Maybe we would meet another friendly 'sandwich artist' like the one in Minnesota the week before. We walked in and got in line behind a couple and a single woman. We soon learned that if the Minnesota Subway employee was, indeed, a sandwich artist, this particular employee must have flunked out of art school.

He first messed up the couple's order. It was not a crisis; he remade the correct subs and began to apply a white condiment. Naturally the squeeze bottle was almost empty, which resulted in another lost minute or so in the act of trying to shake it down while smacking the bottom. When that failed, he excused himself to leave to get another one from the storage room. The couple smiled understandingly. The new squeeze bottle then required its own round of coaxing, until it yielded a trail of white glob. The couple smiled again, a little less understandingly. It was about this time that one of involved parties realized that the mystery sauce was not, in fact, the requested ranch dressing, but mayonnaise. This set progress back to a point where the couple did not attempt any more smiles, understanding or otherwise. The woman in line behind them looked back at us. "I've been here twenty minutes," she informed us flatly. My eyebrows raised.

As we were debating what to do, another couple came in. It might be too late for us, but there was no point in them suffering. I turned around and told them that we had not moved in line in ten minutes. They thanked me and left. The sandwich-art-school-dropout looked relieved. The patient couple at the front of the line started to look menacing. At that point we left, too.

"Well, where else do you want to go?" asked Senator. The Mexican restaurant next door looked like it was only open for lunch, and there was not much else around, except Walmart. I looked up at Walmart for inspiration-- who doesn't?-- and then I saw it. Of all of the fast food options for Walmart to incorporate into their front-of-store retail space, they had chosen to include a Subway. I would ask how they could compete, but we already knew the answer to that question. Thus, we drove across the street, entered the line behind the couple we had convinced to leave the initial Subway, ordered, and were served all in less time than it would have taken had we stayed in the first location. By that time, we were ready for some mindless television and a good crash.

*   *   *

"Ready to go?" asked Senator. I did a quick glance at the overnight bag and the backpack.

"Yeah, I guess so," I answered. I was not exactly enthusiastic about another trip ending, but since there were no more interesting stops between Eau Claire and home, I was ready to hit the road.

"Okay, give me the bags, and you can check out. I'll get the car," stated Senator, commencing our usual routine. I nodded in agreement, and he ushered me out into the hallway. I paused and kissed him. Neither one of us said anything else. Senator was missing his coffee. I was already missing the far north.

Our drive under the mostly clear sky was easy. It left plenty of time for a passenger's mind to wander. It wondered as it wandered. Who knew what I would be getting into when I returned to work? My partner had quit two months earlier. I had heard nothing about a replacement or even any interviews. No partner meant that I also currently had no students enrolled in the program I teach. *Not a stellar beginning.* Normal routines would be further interrupted by a $38,000,000 construction project taking place in the main building on campus. Supposedly they had found us somewhere to park, but it was equally possible that I might be walking two blocks every day. Then again, I had not checked phone messages in over a week. Maybe I did not even had a job. Working for the most financially dismal state in the union leads one to such thoughts.

Nevertheless, off we went. The greatest prayer I taught myself that summer was, "I'm not dealing with this, God. I can't handle it. It's your problem." His response was and is always the same: "Yeah, I know. That's what I keep trying to tell you."

Chapter 3
With Malice Toward None: Early April 2018

Note: All facts, figures, and quotes in the following chapter are attributed to and verified within the United States National Park Service visitor centers, battlefield sites, and literature at Manassas, Fredericksburg, Chancellorsville, Wilderness, Spotsylvania Courthouse, Appomattox Courthouse, and Shenandoah.

In August, I returned to work. Remarkably, the semester came together, assisted greatly by the new employee who replaced the coordinator who had quit. In January, a new semester came together... and then gradually proceeded to fall apart. Related events included losing space due to behind-schedule construction projects, one of my students getting expelled for drug possession in school, a mid-semester curriculum change (sans notice), an entire basketball hoop structure falling down on another one of my students, and a general state of non-productivity and overall disinterest in graduation.

Other than that, things were going well. Senator and I continued to record live music and balance out our winter by spending more time with family. We even got out several times to enjoy the snow, which had finally made a comeback after a few lame winters. When March rolled around, however, I was very grateful that we had planned a trip for spring break.

For many years I had wanted to travel to Virginia with the specific intent of visiting various historical sites. After completing the Canadian provinces in 2017, spring break of 2018 seemed like a good time to plan such a trip. Going in April would also (hopefully) prevent the misery of southern July heat indices. As I started brainstorming my list of major Revolutionary and Civil War era battlefields, homes, and historical parks, it became apparent that we would need much more than the allotted week. Rather than compromise on places I wanted to visit, I decided to break the trip into two parts: Revolutionary War and Civil War. When we thought about it further, we decided it would also make more sense from an academic standpoint, rather than trying to mentally jump back and forth between two immensely significant time periods.

Chronologically, it might have seemed obvious to start with the colonial era, but current events surrounding gross misunderstanding of the Confederacy and a new-found interest in Shelby Foote's *The Civil War: A Narrative* trilogy[*] on Senator's part pushed us both toward the 1860s. On New Year's Day, I sat at the computer, committing us to the planned itinerary via hotel reservations. "Hey, we

---

[*] 2,800 pages; Yes, I have read it, and yes, I have forgotten much of it. Yes, I hope to tackle it again-- probably in retirement.

earned a free night!" I told Senator, delighted.

"Oh, good," he responded casually.

Upon a moment's further reflection, I added, "Although, I guess *free* might not be totally accurate, since it means we have paid for ten nights in hotels to earn it..." Senator smiled. He knew that it would not be the only 'free' night we earned. At any given time, I admittedly have at least rough outlines for the next three or four trips up my sleeve.

For about two months before leaving, Senator and I prepped for our on-location education. He plunged into reading the first volume of *The Civil War*, making some headway into 1861, while enjoying Foote's extensive knowledge, uniquely comfortable voice, and mischievous humor. I picked up a collection of odd facts and tales from the Civil War. After devouring that, I read another 600 pages of newspaper accounts, diaries, and folk tales reflecting on major battles, soldiering, civilian life, famous lives, and not-so-famous lives. Meanwhile, Senator ordered an oversized Civil War atlas and found a Manassas documentary for us to watch. "What have you *done* to me?!" he asked mockingly, referencing his conversion to the type of person who orders oversized Civil War atlases and historical documentaries. Likewise, we could only take it as a positive sign when, one night while visiting my parents, I noticed a copy of the movie *Shenandoah*[*] on their shelf. What were the odds that they had a movie focused on the Civil War in the very region where we would be traveling in a few weeks? So we watched that, too. To round it all out, Senator surprised me with hours of old

---

[*] 1965, starring the unconquerable Jimmy Stewart

Civil War-themed radio shows and a recording of a heavy metal tribute to Gettysburg.* We were now ready.

* * *

Monday morning we were up and on the road ten minutes earlier than planned, which is noteworthy, considering I was pushing for a 6:00am departure time. We had a long drive ahead, and there would be the temporarily inconvenient loss of an hour while traveling into the Eastern time zone. It was still dark when we left, but before long we were staring down an increasingly brilliant sunrise. "Wow!" I exclaimed. Both of us instinctively grabbed for our sunglasses, which we already had on. "Only about three more hours until the sun is above the visor," I estimated. "Maybe even less for you, since you're taller."

Based on too many bad experiences on I-80/90 near the Indiana border, we finally decided to alter our route. Instead of staying on the interstate straight east into Indiana, we exited south to a major highway, leading to a parallel detour. It only added about a half hour to the trip, and the drive was fine, but the jury was still out on the new route. On one hand, it was wonderful avoiding the crazy drivers and the mess of lane changes and toll plazas. On the other hand, as Senator pointed out, one of the towns we drove through probably would not be prudent to transverse at night. *Hhmmm, tough call.* (I took the opportunity to point out the fact that we would not even have to make the choice if we simply moved East.)

When we reached I-65, we started north to rejoin

---

* by Iced Earth; Yes, I can listen to it on 'repeat' for almost as long as Pickett's charge took.

I-80. Senator started up the first radio show. As we cruised eastward, we were transported back in time to a battle we recognized from our reading. I was amazed at how accurate the details were. Much of the script was taken directly from primary sources with which I was familiar. Mile after mile, we continued to be drawn into emotionally moving and suspenseful audio presentations. It set the tone appropriately for the forthcoming experience.

By the time we were about to leave Ohio, I had done more than half of the driving, which made me feel good. I had sort of been dreading the long-distance drive, but now it was going fast. Despite Senator's offer, I decided to keep the wheel into Pennsylvania. That meant I was the one to hand our eight bucks over to the attendant, just to get on the Million Dollar Turnpike*. I was also the one to hand over another $20.35 when we exited the pike, having only traveled halfway across it. Partially in protest, and partially to get rid of change, twenty-five of the coins were pennies.

"Really?!" snapped the bearded and highly annoyed hipster attendant as I handed him the handful of change.

"Yep!" I beamed, cheerfully. He didn't bother to count it. I'm sure he was paid hourly, so I don't know what his problem was. Had I known how pissy he would be, though, I might have also handed him twenty singles, instead of one twenty. Senator just laughed.

On we rolled, through a few twists and turns which brought us into and took us out of Maryland. I think we were only there for about three miles. "I didn't even see the sign," I told Senator.

"I mentioned it, but you were distracted," he replied.

---

* also known as the Pennsylvania Turnpike

That was true; I was afraid of missing my turn. Suddenly we were in West Virginia. I leaned over and kissed him twice, keeping our state line ritual while simultaneously making up for the elusive Maryland crossing. Settling back over to my original position, I started the next radio show and began our final stretch toward Manassas.

West Virginia is an odd-shaped state. Prior to this trip, our only venture through it saw us cross its needle that pierces between Ohio and Pennsylvania. This time we drove down through the eastern portion. Immediately upon entering the state, there was a more relaxed feel on the road. Small towns and sane drivers ushered us deeper into a picturesque and simple landscape. The trees were bare, but not ugly. Likewise, among the towns and rural areas, no wealth was on display, but neither was anything impoverished. Overall it was a welcome reprieve from the antsy 'friends' we had in Pennsylvania.

We followed Route 522 into Virginia, which was just as appealing. Though it was a little more crowded, we were struck by how neatly kept everything seemed. For a while our route took us onto I-95, and even the interstate appeared cleaner. It was a very different impression than Richmond had left on us years before.[*] I started to get really excited when Jingles declared that we were only moments away from our destination. As proof, I saw the first sign for Bull Run, the famous creek (or skinny river, in

---

[*] Coincidentally, in 2006 we were on another Civil War-related excursion, the object being the Museum of the Confederacy. The museum, in fact, was wonderful. The parking, in fact, was dreadful. As such, I will always associate Richmond with a dilapidated parking deck bejeweled with broken glass and gang graffiti.

some parts) for which the Yankees named the first major battle of the War Between the States.

Manassas was bigger than I had pictured. Our hotel was just off the main drag, but we had driven far enough to know that every major chain and a few minor ones were well represented. There was also a mall, leading me to wonder if the twenty-first century would distract us too much from our serious attempt to further understand a nineteenth century war. It wasn't as though I expected Stonewall Jackson to greet us at the city limits; I was just surprised.

We checked into our room and situated a few necessities before heading back out to grab a bite. While getting our bearings, I realized that Bull Run actually ran right past our hotel-- no bull! With carry-out sandwiches in hand, we drove the mile or so back to our room. The next morning we would venture to the battlefield. According to my maps, it was just five minutes along the same main road, but in the opposite direction. I was skeptical as to whether it would be as well-preserved as other, more remote battlefields, but we could figure all of that out in the morning. It was currently time to unwind from a long day on the road.

*   *   *

Tuesday morning was delightfully chilly. Spring was coming late to Virginia as well, but the dry, cool weather was invigorating. As we claimed a table and cups of coffee in the hotel's breakfast nook, we could see Bull Run quietly flowing by. Eager to tackle our first stop in this quest to gain knowledge and perspective, we gassed up and started down the road.

In just a few moments, the landscape changed dramatically. Gone were the chain stores and fast food restaurants. Open rolling spaces, random groves of trees, and the signature lines of ragged criss-cross fencing announced our arrival at Manassas. We were now on the soil of the first major battle of the Civil War.

Manassas (July 1861)* was a wake-up call. Instead of ending within a few months, the War Between the States took that long to ramp up to a full-scale bloodbath. Union and Confederate soldiers alike were slapped with the realization that war meant confusion, devastation, and irreparable loss. Civilians, though not directly targeted, learned this lesson as well-- in some cases, firsthand. Washingtonians packed their picnics and drove their wagons from the capital to view the battle, much as one would watch a sporting event. By the time it was over, Union soldiers and civilians alike were racing back to D.C., jamming the road in one massive retreat. The South had won that round, but with about 2,000 casualties among Beauregard's and Johnston's forces, in addition to McDowell's almost 2,700 casualties in the North.

We entered the visitor center to get more details on the story we had been studying. Inside, a chart caught my attention. Though I had heard statistics, the graph's visual depiction of American war casualties left a lasting impact on me. Rows of stick figures associated with each war made it very apparent that the Civil War alone garnered more casualties than all other American wars *combined*. It was truly astonishing to consider.

---

* also known as Bull Run in the north, where battles were often named for the nearest body of water, as opposed to the nearest town

Meanwhile, Senator was engrossed in reading another display. Part of it contained a quote that posed the question asking who "we the people" are. Does it refer to the country, the states, or individuals? What did it mean originally in the eighteenth century? What did it mean leading up to the Civil War? What does it mean now? It is a question worth pondering.

"The movie is just about to start," said Senator, indicating the entrance to the visitor center theatre. We walked into the silent room and found a spot on the carpeted bench. While we waited, we whispered, and I tried to decipher the park's map in the dark. Since we had the entire day to spend there, we planned to take the walking tour that highlighted sites from the first battle at Manassas, and the driving tour that followed the critical points of the second battle of Manassas, which took place just over a year later.

The film started, and we were instantly hooked. Fortunately, so were the others in the theatre. No one made a sound as the narrator took us through a gripping drama centered around the first battle. In addition to the facts and figures, an impressive cast recreated the scenes with surprising realism. The movie had been shot on location, bringing to life famous figures like General Thomas "Stonewall" Jackson, (who picked up his nickname there when General Bee noticed him holding fast, like a "stone wall",) as well as lesser characters, like Judith Henry. Though eighty years old and ailing, she refused to evacuate from her house to safety. When the cannons started bombarding the field, she became a civilian casualty.

When the movie ended, we filed out of the theatre

and left the building. Just beyond the back door was the beginning of the trail. In view was the Henry House, restored after being demolished by artillery and ravaged for fire wood. We walked up to it, comparing it with the vivid images from the film. Then we turned around and saw the lone grave of Judith Henry. History was alive.

We continued to walk the loop, stopping to read informational plaques about the landowners and soldiers whose paths crossed unintentionally. Clumps of wild chives grew all over the fields. About halfway around the meandering loop, we crossed a small stream by stepping across a few boards that had been placed there. "Is that Bull Run?" asked Senator.

"I don't think so," I responded. "I think it's bigger. We should come across it later, though." The steady breeze now whipped up to a solid wind. I shrugged my hood up to cover my ears, and Senator blew his nose. By the time we reached our car, it was definitely chilly. That was great-- not a bug for miles around.

Shifting into 1862, we pulled out the map to begin the driving tour. At each stop we encountered another aspect of the Manassas story. A few remaining homes and a church stood as reminders of their immediate necessary conversion to hospitals. At the main intersection, the iconic stone house still stood. Spanning between other sections of the battlefield, an unfinished railroad bed ran through the woods, providing a convenient trench for Stonewall Jackson's men. Elsewhere, the brave and always colorfully dressed 5th New York Voluntary Infantry Zouaves were honored with twin monuments for their bravery. Fighting wildly to buy the Union time, they lost 332 out of 525 men within minutes. On the other side of the road, stones marked southern states in the peaceful Confederate cemetery.

Raindrops began to speckle the pavement as we walked back to the car. We had just one more stop, which I did not want to miss, but it was raining harder. Senator pulled the car into yet another empty lot, this time by the famous arched stone bridge. Throughout the engagements, the bridge served as a key imperative crossing. It was destroyed and rebuilt, and it now sits quietly parallel to the highway, guarding Bull Run.

The light rain had graduated to a full-on spring downpour. "There's no point in getting out to walk now," said Senator. I agreed, especially when he suggested we listen to another radio show. We simultaneously flipped through a newspaper guide to other Civil War sites in the state. The amount of significant historic events that took place on the local soil was staggering. Virginia is for lovers... of history. If it wasn't for too much heat and humidity most of the year, I think I could live there.

Eventually the rain let up, and we took our opportunity to hop out of the car. We walked to the edge of the bridge and surveyed the stream, which thinned slightly as it disappeared into the curve between the budding trees. It was peaceful, yet remnants of the war still lingered. We stood for a few more minutes, looking north and south. Just as our thoughts were winding down, the rain was picking up again.

We left Manassas, having spent a solid six hours engrossed in physical exploration of what was arguably the first major battle of the American Civil War, as well as its 'encore' the following year. It was a lot to take in. The story would continue the next day. Now it was time to bow out of the past and return to the present, but our minds were only halfway transitioned, as we drove the brief commute to the hotel. In less than five miles, the buildings were once again modern, there were no more split rail fences, and the vast greenish-yellow fields were replaced by cement and strip mall parking lots.

Originally we had planned to go to a sleek indoor shooting range for the evening. We had checked their legal requirements online and come prepared. When I asked Senator if he still wanted to go, however, he unenthusiastically left it up to me. Curiously, I had lost my interest, also. It was not that we had suddenly given up an interest in improving our marksmanship, but our minds were too preoccupied with things we had learned and absorbed. Switching gears and being in a busy public place had no appeal to our mutual quiet pensiveness; a slow-paced dinner at a local Indian restaurant was more in keeping with our mood. The fact that we arrived right as they were opening for dinner, and remained one of only three tables during the pre-rush period, also fit. We continued to discuss our thoughts between mouthfuls of curried vegetables and garlic naan. All the while, the rain rolled down the window beside our table.

On our way back to our hotel, we passed a massive used book, music, and movie store. We needed any of those items like we needed a another hole in our heads, but we agreed to browse, just for fun. Unlike most such places, this one was completely organized, with multiple quantities of an impressive amount of titles. Within a half hour, I had five books picked out, not including the ones that the practical and frugal voice in my head had talked me out of. Among the stack was Stephen Crane's classic *The Red Badge of Courage*, set in the Civil War. It was a novel I probably should have read in high school, but somehow it had evaded me.

In our room we relaxed, and I went over itinerary notes for the next day. I wondered if Wednesday's sites would be as meaningful as the first battlefield of the trip. We would see. In the meantime, we were tired enough to fall asleep by 11:00pm, despite the loud chaperones of a school group in the hallway. Ironically, the teenagers were reasonably quiet and well-behaved, but the act of adults checking on them apparently involved lots of loud knocking and unnecessarily grandiose reading of their names. *Go away. We're not even in your century.*

* * *

The school group woke us up half an hour before the alarm, but it was no big deal. Still, after ten minutes of their raucous chattering, it warranted a response. Bleary-eyed, in sleep shorts and a wrinkled tee shirt, I opened the door (which was blocked by a mob of twenty people) and addressed the group, particularly the yuppie mom who appeared to be the leader. I did not want to be menacing, but I did want to make a point. "You guys do realize you're not the only ones in the hotel, right?" was all I said.

Before I could close the door, Yuppie Chaperone responded. "We're leaving right now," she said, clearly startled. *Good.* Thankfully, there was no trace of them by the time we came down to the lobby to grab some breakfast. Our peace was once again restored.

The weather forecast was completely wrong. They had predicted rain all morning, claiming that it would end by early afternoon. Instead, the sun gradually muscled its way in front of the clouds as we drove the hour south to Fredericksburg. It was brilliant against the apple blossoms and daffodils that had just started to bloom there, weeks ahead of our more northerly ones at home.

In mid-December of 1862, General Ambrose Burnside, new head honcho of the Union's Army of the Potomac, led an attack on General Robert E. Lee's forces at Fredericksburg. The Confederate troops were outnumbered vastly, and they were attacked on two flanks, but they had the crucial advantage of higher ground and a wiser general. Throw in an extended stone wall for fortified protection, and the northern soldiers were left with an almost impossible task. Trying to construct a delayed bridge, under heavy fire, partially in the dark, did not help matters. In the end, it was a demoralizing bloodbath for General Burnside's army. Lincoln, upon hearing the news, responded dimly, saying, "If there is a place worse than Hell, I am in it."

We stepped into the visitor center to obtain a map and check out the exhibits. Immediately a smiling pair of park rangers greeted us. One was a younger guy, probably in his first professional job. The other one may have been recently retired from a less satisfying job. Before we could say "Hello" and request a map, he jumped right into sharing his expertise with us. Indicating key sites on the opened driving map that now covered half of the counter, he retold the tale of the battle, carefully explaining the background, challenges, and events that led to the South's undeniable victory. When he felt that we had sufficiently grasped the narrative, he turned us loose to the parking lot, where the walking trail began. "That's the stone wall right there," he concluded, pointing through the visitor center toward the direction we would take once outside.

We knew the one; we had parked right next to it. Now, however, it took on unprecedented meaning. It was not just a property divider or a decorative border; it had meant the difference between life and death for so many. Not coincidentally, the walking trail paralleled it perfectly for about two blocks. One house was still riddled with Minié ball[*] holes in its exterior as well as interior. How anybody could have survived being hit with one of those is a true mystery. Another nearby home was converted to a hospital, particularly when its aged, corncob pipe-smoking 'Ma' refused to evacuate. Instead, she drew water from her well for the wounded. Other buildings and sites told more of the story, bringing us face to face with the impossibility of the Union's mission, especially for the Irish Brigade. Appropriately, the walk ended at the cemetery, located on a hill that overlooked the once-devastated town.

The visitor center further explained the engagement through exhibits, artifacts, and another excellent film. Prior to the battle, the Union had enjoyed a an epic pillaging of local homes and businesses. Most civilians left or at least hid, as Yankees carried off everything that was not nailed down-- up to and including an attempt to take a piano. By the time they were ordered to charge the Rebels, the South was good and aggravated. Despite the horrific failure of the attack, General Burnside had to be talked out of another

---

* soft lead, conical bullet made to expand; cast in .58 or .69 caliber

day of a hopeless charge. The outcome may have been significantly different, however, had a necessary bridge not been days late. At any rate, it was not the victory the North needed to sustain confidence in its success.

At least one good tale came out of the clash. Slave John Washington, along with two others, walked to the edge of the Rappahannock River, where they could see the Union soldiers. Whether for mercy's sake, or just to stick it to the enemy, the soldiers asked them if they wanted to cross over. Washington's life-altering response was a simple and honest, "Yes, I want to come over." So he did, marking the first day of his life as a free man.

Before leaving Fredericksburg National Battlefield, we needed to stop in the gift shop. This was not so much to shop as it was to pay the requested $2.00 per person fee for the film we had seen. That's right; we were instructed to pay *afterward*. As I pulled out a five-dollar bill, I remembered where I was. "Will you accept a note with Lincoln's face on it?" I asked the cashier. She smiled, and at least pretended it was the first time she had heard that joke.

As we walked to the car, Senator announced that he might have picked up a hitchhiker. "I think I have a tick, maybe."

"What? When did you notice that?" I asked, mildly alarmed, but somewhat skeptical, as we had not been in any woods.

"I'm not sure, but it feels like something..."

I launched a meticulous finger-driven investigation that portioned his head into zones on a grid. After taking my time, I pronounced my results. "As a former ticked victim, I am declaring you tickless. I can't find anything, and it would be very rare to pick one up out in this type of landscape."

"Well, maybe it wasn't a tick," Senator reasoned, brushing his hair back into place.

Crisis averted, we consulted the map for the driving tour. Artillery and flank positions were marked, as well as a spot where the Union temporarily broke through the Confederate lines. The highlight among the stops was the hill where General Lee watched the unfolding battle. The short, steep, paved path led to a kiosk and a narrow lookout point. As we surveyed the land, an osprey flew overhead, marking the spot where General Lee consulted with his "right arm", Stonewall Jackson.

It was midday and time to continue the story further west at Chancellorsville. Taking the same Plank Road that the Victorians had used, we arrived in less than half an hour. Ironically, it was a lovely drive among rolling farms and groves of trees, between two towns that will forever be associated with devastating loss. Unlike Manassas and Fredericksburg, the Chancellorsville visitor center had about fifteen cars in the lot. Inside, however, there was no one around except two rangers behind the counter.

Senator broke off to make a pit stop, while I inquired about the film. Like the last one, it had also been advertised with a $2.00 fee. I paid for our tickets, this time omitting my lame joke. Senator then met me, and we stepped into the empty theatre. As we had come to expect, the dramatic reenactment was gripping, having the added impact of being filmed on various parts of the battlefield.

In spring of 1863, still reeling from the defeat at Fredericksburg, the Union Army of the Potomac was now under the command of General Joseph Hooker. Again outnumbered, the Confederate Army of Northern Virginia, by order of General Lee, split into two and attacked. Stonewall Jackson's surprise offensive was successful, but it drove the action into the dark night. Amid the confusion, he was accidentally shot by his own men, necessitating the amputation of his left arm. Lee lamented that though Jackson had lost his left arm, *he* had "lost his right". This time Lincoln, upon hearing of the Union's defeat, could only lament, "My God! My God! What will the country say?" Ten days later, Stonewall Jackson succumbed to pneumonia resulting from his wound. One of the Confederacy's greatest heroes was dead.

We took some time after the film the roam the rest of the visitor center. In one corner, we saw a model of the home at the crossroads of Chancellorsville, complete with its family, slave population, and myriad farm animals. The same home would witness plenty of bullets and bloodshed during the battle. In fact, during a five hour period on one morning, overall casualties averaged one per *second*.

Losses were indeed staggering. One display featured reference to Stephen Crane's *The Red Badge of Courage*, whose details and mood some believe was inspired by Chancellorsville. Though Crane was not even born until a decade after the War Between the States began, many people held fast to the notion that the riveting accuracy of the novel could have only been conjured up by a veteran who was there. I don't think it was a coincidence that I had just picked up that book the night before.

Other exhibits detailed the events surrounding the battles of the Wilderness and Spotsylvania Courthouse.

We would be traveling there the next day. Those locations had no centers, so we drank in as much knowledge as we could.* In the meantime, I was already missing Stonewall Jackson.

Outside the visitor center, we walked the short path around the sites of General Jackson's wounding and initial care. Naturally there was a monument. On it were inscribed his final words: "Let us cross over the river and rest under the shade of the trees." Though the quote is usually lumped in with his incoherent and random delirious orders to an absent General A.P. Hill, I firmly believe that the devoutly Christian Jackson saw a glimpse of his place in Paradise.†

After our walk, we climbed in the car, noting that the forecast had been completely wrong all day. Only a few random clouds floated across the sky. As we each put on our sunglasses, I consulted the map we had received in Fredericksburg that morning. We now switched to the green route for the driving tour, driving from station to station and reading interpretive information in between walking more of the grounds.

It did not take long to find the long lines of earthworks that trailed the countryside. I knew that the Civil War saw the invention of trench warfare, but I thought it was an uncommon occurrence and only in isolated areas. The countryside at Chancellorsville set me straight on this fact. There were still so many mounded

---

*It was only after choosing the six battlefields of this trip that I learned that four of them were part of the same national park.

† Interestingly (to me, at least), as I write this portion of the book, I realize that today (May 10th) is the anniversary of General Jackson's death.

151

lines left from both Union and Confederate attempts to build up a natural shield that the county sometimes looked as if it had been invaded by giant moles or groundhogs. In many cases, the lines butted up to or even ran through private property. Soon we did not need the short identification signs that sometimes appeared randomly along a line in order to recognize them. We were in awe that, through a century and a half of climatic cycles, ground shift, and development, these breastworks remained. I also found it interesting that at least one soldier felt the need to defend the construction of such obstacles, claiming that it was "not cowardly" since they had "suffered so much".

It was no wonder that building earthworks became part of the regular defense at places like Chancellorsville. Stepping onto one artillery field that looked down over an open field explained the need fully. There was nothing else the men could use for cover. The odds were bad enough when rifles were going against cannon. The ground itself was the only potential ally.

The next section of the drive entered thicker woods. Turning the curve revealed what used to be Catharine Furnace, a busy iron production site during the war. The main brick stack still stood as evidence to the bustling activity that had taken place there. No longer standing, however, was any sign that it had been on the route that General Jackson's men took as they circumvented General Hooker's troops.

After following so many military movements, we halfway expected to look up and see an infantry charge coming toward our position near the small graveyard at the edge of the meadow. None came. We did not hear any sounds, except for a few birds chattering. We did not have to resort to using a tin plate or bayonet to scoop earth into a short, shoddy fortress. The only task at hand was waiting to discover the answer to the persistent question of what in the world "we the people" meant and means. None came.

Senator and I drove back along the main road to Fredericksburg and found our motel. The outside looked like it had not been touched by a renovator's hand since the Reagan administration, but the inside of our room was clean and new. "I guess they haven't gotten as far as fixing the uneven stairs," I commented, referring to the metal outdoor staircase with the wavering concrete steps.

"...Or fixing the cracks," added Senator, pointing out the oddly-toned yellow exterior walls.

The rain never came, but the wind sure did. Our hair flew around wildly as we stepped out of our second-story room to leave for dinner. The original plan of getting some sandwiches for a picnic in a park was instantly nixed, as it would have only resulted in flying debris and wearing more vegetables than we would be able to consume. Instead, we decided to pick up some burritos to take back to the room.

A few miles away, we found our tiny restaurant and placed our to-go order. To kill fifteen minutes, we walked around the historic part of Fredericksburg, noting the rows of federal-style buildings, many of which claimed to still have bullet holes and damage in attics and under updated exteriors. When time was up, we collected our supper and tried to take the same road back to the hotel. As we were driving, however, a narrow road and an unexpected one-way street led us to a dead end. Since the road ended at a riverside park, we pounced on the second chance to have our picnic. Senator parked facing the water, and the emergency picnic kit was raided for extra napkins. We then ate our dinner while listening to an old radio show that took place just *after* the Civil War-- when the heart of the South had far from surrendered.

*   *   *

Thursday was bright and nippy. Both the wind and the temperature had dropped significantly, making it a perfect day to explore two more battlefields. Senator and I brought our gear down to the car, using extra caution on the lumpy stairs. In the motel's breakfast room there were only two other people quietly sipping their coffee and finishing their toast. One watched the television news, while the other read a newspaper.

We tried to be relatively quiet too, but I was buzzing in anticipation of our day. I had known the trip would be concentrated, and that we would learn and experience a lot of Civil War history in a short amount of time, but it was even more gripping than I had imagined. We were both sucked in. Our conversation, whatever the topic, inevitably seemed to roll back around to generals, battles, soldiers' lives, strategies, and ultimately more questions. What started as a glance at the weather forecast morphed into considering climate differences between the battles at Fredericksburg and Manassas. A mention of the upcoming month's schedule back home led to plans to read more biographies and invest in Ken Burns' grand documentary, *The Civil War*.

As we drove west again past Chancellorsville, we did our best to remember details and exhibits from the visitor center there, which also covered the Battle of the Wilderness and the Battle of Spotsylvania Courthouse. Ironically, as we passed fields dotted with the dainty yellow and white cups of wild daffodils, what I most recalled learning about the Wilderness* was that it was one of the most miserable landscapes upon which an American battle has ever been fought. Diaries and oral accounts used terms such as "wild, weird", "place of gloom", and simply "hell" to describe the terrain. Basically a sprawling network of dense forests, it had been worked, and in some places, mined out for years, leaving thick, scraggly underbrush to grow in the mostly unfarmable soil.

About a year after Chancellorsville, following a few months of relatively small battles, the Union and the Confederacy clashed in this harsh landscape. After a long string of dismal mismanagement by other generals, Ulysses S. Grant was now in control of all northern armies, steadfastly leading his Overland Campaign against the Army of Northern Virginia. On the southern side, General Lee still held the reins, despite a brief attempt at resigning over his grave error at Gettysburg the previous summer. While woods can often provide some cover under the right circumstances, chaos and confusion as the two armies met among the tangled growth resulted in another almost 30,000 casualties. Ammunition struck men and nature alike, many times igniting the forest in raging fire. In many cases, those not hit directly succumbed to burns, smoke

---

* I use the capital 'W' to refer to the specific Wilderness of battle fame, as it was designated as such on maps during the Civil War, and it has maintained its own reknown apart from general areas of geographic wilderness.

inhalation, or suicide to prevent being burned alive. Others were victims of their own ammunition, which was vulnerable to the intense heat as well. Among the wounded was General James Longstreet, who was hit in the shoulder and neck with friendly fire. General Lee's "Old War Horse" was now out of the equation until the following October.

Senator and I pulled into the parking lot for the first stop on our driving tour. A path led into the woods, so we could check out the Wilderness for ourselves. There was one other family starting up the same path, but we quickly passed them and kept up a fast pace to place some distance between us and them. We did not want our thoughts interrupted during this next phase of our exploration.

My first impression was that the forest seemed inappropriately amiable. We did not initially encounter any tangled masses of bushes or dense trees. Instead, the sun streamed through the mostly bare branches, occasionally lighting up more mounded lines of earthworks. It felt wrong, in a way, that it was as pleasant of a walk as if we were traipsing through our local state park at home. Later along the trail we did find some thicker growth, but we learned that much of the forest was currently sparser than it had been in the 1860s. Even so, near the end of the trail, we almost got turned around, despite a cleared path. It did not take too much imagination to picture the horror that led to animals routinely digging up skulls and bones during the years following the battle.

Our tour then took us along a curvy road that led to a few farmlands that saw heavy fighting. One of these was the Higgerson property, where a feisty Mrs. Permelia Higgerson was happy to taunt the Yankees as they retreated. "I think she may be taunting us, too," observed Senator. Though we had taken the short path up to the clearing and looked in all directions, neither of us could see the home's chimney that supposedly still stood. We rested on the hill for a few minutes and then marched back down to the car to see the next stop.

A mile or two down the road we reached the Chewning Farm. Like the Higgerson farm, the field was bare. The interpretive sign had not even promised a foundation or lone chimney, so we did not have false expectations. The gravel road leading to the hill top was an easy walk, though, so we took it. "We might as well, as long as we are here," said Senator. I nodded in agreement, and we started up the drive, noticing more of the wild chives growing in little clumps all over the open field.

In ten minutes we reached the end of the path. There we read the national park's posted information. Then, having no reason to linger, we began our brief walk back down the same gravel road. Just as we were reaching the end, perhaps twenty feet from where we had pulled over on the side of the road, we were both hit with an overpowering and absolutely putrid smell. "Did the wind change?" asked Senator, as we both involuntarily tugged our shirt collars up to our noses. As soon as he said it, we both knew there was no way any wind could bring something that awful our way without any hint of it anywhere else.

Before I even realized what I was saying, I blurted out my response. "No, that's the smell of rotting, killed flesh." I looked up and saw Senator staring at me as my words sank into both of our minds. There were no dead animals anywhere in the vicinity. Likewise, we had only been gone twenty minutes, and no vehicles had passed by in that time. We could see the car, the whole gravel road, and the main road during the entirety of our walk. To recreate a smell that horrible, one would have to kill an animal, leave its body in the hot sun for a few days, and then bring one's nose to within a few inches of the decaying result. In other words, we surely would have noticed it when we first walked by. Make what you will of the incident, Reader, but we are both firmly convinced that we were given just a glimpse of the terrible loss of life, not just in the Wilderness, but throughout the four years of disunity. It was a reminder we will not forget anytime soon.

The Battle of the Wilderness was officially a stalemate. It did, however, provoke General Grant's determination to pursue General Lee all the way to Richmond. Unlike previous northern military leaders, he was not about to retreat or even pause. As soon as the battle was over, he was already rallying the Union to race to Spotsylvania Courthouse. Both generals beat us there.

After traveling the same route as the armies, Senator and I arrived at Spotsylvania Courthouse battlefield. We made a brief stop at the shelter that served as an overall exhibit. Scanning the narrative and artists' renderings, we reviewed the summary of the engagement. Just days after leaving the Wilderness, a prolonged combat series took place on these grounds. The climax occurred when the Union attacked the Confederacy at the infamous Bloody Angle. Counterattacks surged, and relentless, ferocious fighting raged for twenty hours straight. After another

30,000 casualties, two generals killed, two generals mortally wounded, and two generals captured, the battle broke up inconclusively, and General Grant pressed forward toward the Confederate capital at Richmond.

Our driving tour led us among intermittent forests and open fields. Silently snaking their way around the countryside were more trenches and earthworks. After a short while we found ourselves at the Mule Shoe salient. Unlike most of the other stops along battlefield routes, this one had a sizable parking lot of perhaps fifteen or twenty spots. Even so, there were only four other vehicles there. From the car, I thought I could already see the giant formation.

Senator parked and we got out, grabbing our sunglasses, since the sky had gradually brightened. Before walking the long trail along one side of the Mule Shoe, we stopped to read the interpretive signs. The salient supported curved flanks that stood ready to fight on multiple sides. As we learned more about the fight, I heard some noises coming from the woods to the left, where a trail started near our parking spot. I assumed that a family was exiting the trail, possibly with a small boy who had found a suitable stick with which to smack around the ground and trees. At least, that is what my brothers would have been doing to make the familiar sound.

I continued to read the next panel of information, and I heard the sound again. The imagined family probably belonged to the mini-van parked a few spaces away from us. I finished the sentence I was reading and started to pose a thought-provoking question to Senator, as had been our habit the past three days. All of a sudden we heard a very loud crack, followed by the pronounced swoosh of a tree falling. Where we stood, we were not in any danger. It was close enough, however, that I did peer across the parking lot to see if our car had been crushed. It had not, but with our record of vacation site destruction, I would not have been surprised.[*]

"Wow!" I interrupted myself. "I don't think I've every actually heard a tree fall naturally-- I mean, when someone was not purposely cutting it down. Have you?"

"No, I don't think so," replied Senator. Chalk that one up to a new experience for both of us. I always wondered if we would ever witness that. I think about it when we walk the trail in the woods outside our town and notice trees down that were erect a week before. *Hhmmm...*

We drove on, meandering among more farmland that had seen intense combat. After the battle, one farmer's land was littered with hundreds of thousands of rounds. As in the case of other bloody countryside, choices for civilian survival came down to evacuation or hiding in cellars and hoping the house did not burn down. From vantage points on some farms, we could see other perspectives of the Mule Shoe and Heth's salients. All of the land now looked so peaceful under April cumulus clouds.

Most historians call Spotsylvania Courthouse a draw. Others claim that the South won via maneuvers. Ultimately, though, by June 1864, it was clear that the North was going to come out victorious sooner or later. General Grant employed simple, if cold, math. He recognized that the North was better supplied with provisions, clothing,

---

[*] See various sections of Books 1-7.

firepower, and most importantly, soldiers. With this knowledge, he famously promised to fight it out in the region if it took "all summer".

Though we had covered two battlefields extensively, we were still ahead of schedule. Our hotel was only a fifteen-minute drive away, but it was not even 1:30 in the afternoon. It seemed a shame to waste the rest of the day. Before rejoining the main highway, we paused for some fruit and schedule adjusting.

"Where are are we going tomorrow?" asked Senator.

"Our last Civil War stop is at Appomattox, but it's about two and a half hours away. If I had known we'd be done this early, I would have reserved a hotel down there."

"Well, why don't we go now?"

I instantly liked the idea, but I wanted to think it through just to be sure. "It's up to you. It would mean five more hours of driving today, but it's open until five. I think we'd only need about a half hour there, so we could just make it."

Senator easily settled the matter. "We've got nothing else going on. Let's do it." I was glad. Plus, it would give us more time at Shenandoah National Park on Friday.

At one point along the lovely drive, Senator pointed out that we sometimes have commutes to Chicago that are as long as our drive to Appomattox was. This drive was considerably easier, too. Instead of overcrowded traffic conditions and angry or distracted drivers, we drove at a comfortable pace around people who generally paid attention to what they were doing. Likewise, rather than ugly miles of cement, modern architecture, and pollution, we were rolling amid green pastures, more immaculately kept homes and farms, and budding trees planted among unassuming rocky streams. "Gee, I don't know," I started, sarcastically, "I sort of miss the gang graffiti. How will we know which neighborhood we're in?"*

We arrived at Appomattox Courthouse at 4:00pm. For those of you who appreciate arithmetic, that left us precisely one hour to explore the grounds where the Civil War effectively ended. As we parked the car, I opened the guide brochure and looked around to plot our remaining fifty-six minutes. Naturally, I had somehow underestimated the time needed to properly explore Appomattox, but I was confident we could still hit the essentials before the park rangers kicked us out.

By April 9, 1865, General Lee's Army of Northern Virginia was surrounded, starving, demoralized, and deserting. Realizing with great regret that he had no other option, General Lee began correspondence with General Grant, initiating a meeting of surrender. That afternoon, the two met in the most suitable location of the tiny town-- Wilmer McLean's parlor.† General Lee was the picture of southern dignity and decorum, dressed in a spotless new uniform. General Grant was every inch his opposite-- muddy and disheveled. After some small talk, the two gracious men began the solemn task of formalizing the surrender. Per President Lincoln's wishes, Confederate soldiers could keep both their personal weapons and their

---

* I don't know which makes me hate Chicago more: every time I have to go there, or every time I am far away from it.

† Ironically, almost four years earlier McLean had moved his family southwest to get away from the war, which had seen his land trampled and his home taken over as General Beauregard's headquarters during the first battle at Manassas.

horses, as long as they would swear to never take up arms against the United States again. In the spirit of "malice toward none", Union rations were immediately shared, and General Grant forbade any heckling of the losers. As the news spread throughout the country, Appomattox Courthouse became a thriving camp dedicated to printing parole passes and working out other immediate logistics associated with reunifying a nation.

"I thought you said this place was only one building," Senator said, hoofing it up to the main intersection of the small restored village.

"I don't remember why I thought that," I replied, becoming breathless and wondering when I had become so out of shape.

With time at a premium, we agreed to start at McLean's home. Though the original home had been dismantled, the National Park Service had reconstructed it on its foundation in the 1940s, using archaeological evidence. Inside, a young volunteer told us the basic information and a bit about each room. As soon as she finished, we zoomed around the less important rooms and then stepped into the parlor together.

We halted, synchronized, and no one else was around. The room was silent, but as we viewed the scene of what must have been one of the most forgiving surrenders in history, our thoughts were loud. Unbeknownst to each other, after spending a few days of concentrated study of several of Virginia's major Civil War battles, we had both expected to feel some sort of closure upon reaching McLean's home. We had followed two incredible armies who fought within horrendous conditions, rending a country. The end of it was supposed to feel peaceful and calming, like an overdue exhale. Instead, we were both struck with an intense sorrow. There was not one player who had been in that room or outside waiting on the grounds whom I did not deeply pity.

We left the McLean house slower than we had entered it, but we were still aware of our time constraints. Senator wisely grabbed the first ranger he saw. "If you had only thirty-seven minutes to see Appomattox, where would you go?" he demanded.

"Well," he began, "I would definitely see the McLean house..."

"Just did," I interrupted.

"Then I would make sure to see Clover Hill Tavern, the oldest building in the village... and I would stop by the visitor center, too." As we were thanking him and just about to sprint off, he added that we might also want to check out the store and maybe the law office.

I knew we would not have time for those, but I had seen enough similar structures throughout my years of touring old buildings. Clover Hill Tavern, on the other hand, had a specific role in the story at hand. Knowing his boys would never be able to return home uninhibited without proper paper work, General Lee requested parole passes for each soldier. Upon signing the terms of surrender, the Clover Hill Tavern was instantly converted into a printing press, cranking out the necessary 30,000 passes. In the main room, we could see the heavy presses and ink. Strung across the room on what looked like laundry lines were drying passes, ready for the next batch of distribution. The efficiency with which the process took place was impressive.

From there we had just enough time to run across the street to the visitor center. Inside I noticed a sign that said a film ran on the half-hours. We had missed the 4:00pm, but we could still catch the 4:30pm. Up the stairs we trod and plopped down in the small, dark theatre. As we waited for the docudrama to begin, I tried to figure out why I had thought that Appomattox Courthouse had only a small display. Who knows? Points deducted for Wendy V.

The film began with the familiar back story leading up to the inevitable surrender. It set the stage, depicting those in attendance on both sides. Then the days immediately following the surrender were reenacted. Seemingly endless lines of men disarmed and stacked their rifles in conical groupings. They removed their signature C.S.A. belts. I do not usually get emotional in movies-- I have been called a 'rock' by female friends in particular-- but by the time they were were folding up the Stars 'n' Bars, I was misty-eyed. I'm probably the only person to ever have gone for the tissues during a fifteen-minute visitor center film.

After the film, I stuffed my crumpled tissue in my pocket and quickly moved through a few exhibits. Senator was monitoring the time, reminding me that we did not want to be "those people". He meant the kind that we detested when we worked in retail. They would stay at least five minutes after closing time, acting oblivious to the thinly veiled announcements asking them to leave. He was right. By 4:58pm we were in the car, turning onto the main road. Upon crossing the county line, I noticed a sign in the rear view mirror that read "Where Our Country Reunited".

I hope so.

On the way back to our hotel, we discussed all we had seen and felt at Appomattox. The conversation naturally came around to discussing the two sides of the war. Because all of our ancestors were still in Europe at the time, we had no genealogical ties to either the North or the South. I decided to put Senator on the spot. "...But if you *had* to choose?..."

He thought for a moment. "I'd be Jimmy Stewart!" he responded, referencing the main character in the movie *Shenandoah*, who did his best to avoid the war, until the war came to him. It was a solid answer. I could not disagree.

The rest of the night involved sloppy sandwiches and television comedy. We needed some balance. Apparently I had not completely given my mind a rest from the War Between the States, though. That night I dreamed that General Grant had assigned me with the momentous task of organizing the surrender ceremony of the armies in the Western Theatre. This vacation was getting to be a lot of mental work.

*   *   *

Friday was another chilly, sunny morning. I was glad that we had driven down to Appomattox on Thursday, instead of going there Friday morning as intended. It freed up the entire day for Shenandoah National Park. We would get there about four hours earlier than scheduled, leaving plenty of time for hiking. Other than one minor scuffle between Jingles and myself, it was another beautiful drive among more pretty farms and small towns, this time with approaching bands of various hues of blue mountains.[*]

---

[*] Why the heck can't she just call a route or highway by its nationally

Shenandoah National Park is long and skinny. That is not a cartographer's terminology, but it is an appropriate description for the average person looking at a map of western Virginia. Running through the park is a 105-mile road called Skyline Drive. We entered the park at roughly the center of Skyline and began heading north.

I had done my homework ahead of time and chosen about ten potential hikes. From the past several years of experience, I was fairly adept at picking trails that worked well within our abilities, interests, and available time. After climbing up into the forested hills, we reached the first trail at Bearfence Viewpoint. It was a steep, rocky climb to the top, reminding me that it would soon be time to start thinking about the White Mountains again. A constant, prevailing wind chilled us in the shadows on our way up. On the way down, we were glad for it; returning on the sunny east side was about ten degrees warmer.

While hiking, I realized that the winds sounded different than we were used to when hiking in mountains. Then I figured out that I was missing the sound of rustling leaves. Most of our elevated hikes take place in summer, when the trees are in full leafiness. Due to the late arrival of spring, the trees were still completely bare. In retrospect, we had probably visited Shenandoah at the worst time of year to appreciate its splendor. Not only were the trees bare, but no wildflowers were blooming yet. The bears were still asleep, too, so no exciting wildlife sightings were in store. (That is, unless you count the occasional

---

recognized number, instead of its local street name? If we were locals who knew the name, we wouldn't be appealing to you for assistance in the first place, now would we, Jingles?

squawking bird.) On the other hand, we were too late for the snow that would have undoubtedly turned the landscape into a whimsical, white wonderland. As for an autumn palette of brilliant color... that was at the exact opposite part of the calendar. Learn from my mistake, Reader.

Senator's feet were hurting, and we were both ready for a bathroom stop, so we decided to drive up to the visitor center before attempting another hike. After five miles of scenic overlooks of the lowlands, we arrived at the busy parking lot. It was not overcrowded, but it was still more people than we had encountered anywhere else on the trip. It had to happen eventually, but I did not care for the mental transition that took me fully away from the 1860s. I was not ready for it yet.

After the necessary business, we started to walk the circular exhibit that told about the park. We had expected the usual explanations about geology or perhaps a wildlife video, but we got an uncomfortable history lesson instead. Essentially, Shenandoah National Park is the result of scamming and cheating.[*] In its earlier days, wealthy vacationers enjoyed a portion of what is now Shenandoah National Park as their fancy lodge resort, called Skyland. About that time, President Coolidge was convinced to sign legislation to create a national park in the east, making it more accessible to the majority of Americans than the national parks out west. This dovetailed nicely with the aspirations of Skyland's owner and other investors. When President Hoover took office, they courted his presence, ultimately getting him hooked on the region's beauty. He

---

[*] In the words of our current president, "Not good!"

established a remote camp there, and the media latched on to its popularity as a "pristine" and "undeveloped" place. The next president, Roosevelt, closed the deal, officially creating Shenandoah National Park.

It would have been a nice story if it ended there. Whereas most national parks are developed from existing public lands, however, Shenandoah was derived from privately held lands. The reality is that it was not, in fact, the uninhabited wilderness the public was led to believe it was. No less than 400 families were kicked off of their homesteads and forced to resettle. Some of them had been there for generations. To lend bogus credence to the removal, a teacher and two sociologists were employed to assemble a false propaganda report stating, in essence, that the residents were stupid, uneducated, and incapable of being proper citizens. Therefore, they argued, the government was actually doing them a favor by bringing them out of the mountains. Sadly, many of today's stereotypes of 'hill people' trace their roots back to this 'study'.

We watched a brief film and perused a display about ecology, but we were soured on Shenandoah. As a national park, it was pretty, but so were all of the others we had visited. This one lacked the majestic peaks and colossal canyons of the west. It did not boast any especially rare features like the volcano or fjords we had visited. The trees were lovely, but of average height, and the palette, though partially excused by the time of year, was dull, unlike the colorful hues of other places we had seen. I knew all of this beforehand and set my expectations accordingly, but learning the shady history of the park further lessened my interest in it.

Even so, we wanted to do more hiking, so I glanced at my prepared list of options. After a quick review, I chose the trail to Dark Hollow Falls, partly because you can never go wrong with waterfalls, and partly because I liked the name. The hike was classified as "moderate", which seemed reasonable, as it was only midday. Conveniently, it connected to the visitor center parking lot.

It was still chilly enough to keep lightweight jackets on as we started, initiating a pleasant spring walk. There was no one else around as we easily stepped along through the trees to the trailhead. As we crossed the road to the paved, downward path, that changed. "Oh, here's where they all are," said Senator. It was true; our private walk had merged us with middle-aged and senior citizen couples, whole families, and a few overly serious and expensively outfitted hikers. It was easy to assess the latitudinal regions from which each group hailed: shorts and tee shirts= Northwoods; parka, mittens, hat, and scarf= Deep South; sunglasses and light jackets that were quickly being shed= Midwest.

It was getting hot quickly (for us). The downhill walk was not hard, but it was steep and rocky. When we first glimpsed the rushing water, I figured we must be close to the end. This was not so. Back and forth we switched along the deceptive trail, driving further downward. At least the cool water was in view the entire time, but we were dreading the march up and out. Already the categorization of the route as "moderate" was in question. The estimated length of time was suspect as well.

"Do you want to rest a while?" I asked Senator.

"No, let's just keep going a little further," he answered. "I think we're almost there." The nerves in his feet had started to pulse in pain, due to an emerging condition we had not yet diagnosed. For some reason, he wanted to press on.

He was correct, though. Soon we found the bottom of the rocky falls. By comparison, I suppose it was dark and resembled a hollow, but we only paused enough for a quick photograph. We both knew that if we stopped too long, it might be our new permanent home. Besides, how many pictures did we really need of us next to water, trees, and rocks?[*]

The climb out was sweaty and breathless, but we actually made it in less time than anticipated. At times I felt like warning some of the people near the top not to bother. There was no way some of them were going to make it, especially given their inappropriate attire, but they seemed content to try. I passed Senator the rest of the water bottle, which we had properly rationed. At least we were not dehydrated. "So that was not considered 'strenuous'?" asked Senator in disbelief.

"Surprisingly, no, and I think I could be done hiking for the day," I suggested.

"Oh, yes," agreed Senator. "My feet are on fire." *Hhmmm.* This was not a good sign. We would have to get serious about the research and plan of attack for this matter when we got home.

We spent another hour or so driving Skyline Drive.

---

[*] It is not the first, and surely not the last time I have asked myself this question. In our defense, we dump at least half of the photographs we take, and we are rather selective to begin with.

At a few of the overviews we stepped out to stretch our legs and catch a swift breeze. As often happens, Senator was asked by a family of foreign tourists to take their picture. He obliged, and they motioned, offering to return the favor, Politely, we declined. We were getting tired, and the baggie of nuts and raisins was not doing much to tide us over. After a few more miles, we pulled around and drove back southward to the park's central gate, where we had first entered. Perhaps we would return for another hike or two in the morning, but it was time to find our room for the night.

 Not many hotels options came up when I searched online in the area near Shenandoah National Park. Instead, I located and reserved a nice room in a quiet bed and breakfast on farm property. After all of our Civil War-related travels, I thought it would be special to stay in a home that had weathered the war years, having been built a generation earlier. It was located less than half an hour from the park, so we entered the address, sat back, and enjoyed the ride through a few small towns before reaching the pastureland.

 Senator looked up at the small home Jingles had led us to. I guessed it to have two or three bedrooms. It appeared to have been built in the '60s-- the 1960s. "Are you sure this is the place?" asked Senator unenthusiastically.

 "Well, I'm assuming maybe the owners live here, and the b&b is elsewhere. I'll go up and see if this is where we check-in." *Please don't let this be it*, I thought, as I gingerly stepped my way onto the porch. No one was around, and it looked virtually abandoned. I got braver and moved around to the back porch. By this time Senator was closing his car door and approaching as well. There was still no sign of life, which was both annoying and a relief.

We scanned the horizon to determine our next step. About a block away several dozen cows were contentedly shuffling between trees and a water trough, pausing occasionally to munch on grass and bugs. "That's got to be the right place," I declared, pointing to a large, federal-style home past the cow pen. "I think I remember the website picture looking like that."

"If it's not, we're staying with them anyway," announced Senator, nodding in the same direction.

"The owners or the cows?..."

Fairly confident that we had the right place this time (no thanks to Jingles), we walked up to the door and prepared to knock. "Wait-- there's a note with my name on it," I said. I pulled the taped envelope off the door and opened it. Inside, the paper briefly explained that the owners were not able to be there, but we could make ourselves at home in our room. It went on to say that they do not issue keys, but they lock up late at night, once everyone is in.

I held the empty envelope upside-down. Sure enough, nothing fell out. "Well of all the stupid..." We had never heard of a room of any establishment not giving the guests a key to their own room. We decided to check it out just the same, but not bring in any luggage until we were in for the night.

The room was very pretty. Its Victorian dressiness was accented with plenty of antiques. A plaque explained some family history related to the room and the home, which had been passed down through generations. Unfortunately, no directions explained how to work the gas fireplace, which neither of us could figure out. Most important, there was a functioning dead bolt on the door. It was not that I anticipated any murderers or thieves on a farm in the middle of nowhere, but we are, after all, from Chicagoland. The situation would serve us fine for the night, but it would be a pain to bring our gear back and forth to the car if we had planned to stay several nights.

As we were about to leave the home to go find some dinner, I remembered another note I had seen in the room. It invited us to explore the small museum in the basement. Either we would have fun nosing around the big house, or no one would ever hear from us again. Happily, it turned out to be the former. Farm and domestic items that had accumulated over the past century-and-a-half were tucked in corners and on shelves, usually accompanied by an interpretive sign or note. Most impressive was the collection of antebellum pots, pans, and kitchen utensils. That reminded us how hungry we were, so off we went.

After perusing the local options, and taking into account the fact that we still smelled like we had been hiking, we opted to order a pizza. Taking it back to the room sounded good, and we could eat casually in front of the television. As we waited in the parking lot of the carry-out joint, we attempted a round of Farkel. It proved overly ambitious. Dice slid to inconvenient places between seats. Deciding it would be too easy to lose them, we soon gave up. Our gooey pizza was ready anyway.

Back to the farm we drove. Still no one was around. As we got out of the car, the cows gathered, interested in what was going on. Perhaps they just wanted a slice.

Just before we reached the front door, I laughed out loud. "What did you see?" asked Senator.

"I just noticed the sign in the yard." Senator looked down to where I was pointing and nodded at the irony. He held open the unlocked front door for me, as we both acknowledged the home security sign poked into the grass.

Once inside, we bolted ourselves in from any potentially menacing cows. It was time to get down to the business of eating mediocre pizza. Afterward, we cleaned up and took some time to relax. Nothing interesting was on television, but we were absorbed in other tasks, anyway. I found a better, more rural route home. Senator found reviews on a multi-volume biographies of Robert E. Lee, Abraham Lincoln, and Jefferson Davis. So much for light summer reading.

*   *   *

Throughout the night, Senator did not sleep well. When he was asleep, he gasped too often. This woke me up, and led me to nudge and try to rearrange him. That, in turn, woke him up. It was a miserable and vicious cycle that culminated in him getting up somewhere between 3:00am and 4:00am and declaring he was ready to leave.

I could appreciate his frustration, but there was no way I was getting up in the middle of the night to get on the road for a long, tired drive. I had been down that road before; it was absolutely not the correct solution. He was irritated, but I covered my eyes and tried to grab a few more hours of sleep. For once I was standing (or lying) my ground. Despite the tenseness, I managed to snooze until 7:00am.

"I'm up now," I announced vaguely, and started my morning routine. The previous night's fake garlic butter on the pizza crust was reminding me of its poor chemical composition. I was soon ready to go, but I hoped it would not involve numerous rest area stops. Senator was ready. He only needed to put his shoes on and grab two bags. I already knew the answer, but I asked to confirm. "I assume we're not going back to Shenandoah for any more hiking?..."

"Correct," he answered flatly.

"Can we sit down and have breakfast first?" I asked, halfway wondering if there was even any host in the bed and breakfast to cook it.

"Alright," he reluctantly agreed. We went down to the dining room and met the only other couple who had stayed at the house that night. Like us, they had been wondering about the mystery-owners and the lack of room keys. Also like us, they had done the hike down to Dark Hollow Falls, and had the same reaction about the trail's unexpected length and rigor.

Soon our host came out with coffee. She looked about twenty-three. In the background, we could hear a baby crying. A few minutes later, her husband took a break from cooking and took the baby out of the house. (He was much older-- maybe twenty-five.) As the woman poured, she told us about the history of the home, explaining that its current owner was a descendant of the original family, but that he was in his 90s. It sounded like the young family may have been caretakers. Or perhaps the cows were really in charge.

We finished our breakfast and bid our companions

happy travels. Since there was no key to return, we yelled a "good-bye" and "thank-you" toward the kitchen. On our way out, the woman wished us well. We nodded and exited, again noticing the security sign in the yard.

Senator was tired but determined. "I can drive," he stated, before I could offer. The sky was dreary, but it was nice not to have the sun shining in our faces. After a quiet period of getting to the main highway, Senator put on the next Civil War radio show. I knew that his intention was to do the entire stretch, as opposed to stopping overnight on the way, as originally planned. I was glad.

In the hills of West Virginia we made our first gas stop. Senator pumped and then went inside for coffee. I glanced at the map as I waited. I looked up when I heard commotion behind the car at the next row of pumps. It sounded like a raised voice, so I thought there might be trouble. Thankfully, there was no trouble. When I craned my neck back, I saw Senator smiling and chatting with a woman who was excited to recognize the dealer name on our license plate surround. We were all amazed to learn that she lived only eight miles from us. She, too, was on her way home, after visiting Shenandoah National Park. *How do these coincidences keep happening, in a country of 330,000,000 people?*

As we crossed deeper into the mountains, it started to snow heavily. Big flakes blew across the entire state, but there was never much accumulation. Visibility was still decent, too, so it was really a nice diversion. April snow has always had its own distinct appeal to me.

In Ohio I took the wheel. Senator dozed on and off, making up for some of his lost sleep Friday night. The snows had been left behind, but it was still cool. We continued along into Indiana, where we would turn north to ride I-65 up to I-80.

Senator was playing with Jingles, zooming in and out on her screen. "Whatcha' doin' over there?"

He looked thoughtful. "Are we going through Richmond?" he asked.

At first I thought of Richmond, Virginia. It was a little late for that. Then I realized that he meant Richmond, Indiana, home of historic Gennett Records. "I don't really know, but if it's showing up close by, we can..."

He studied the route line on the screen for a moment. "No, that's okay. Never mind." Being together for almost fifteen years has taught me that that actually meant, "I would really like to stop here, Wendy."

"Does it show an exit number?" I asked. I glanced over to sneak a peek at the screen while watching the road.

"I don't think so," he answered.

I had caught enough of a glimpse to make a reasonable guess as to where to get off the highway. "Well, based on the position of the purple dot, I think I'll take the next exit and head south," I planned out loud.

"If you want to. I don't know. We can skip it..." Now I was certain he wanted to go. In five minutes, we were off of the interstate and driving south toward Richmond. We had no plan beyond that.

Five years earlier, we had stopped in Richmond (population 35,000) for an afternoon while staying in Indianapolis. We had parked and walked around an area that eventually led us to the remains of the building that once stood as the home of the Starr Piano Company. As part of a ploy to sell phonograph players, Starr started recording musicians and singers. As a result, they unintentionally captured early American jazz and blues, leaving historical gems for future music lovers.

It had been a very enjoyable experience for two people whose love of history, music, and recording overlapped. The only problem was that we had absolutely no idea where it was located. Not having internet access, we could not look up any information, either. Senator again looked doubtful, but I was also thinking of the fact that, for the five years since, he has regularly lamented the fact that he never took a brick from the neglected pile of rubble by the Starr building. "We're going to at least try to find it," I announced. Senator smiled. In the parlance of Sherlock Holmes, the game was afoot.

The first thing we saw after we exited the interstate was a sign referencing Richmond. At least we had the right city. A few blocks down the main road took us to a major intersection. For no particular reason, we turned right. "This is starting to look old," said Senator, observing streets lined with homes built in a much earlier time.

"That's good!" I replied. It was encouraging. A factory from the 1920s would not be in the modern section of town, near the Starbucks. "Let's turn into this block."

We drove around a neighborhood for a while, but it was too residential for our purpose. It was time for some strategy. We might roam around aimlessly on a wild goose chase, but we were not giving up without a fight. "What do we actually remember?" I asked.

"I know there was a smokestack," started Senator. That could be very helpful, provided it was a tall one.

I racked my brain. "Yes, I seem to remember walking westward, toward a park. Maybe there was some sort of barrier, too..." I was getting excited. We had some mental pictures to work with.

For the next fifteen minutes or so, we focused our efforts on an area around an overpass. I thought that was the barrier I remembered. Just as I was reconciling it with my memory, Senator spotted the smoke stack. For the first time, it seemed realistic that our search was not in vain. Like many older cities, though the streets were in a grid pattern, "You can't get there from here," as they say. After many baffling turns, we lost sight of our beacon.

I pulled back onto a main road and turned down the next street we saw. There was a vacant lot, so I parked the car facing west. We were a little discouraged, but I was sure we could find it. We reassessed. "Okay, we have narrowed down a good-size city to about six square blocks. The place didn't just disappear, so it has to be somewhere. You mention that you think it was sunk down somehow..."

Senator picked up my idea and ran with it. "So, we have to find some turn that goes down, maybe from a side street. It must not be very noticeable." With that, I pulled the car back to the main westward road. We agreed to watch for any inlet that looked obscured. The very next street matched that description. We both spoke over each other to say we wanted to try it. At the same time, Senator pointed to a large mural of a record, with an arrow pointing down the road. We had found it.

Though there was a sign, we could hardly be blamed for missing it, as it was on the side of a low cement wall. They were not going out of their way to assist the tourists.

It was okay; we were just happy to be there. We parked in the empty lot and took our time surveying the multi-story, empty brick building. Stoic open arches were the predominant feature, along with the nearby elusive smoke stack. In the park in which it was situated, a walk of fame illustrated artists like Hoagy Carmichael, Louis Armstrong, Gene Autry, Charlie Patton, and Duke Ellington in mosaic.

We walked around and read a few humble plaques. Then I stood in front of the building as Senator disappeared behind it. I heard mild rustling. *I sure hope that's him, and not someone or something else*, I thought. My suspicions were confirmed when he emerged with a plastic bag in his hands. Its awkward swinging movement made it clear that a heavy object was inside. He had finally obtained his brick.

The rest of our trip was non-eventful. We drove north and caught I-80, forgoing the side route we had taken out. Traffic near the Illinois border was not awful, or at least not as awful as it typically is there. Before midnight we were home.

We had fun in Virginia, but we have certainly had more laughs elsewhere. We appreciated the serene landscape, but there are far more visually stunning places. Next to our other vacations, this one probably falls somewhere in the middle of the pack. Nevertheless, visiting these Civil War sites and walking such hallowed ground after months of dedicated study of the battles and associated events made this the most impactful trip we have taken thus far. In fact, I am already blocking out dates to visit battlefields in Tennessee next year. Yet, we still had unanswered questions. We still did not believe either side was completely right or completely wrong. Having many sympathies with the South's desire to defend its land, I also recognized the North's role (intentional or accidental) in crushing slavery. Considering the miserable conditions of soldiering, though, I probably would have just been shot as a deserter, whichever side I was on. The one solid conclusion Senator and I reached was a renewed vow to act "with malice toward none". In today's world, this is not always easy, but we are getting better at it. Thank you, Mr. Lincoln.

Chapter 4
The Eyes Have It, (or Vertical): Late July 2018

Yes, with malice toward none. Not even illogical administrators. Not even an unhinged and violent political party bent on destroying the greatest country on Earth. Not even the neighbor who waits until perfectly dry, lovely days to burn garbage. Not even the guy who just cut us off in traffic. We instead channeled our would-be malice toward the mounting heat and humidity.

From May on, it was a wild ride of moist summer misery, punctuated by the odd cool, dry day that teased us into internet searches for homes in better climates. It was quite a roller coaster, with the highs consistently landing on holidays. The Memorial Day service in our little town canceled the cemetery portion of the itinerary, due to heat indices that had become excessive by 9:30 in the morning. Likewise, our family's Independence Day picnic was moved inside to prevent the 100°F+ temperature and soppy humidity from taking out the children, the senior citizens, and yours truly. By nightfall, it had cooled down to a balmy 90°F or thereabouts, but the downpours that had plagued June continued, canceling the fireworks that we were going to watch by the river (from our air-conditioned car, that is).

Major renovations at my job placed our staff on an extended summer vacation. Senator's recording engineer job, however, showed no sign of letting up. That meant more moving heavy gear in an out of buildings and up and down stairs. I was very hot and counting down days until fall.[*] He was beyond hot and counting down the hours until he could take his next cool shower. I was glad he was no longer the heat-loving guy I started dating fifteen years earlier, but I felt bad for him. He was really having a rough time with it. The entire uncomfortable mess that was May, June, and July pointed our thoughts toward the end of the month, when we would escape together to the higher,

---

[*] For many years I have argued that September, at least in our part of the country, is a summer month. Though I offer consistent quantitative data as evidence, I am regularly refuted by people who erroneously cling to the myth that autumn begins in September. My mother was among such folks, gently presenting her case that went something along the lines of, "Well, the temperatures do drop off just about Labor Day, and there are some really beautiful days." "No," I counter, "you're thinking of something else. It is called 'October'." I attribute her and others' mistake to a nostalgia for returning to school during crisp, autumn days of yesteryear, which happened to occur in September. Sadly, those days are gone, and back-to-school now means sweaty staff and students, regardless of whether the weather takes place in August or September. This year, my mom finally conceded the point, on a mid-September day of 96°F. I did not gloat; I wish she was right.

cooler, drier northern New England climate.

This time we were not just going to New Hampshire; we would hit coastal Maine to take in Acadia National Park as well. It was another one of those places my parents had taken us to during the grand tour of the U.S. and Canadian Northeast when I was sixteen. The same trip had introduced me to Cape Breton and Prince Edward Islands, where Senator and I had roamed the previous year. I do not feel compelled to visit every national park, but Acadia's rocky Atlantic shoreline and soaring, windy peak earned it a prime spot on my list.*

Oceans and forested mountains were again the backdrop for what I hoped would be two weeks of outdoor paradise. In addition to the impending joy of better weather, I had another pleasantry up my sleeve. Months earlier I had booked a marine life cruise out of Bar Harbor, Maine. It would not be as intimate as the one we took in Nova Scotia, but this one promised puffin-watching as well as whale-watching. For some reason, I determined that we needed to witness puffins doing whatever it is that puffins do in the wild. A boat ride that left the shoreline twenty or thirty miles behind seemed sufficient to do the trick.

Of course, there were also planned hikes in the White Mountains. It would be our fourth time in the area,

---

* There are not too many more that I want to see that I have not already seen. I suppose Yosemite would be interesting, but it might pale in comparison to Yellowstone and the canyon parks of the West. At some point, we will probably see Smoky Mountain National Park (the country's most visited), but I imagine it is similar to Shenandoah. Years ago, I used to think I would like to see the Everglades, but now it just seems like it would be a giant mosquito nighmare.

and by now we were fairly confident that we could re-attempt one of the majestic 4,000-footers*. Unlike the first time we had tried, Senator was not sporting a broken toe this year. Just in case of a non-cooperative weather day, though, I also researched and compiled a list of local town museums and historical societies. After all, we might someday be residents. We might as well get to know the real history behind some of these quirky and inviting little towns.

By the time I threw all of the plans into the mix, (and added a dash of the Civil War once I realized how close we would be to Joshua Lawrence Chamberlain's home,) I had a substantial journey outlined. I explained to Senator that we could either drive two very long days or three seven-hour days. To my delight, since his schedule allowed, he opted for the latter. Eagerly we counted down the weeks and then days until we could escape Illinois.

*   *   *

Knowing we had only a seven-hour drive made it a fairly easy departure. We did not need to fight early commuter traffic or dread a seemingly endless day on the road. Pulling onto the highway in the pouring rain, however, added a dose of stress. For the first hour and a half, which included the busiest part of the drive (south suburbs of Chicago and Indiana border), the deluge continued. Thankfully the traffic and the weather settled down majorly afterward, leaving us with partly sunny skies, if still too much summer heat.

It was early evening when we exited the interstate in

---

*   local speak for mountains in the White Mountain range that are over 4,000 feet high

Ashtabula, Ohio. In honor of our not being on a tight schedule, and because there was a surprising lack of hotel availability, I had booked a bed and breakfast. My anticipation grew as we drove through an attractive part of town, where historic homes were woven together with ivied trellises and shady, flowered gardens. I recognized some of the same lilies and roses that I had at home, but theirs looked happier.

I was happy, too, but I was admittedly disappointed when our route took us steadily away from the lovely neighborhoods and over a bridge that sent a message without saying a word. Just beyond the brief descent, we were clearly in a different part of town. I won't call it dumpy, but the homes and businesses definitely looked like they had their share of woeful tales. Though not dangerous, it is also true that it probably was not the best place we could have made a wrong turn.

Knowing we were near our intended address, we simply misjudged by a street or two. Turning just a moment before we should have, we were suddenly aimed at a dead-end. Appropriately, the terminus was a biker hangout. Leathered and braided men and women half-sat on their bikes and began to take notice of our car, (which probably has a smaller engine than some of their rides,) coming down the street. A few still clutched their adult beverages. Senator and I each scanned the road for the quickest exit. There was no alternate side street, so Senator made a u-turn before we reached the cul-de-sac. This move, I believe, resulted in the mutual satisfaction of all involved parties. The bikers got to keep their secret spot-- unintruded upon, and we got to keep our limbs.

A few minutes later, we were at the bed and breakfast. As we waited on the porch for our host to answer the door, I could not help but notice that the biker hangout was still within view if I craned my neck and peered beyond houses across the street. "I suppose it's okay?..." I ventured, inviting Senator's opinion.

"Yeah, I think it's fine," he said. "The street's quiet and clean, and there's some children playing over in that yard." He was right. Overall it was not a bad feel. For better or worse, there was also a gated parking area.

"Welcome!" came a voice from the doorway. The home's owner let us in and allowed us to peruse the main level before leading us upstairs. Victorian antiques, including an Alexander Graham Bell telephone, unusual paintings, and plenty of glassware filled the parlor, library, and dining rooms. The home's swan theme was carried throughout.

Upstairs, our room sported a nautical theme, with plenty of lighthouse references and a roped border. In the bathroom was large whirlpool, whose water poured in through a swan's mouth. "This reminds me of Neuschwanstein," Senator remarked, remembering the German Castle of Ludwig II, the Swan King. It did indeed.

The only problem was that there was no shower. A bathtub might work for people with short hair or mad Bavarian royals, but it would be tricky for me. Senator opted to use the shower in the bathroom next door, but I did not want to parade out into the hall with all of my necessary gear. Instead, I sat in the tub, leaned my head back at an uncomfortable angle[*], and did my best to imitate

---
[*] smacking it only once

a shower and wash a mass of hair. I was rewarded for my efforts with a massive amount of water in my ear that plagued me for the next two days.

We passed the rest of our night along the waterfront in another historic part of town. As we ate our falafel burgers, we could see the bridge out the window. An enormous cement weight swung the bridge open for passing boats, which came from two directions. It was funny how the bridges in the town where we used to live were always considered nuisances whenever drawn. Now, on vacation, they were romantic wonders adding to the streetscape.

* * *

Saturday morning we awoke at a sane hour, happy to be facing another day of only about seven hours of driving. We were going as far as Vermont, which would position us unquestionably within New England-- an undeniable boost in morale. By dinnertime, the Midwest would only be a vague memory, or so at least I pretended. For the next hour or so, though, we were appreciating the final corner of Ohio, as we ate breakfast with two other couples at the communal table.

Our host served plates of fruit and French toast, and then exited temporarily to refill the coffee carafe. As I am sure I have mentioned, Senator and I are not big on the sharing-a-table-with-strangers thing, but we seem to make it work. In this case, the two other couples were both easy-going, and everyone seemed genuinely interested in each others' travel tales and advice, particularly when it came to hiking. As an icebreaker, I told my Christian bear joke.[*]

---

[*] (which is completely plagiarized from at least one pastor): One day

Even more amazing than how hard the other couples laughed at the silly joke was how in awe they were of our travel plans. Three of them were from within an hour radius of that very spot. The other was a South Carolinian, but Ohioan by marriage. When they heard we were going out to Maine *(gasp!)*, from Illinois *(gasp!)*, by automobile *(double gasp!)*, we were met with expressions of wonder and wistfulness. All agreed that they had always wanted to go to Maine, making it sound more mysterious than the state warranted. They seemed to consider us real road warriors and adventurers. I bit my tongue rather than pointing out that they all lived closer to it than we did, and they could probably make a Maine vacation a reality rather easily. Once again, though, our experience confirms that people from New England do not leave their boundaries, and rarely do natives of other parts of the country visit them.

We finished a pleasant final round of coffee warm-ups and wished everyone well. I paid our host while Senator brought our bags down to the car. It was a peaceful, if drizzly, morning. The neighborhood was quiet, and no ruffian biker gangs were occupying the streets, demanding that we surrender our hiking boots or extra tee-shirts. We were again on our way.

Before leaving Ohio, we stopped to make some adjustments in light of more restrictive Pennsylvania and New York firearm laws. Accordingly, we separately stowed

---

a lone hiker was out in the woods. Turning around, he was startled and fearful to see a bear quickly approaching him. Thinking quickly, he threw up a brief prayer. "Oh, Lord! Please let this be a Christian bear!" With that, he reopened his eyes to see the bear stop in its tracks. A miracle! Then it knelt down, folded its paws, and declared, "Thank you, Lord, for this meal which I am about to receive!"

our guns and ammunition. These measures were carefully taken lest the bullets magically insert themselves neatly into magazines, which then might bust out of their locked boxes Houdini-style and bust into other boxes equally impressively, prior to loading themselves into our guns, switching their own safeties off, racking their own slides, and squeezing their own triggers. (For the record, this has occurred a grand total of zero times in the history of humanity.) Nevertheless, we comply.

On through Pennsylvania we rode, with precipitation alternating between heavy mist and substantial showers. Next came New York, my least favorite state through which to travel when we go east. It has earned this distinction for three reasons: 1.)Buffalo traffic is always horrific and always stops dead at the toll plaza, 2.)gas is more expensive, and 3.)they consistently have the most disgusting restrooms on the interstates. All of these are meaningful statements coming from a girl who grew up in outer Chicagoland.

At some point, though, people who drive toward exotic places like Maine have to use the facilities, so we made a pit stop somewhere in the middle of I-90. Parting into our separate regions, I told Senator to wait right outside the women's bathroom for me. I was certain he would be done first, and as it turned out, this was a safe assumption. The first stall I picked had an unflushed mess in it.[*] The next four had nowhere to hang my handbag, which was too bulky to swing around me. Number six had no toilet paper, which, come to think of it, I probably had in

---

[*] Yes, I know it is simply a matter of pressing a button. Doesn't matter-- I won't do it. Ever. Just can't.

my bulky bag. As that fact did not occur to me then, I went back outside the restroom to hand my bag to Senator, who, of course, had finished his business and was patiently waiting for me. Back in I went and successfully completed phase one of my own business. Phase two, finding a sink with a soap dispenser *not* torn off the wall, took a bit of astute perception. On the other hand, no amount of astuteness could help the barely-functioning hand dryer. Eventually I gave up and exited the bathroom while wiping my hands on my jeans. I don't even think I paused in my stride as Senator transferred my bag back to me. Moments later, we were back on the road.

It was late afternoon, and thankfully we were crossing into Vermont. Immediately the pristine Green Mountains were in view. The rain had let up and gradually quit, further improving the drive. When we reached our motel, neatly nestled among rolling fields at the edge of a valley, the weather fantasy we had been dreaming about for months became a reality. We stepped out of the car into a dry 70°F breeze. It lightly whirled around us as if to welcome us to the serene pastureland of the Northeast. It was deliciously comfortable after all the humidity we had experienced all summer. When we went out for a bite, we took advantage of it by claiming a table near the wide open doorway to the restaurant's patio. Everyone else seemed to take it for granted; we were just taking it in, eager to continue deeper into mountain country.

*   *   *

After Saturday's blissful climate, we were more motivated than ever to reach the coast. If the inland breeze was that sweet and refreshing, the ocean winds would be heavenly. Hiking would be beautiful, too. Plus, we would really be able to maximize our time, since we would not be hopping across provinces daily like the year before. As I finished packing our gear, I thought about how nice it would be to stay several nights in the same location.

"I'm going to take a few things to the car," I told Senator. We were parked right outside the door to our room, so I could drop off those items and easily return for round two. By that time, Senator would be ready to leave, and we could continue east. With one bag strap over my shoulder and another in hand, I opened the door and stepped out.

"Whoa!" I exclaimed. My visions of ideal weather were temporarily put on hold as I tried my best to hold the door against the gale-force wind. The car keys were ready in my right hand, but I still had to fumble with them as I battled the pelting rain. I guess we had not looked out the window as we were getting ready. Nevertheless, we were soon situated in the car, drying our faces, and going on our way.

Crossing southern Vermont, we passed through the town of Wilmington, where we had stayed on our first trip together, fifteen years ago. I was happy to see it had maintained its lovely few 'downtown' blocks of colonial and early-eighteenth century homes and shops. Each was stubbornly and appropriately perched on its foundation among thick trees or the rocky streams that meander around the foothills of the Green Mountains. I still remember our room in the inn there, where the pervasive local mood was friendly, but not impressed. I also remember indulging in cupcakes with maple frosting, an especially decadent treat, considering how much stronger our willpower was in those days.

As you might assume, it does not take long to cross Vermont in an east-west direction. The consolation for it ending, however, is that you enter New Hampshire-- God's gift to New Englanders who can't relate to leftists. I admit to always feeling an odd sense of being home when I enter the Granite State. It is illogical, I know, but it hits me all the same. Of course, the feeling fades somewhat if I realize that I am only being teased. Traveling through the southern part of the state cheats one out of the lakes, mountains, and isolated wilderness of the north country, though there are still some pretty darn scenic spots, even from the busy highway. When one reaches the southeast corner, however, one starts to highly suspect that Massachusetts has finally staged a hostile takeover. For one thing, there are tolls. *What's this?! Are you not aware of your own state motto?* Furthermore, there are more vehicles on the road there than in the rest of the state combined.* Not surprisingly, most of them sport Massachusetts license plates. I could say more, but I am again reminded of my sincere attempt to uphold "with malice toward none".

When we reached the edge of the continent, we turned to follow the coast up into Maine. Thankfully, we were traveling north on I-95. Those in the southbound lane (mainly weekend vacationers heading home) were clogging up the interstate for at least fifty miles. Their pace crawled, slowed further by the steady rain.

Our side was not nearly as bad, but we did have one or two slowdowns. In these instances, I typically pass the

---
* and that includes tractors and snowmobiles

time by reading bumper stickers. On this particular day, there was a roughly even assortment of "COEXIST" or pro-leftist stickers and 2nd Amendment or pro-Trump stickers. None of them were terribly clever, but it did give me a funny idea. During the 2016 election, I would have liked to have seen someone with three bumper stickers on their car: an "I'm with Her", a "Make America Great Again", and a "Feel the Bern"-- with absolutely no explanation. It might have united the country, strictly by way of its non-committal confusion.

In the midafternoon, amid soggy showers and warming air, we pulled into the parking lot of the Joshua L. Chamberlain museum in Brunswick, Maine. We arrived about an hour later than I had hoped, but we still made it onto the second-to-last tour. As soon as I had our tickets in hand, our knowledgeable guide led us through the only home owned by the Gettysburg war hero and his wife, Fanny. Remarkably, the original home was moved from down the block. Later it was raised up, and a ground floor was added beneath it, engineered by shipbuilders. For a time, the home also served as the residence of Henry Wadsworth Longfellow and his wife.

In a less-respected period of the home's history, it was broken into apartments and student housing for the nearby college. Fortunately, it has since been rescued and restored. Now the public can view upstairs rooms, a grand parlor where concerts were once held, and Chamberlain's library, which includes some of his original furnishings, books, Civil War military boxes, and Medal of Honor. Adjacent to the library is Chamberlain's study, which now contains his regal-looking chair, once co-opted as a throne for the local college's homecoming queen. In fact, various other artifacts gradually made their way back to the home, decades after being sold off or even left in the garbage. My favorite story involved a woman in her eighties who recently returned a salt and pepper shaker set she "may have borrowed" when she was a girl. At that time, General Chamberlain was already long departed, but when his family's summer home burned down, some locals found the souvenir shopping too good to resist.

Three more history books found their way into our collection before we left Brunswick. Then it was back toward the coast and Down East.* Though the rain let up a little, it rarely stopped completely. There would be no harbor walks tonight, but maybe we could at least drive through the national park before dark.

A few hours later, we checked into our tiny cabin. As soon as we stepped foot through the doorway, I loved it. It was clean and cozy as expected, but it had an extra good feel to it. It was not until we were checking out a few days later that I finally put my finger on it; the mid-century wooden paneling was the same pattern as in my grandparents' finished basement. Less romantic but equally appreciated was the small window air conditioner. Temperatures were higher than they should have been for coastal Maine, but we were still holding out for great hiking the next day.

Senator and I were getting hungry, but we wanted to make the most of the daylight, so we left the room and drove fifteen minutes south into Acadia National Park. We

---

* nautical term referring to wind patterns along the southern coast of Maine were hoping to see some wildlife while getting our bearings, but we mainly saw trees. The warm air and the wet everything combined to produce a hefty fog. There was just enough time to grab a park map and drive back to the main highway before dark.

On the way back to our cabin, we surveyed the dinner options. Having learned our lesson about the availability of non-seafood on the north Atlantic coast, we stopped at the first pizza place we saw. It was a carry-out window, run by Jamaicans. *Different...* Senator placed our order, and we waited in the car. Fortunately, he had brought a radio show for us to pass the time. Halfway through an episode, he left the car to pick up our crummy New England pizza. We finished the rest of the episode with an open box spanned across the front seat, each of us lifting out and folding our floppy, cheesy triangles while trying not to drip them into our laps.

Back at our cabin, we were each ready for a shower and some time to read. I went first, while Senator cracked into one of his new books. Then it was his turn. While he was in the bathroom, I worked on the computer to confirm the next day's itinerary and weather.

Just as he stepped out to dry himself, the smoke detector went off. There were no signs of smoke or fire anywhere, so he scrambled to get dressed while I opened the door to the outside. Immediately the alarm stopped. Had it been a steamy shower, it might have made sense, but the room did not look cloudy to either of us. I was concerned that maybe something was going on in the adjoining cabin next door, but their alarm had not even gone off. After careful inspection, we never did see any problem, so I think the unit must have been oversensitive. Now we were really ready for some quiet reading time.

*   *   *

Monday morning was Mount Desert Island hiking day. While one might logically assume that means hiking in a desert, Mount Desert is the large island which makes up the bulk of Acadia National Park. Rather than 'desert', as in dry, arid landscape, the name comes from the French *désert*, as in, no one really hangs out there-- French or otherwise. These days, however, Mount Desert Island is overrun with tourists, especially in summer. So claims their website, which seamlessly links the visitor to complex tables of shuttle bus schedules that would give Dr. Watson a challenge.* Cautions abound, highly encouraging the potential hiker, biker, or sightseer to forgo his or her own vehicle in lieu of the clean, green, convenient, free buses.

On the surface, it sounded good. In reality, I knew it would be a pain. For one thing, the matrix of stops, times, and routes was not as easy to interpret as the website would have one believe. There was also the fact that we were not exactly sure of the order of the trails we were going to hike. Terrain and weather dictate those facts for a hiker, despite thorough planning. The overcast sky and on-and-off drizzle were also not solidifying any plans. Thus, at 8:00am, in our own car, we started down the highway toward the park. If the first few trailhead parking lots were filled, we would try other spots.

It was a pleasant discovery when we found that we

---

* You remember, of course, that Dr. John Watson (of Sherlock Holmes fame) had an uncanny ability to memorize train schedules-- times, stations, the whole works.

were one of the few cars on the road. There were some other early-ish birds, and some construction workers, but for the most part, we had the pick of the park. At the park entrance station, Senator slowed to a stop and presented his i.d. to the ranger. I handed over our prepaid pass[*] and dug in my purse for my license. Before I could produce it, the man waved me off saying, "That's okay-- same name anyway, right?"

"Actually, no..." replied Senator.

The man finished glancing at Senator's license before handing it back to him. "Oh, Zuchowski... well, I can trust you then!" he announced cheerfully. He gave no explanation for our elevated clearance status, but he never did require my license. We thanked him, shrugged, and drove forward.

Once inside the park, we drove south toward our first trailhead. A persistent fog gave the island a thin veil of white. Each time a vehicle tore through it, it split and swirled lightly to the sides in mild offense. Almost unbelievably, every so often we encountered bicyclists trudging up the hill of the main road. "That is just plain stupid!" I said, annoyed at the arrogance on display. We

---

[*] During the planning of this trip, the federal government raised the entrance fees for the most popular national parks. A passenger car and its passengers already cost a sizeable $25.00 for one week. They wanted to raise it to a hefty $75.00, but public backlash (including from me) caused them to readjust their figure to a more reasonable $30.00. To be extra sure that no one tries to pull any cost-cutting shenanigans (like the time I gave our Badlands pass to some people we met at an inn), all visitors now have to show i.d., and the vehicle's license plate is printed on the pass, along with the name of the pass purchaser. *All this, but we can't demand i.d.s to vote.*

had come upon a couple crawling their way up, both in the middle of the only lane, risking calamity by riding in the fog. Senator agreed with my judgment, inserting a few key adjectives. We would have similar experiences behind cyclists several more times that day before learning that, in fact, there were beautiful bicycle paths on converted historic carriage roads through the park. No cars were allowed there, and they were further inland and away from the fog. You really have to wonder about some people.*

Our first stop was the ample parking lot at the Sand Beach area. This was ironic, as I more or less detest sand. Avoiding the trail down to the suggested sand beach, one can find the launching spot for a more preferable walk. Climbing up some stairs led us back to the road, where we paralleled it on the Ocean Path.

Soon intermittent views opened up to the rocky Maine coast. The fog still obscured the water, but the shoreline was rough and gorgeous, with nary a grain of sand in sight. When we came to a secluded area, we made our way down to the boulders below. Their color contained a duller hue of the Nova Scotia pink we had seen the previous year. The waves pounded the shore, forcing air from hollow spots and perfectly mimicking thunder. Time after time the surf seemed to rise out of nowhere,

---

* Looking to take a more active role in the production of my travelogues, Senator here interjects a public service announcement for visitors to Acadia National Park: "If you find that you are getting too frustrated with the cyclists who insist on pedaling up the only car road, just be patient until around 2:30 in the afternoon. By that time the roads are clear, as the bikers have either been picked up from heat exhaustion by emergency medical services, or have simply been run over."

organizing its shape just in time to disperse in a grand crash.

We stood and watched as the dance was repeated with interesting variations. At the moment, we were the only ones there, but we certainly were not the first pioneers. Several cairns stood as testimony that others had perched rocks either for informative or entertainment purposes. The air felt clean, but it was still surprising how warm and humid it was. It was only mid-morning, and we were starting to sweat in tee shirts.

We moved on to another beach, enjoying more of the mysteriously emerging ocean waves. Though it was probably just my imagination, it seemed like this place was a little saltier. I mentioned it to Senator. He was not sure about the salinity of the air, but he was sure it was getting even more humid. We both hoped it would improve for our second day in Acadia.

Before we got too far, we doubled back to our car. I checked the map, not to find our way-- there was only one looping road-- but to see what was up ahead. "Oh," I said.

"What'd'ya' find?" asked Senator.

"It says that we are coming up to Thunder Hole," I answered, tracing the red line with my finger. "I assume they mean that the water sounds like thunder there, but I thought it sounded exactly like thunder where we just were..."

"Guess we'll find out," he said, as he pulled the car into the parking lot. It was getting a little busier tourist-wise, but thankfully we were not seeing the throngs of vacationers that the ads for the shuttle buses had promised. I was beginning to suspect a public transportation racket.

On the other hand, that could just be my Chicagoland roots coming through.

Thunder Hole, as it turned out, was not as thunderous as the random beach we had discovered near the Ocean Path. The water still made a throaty *harumph* whenever it hit, but the real wonder was the indescribable blue/green/gray color of the waves as they rolled inward in mounting succession. We watched for a while, pointing out to each other the longest approaching lines. "Ready to go?" one of us eventually asked. We agreed to stay five more minutes, which paid off majorly when we saw the biggest wave of the day come rushing in. By the time it broke and finished pushing its shallow arms toward us, it had reached much further than even the largest waves we had seen. Previously dry land was now soaked in foamy residue.

By this time Senator was hungry, so we decided to hit a Subway in the center of the island. The park road did not go there, so we got a little adventurous with the back roads. We only missed one turn by a few blocks and quickly corrected our error. Even after doing so, there was no Subway in sight. There was, however, a gas station with a deli called Freshlies inside. We surmised that at one time there was a Subway there instead. Perhaps their contract expired and Freshlies swooped in to garner the market of hungry hikers.

Senator went in, but I chose to stay in the car. I was trying to soak up every moment of the outdoors. It was also sort of fun to people watch. By now we had come to understand that service everywhere we go on vacations is slower than at home. As I believe I have mentioned, we are fine with that. When fifteen minutes passed without a sign of Senator, though, I went in to investigate. Just as I stepped into the building, the cashier was handing him the small brown bag that contained his egg and cheese sandwich. At least his food was hot, thanks to the employees at the recently redubbed (by us) "Slowies".

As long as we would be near the west side of Park Loop Road, we turned off to drive up to Cadillac Mountain. Cadillac Mountain holds the distinction of being the highest point on Mount Desert Island, which places it somewhere in the neighborhood of 1,500 feet. By mountain standards, this is not terribly impressive. As we had learned on Cape Breton Island, however, 1,500 feet rising from sea level is nothing to scoff at.[*]

Up we rose, circling around the mountain with increasingly distant views. About a third of the way from the top, the fog thickened. We could tell we were near the top by the amount of cars that were creeping slowly toward the parking lot, hoping for an open spot. When we reached the summit, we did find some cloudy parking spots, despite the many couples, families, and groups coming and going.

Senator parked and we exited, finding ourselves close to a crosswalk. We took it over to the bald summit. A cement path wound around the stony pinkish ground. For exercise and the heck of it, we walked it, even though it yielded nothing but 360° views of fog. Looking at the ground was more interesting; wild blueberry bushes covered large masses atop the peak. Against Senator's

---

[*] Plus, according to the Acadia National Park brochure, it is the highest point on the U.S. Atlantic coast... (and the brochure's in color and everything).

better judgment, I popped a few in my mouth. He shook his head disapprovingly. "No, you shouldn't have any;" I agreed, "someone's got to live to tell 'em what happened!"*

We did not completely give up on Cadillac Mountain, but we postponed spending any more time there in hope of clearer weather later. Back down we looped, making our way to the main road again. Shortly thereafter, we reached the south coast of the island at an intersection. To the left was a sandy beach. To the right the road continued. We followed it to a section of the park we had not seen yet.

This quieter area featured beautiful stone bridges. Their stoic arches were perfectly engineered to accommodate the 100-year old carriage roads crossing at different elevations. They reminded me of the stone bridge at Manassas. For a moment my mind wandered to Civil War battlefields. We were a long way from Virginia, but maybe not so far away from the divided national climate of the early 1860s.

We drove slowly a while longer, taking in more of the forested inland of Mt. Desert. In the lower elevations the sun was making a respectable appearance. Luring us in with its promises of great views, we once again drove up to Cadillac Mountain. I took it as a good sign when I noticed a gift shop that I had not even seen earlier in the day. Either

---

* I have come across a few versions of this joke, each varying slightly depending on region and storyteller. My favorite is the first time I heard it. A family friend (who is not known for his overly-cautious driving) was transporting a van of young men on a road trip to the Grand Canyon. He encouraged the passengers to put on their seat belts, but definitely insisted on wearing his own because, "Someone's got to live to tell 'em what happened!"

the fog was breaking slightly, or they had rapidly constructed the building during the past few hours.

We again found parking and again walked out to the summit. This time it wasn't a total white-out. We could at least see swirls of different masses of mist and clouds, but there were only brief holes that gave glimpses of granite hills across the valley. Soon they and their pine carpets were swallowed up in the white abyss as well.

It was amazing how quickly the views opened up just a few moments' drive down the mountain. At one point we pulled over for a better look. Gazing out over the blue ocean we could see several islands. Each one had a mount of soft white clouds precisely curved over it as if it had been fit with its own custom blanket. Senator and I both instantly thought of a board game we had recently spent many hours of our lives playing. Entdecker's objective was to navigate seas and explore uncharted islands. Now it looked like we were standing over a giant board game, ready to strategically build our empires.

It was late afternoon, so we ducked into the visitor center to see what we could learn on our way out of the park. It was smaller than expected, but I had a memory of being there when my parents brought me to Acadia when I was sixteen. The only fact I learned this time around was that the park was the first national park east of the Mississippi River, founded in 1916. We did have time to watch the interpretive video, which showed us what Acadia looked like on picture-perfect days. "So how long after we leave does the fog lift from Cadillac?" Senator jokingly asked the ranger. He just grinned and nodded, more or less confirming that the warm, humid forecast was not on our side.

Our last stop on the island that day was the overlook (cleverly named "Overlook"). As expected though, it only overlooked more fog. Unfortunately, due to one-way roads, our brief visit to Overlook meant we would have to drive through the densely crowded tourist trap of Bar Harbor. As annoying as the yuppie vacationers were, it gave us the chance to check out the location of our whale cruise, which would depart from the town's wharf early the next morning. Once we confirmed the address, we made our way out of the chaos, through the construction, and eventually back toward our cottage.

Slowies and some snacks in the car notwithstanding, it was time for some real food. Senator searched online for options that did not contain seafood and were not located in Bar Harbor. Those two parameters narrowed things down quite a bit, but we finally found a pizza joint a few miles up the road. We knew that New England pizza was reliably lousy, but they did advertise calzones, which, somehow, they seem to get right.

When we pulled into the parking lot, we knew we had stumbled upon something good. Though it was a Monday night, the lot was packed, and every license plate was from Maine. *Aha... the well-kept local secret!* Most of the vehicles were large trucks with even larger than necessary tires. Many sported N.R.A. decals or bumper stickers of similar sentiment. We were feeling satisfied with Senator's choice.

Once seated, we wasted no time in ordering. As we waited, we talked, recapping our day, discussing the next day's plans, and continuously noting the out-of-control family across the aisle from us. The two parents were in over their heads when it came to managing their three rambunctious and slightly whiny kids. The youngest looked to be about a year and a half old, and she was absorbed in a sort of obstacle course challenge of squirming her way out of the high chair and across the corner of the table onto her dad's lap. He gripped her with one arm, but another kid who was busy spilling a drink commanded more of his attention. His wife was losing her own battle with the brat she was entangled with across the table.

Senator and I continued chatting, aware of all of this and trying our best to ignore it. It was too much, though, when the dad lost his grip on the youngest kid, allowing her to slide/fall down to the floor. She was not hurt, but it was enough of a shock to send her reeling. She screamed like mad, and the chaos heightened.

Mid-sentence I interrupted myself, without removing my sight from Senator, and flatly and quietly interjected, "You dropped your kid." I figured Senator would think it was funny, since we have always had a shared warped sense of humor. I did not count on him laughing so hard that he practically spit out his water. It had not been that funny, but him laughing hard is extremely contagious to me, so I started. By the time our waitress came with the food, I had used both of our napkins because I was tearing up so badly that my nose was running. I could not stop. Every time I looked at Senator, I lost it and started laughing all over again. It was so stupid. My guts hurt. It was great.

We were about done with our dinner, and though I was honestly full, I was thinking about dessert. Ever since I had seen the blueberry bushes along the coast and on Cadillac Mountain, I had it in my head that I wanted something made with local blueberries. It was still too warm for a New England July, so I was leaning toward something cold-- maybe blueberry cheesecake or blueberry ice cream. Senator supported this fancy, so he asked our server how the blueberry cheesecake on the menu was. It was more of a formality; he expected her to rave about it, if for no other reason than to upsell our bill.

She gave an unexpected though characteristically honest New England response. "I don't know..." she started, giving serious consideration to the matter. "I usually just get my sweets from Blueberry Hill..."

"Blueberry Hill?!" we asked in unison. *Do tell us more.* "Where's that?"

"Right over there," she answered, pointing vaguely north, and explaining that it was right up the highway. Her mild disbelief that we had never heard of it further confirmed our suspicion of this being the local hot spot. We were sold and tipped her as if she had sold us the desired treats.

A few blocks away, we pulled into the gravel parking area for Blueberry Hill. A line was already forming at the walk-up window, despite the drizzle that had set in yet again. I looked at the common overhead menu. It only took a few seconds to make my choice. There was, in fact, a blueberry cheesecake flurry, combining the best of all worlds. Reasoning that four days of dessert abstinence on vacation was enough self-denial, I went for it. Senator did the same, and then finished part of mine as we listened to radio shows in a steamy car.

We were stuffed and satiated. As we drove back to the room, I surveyed the sky. I could see nothing to convince me of fair weather the next day, but who knew? At the moment, we just wanted to get back to our room, shower, and get to bed before our early morning. Thankfully, no smoke alarms were triggered in the process.

*   *   *

Tuesday was the day. I was so excited about our whale and puffin cruise. Months earlier I had researched the best company. I then booked our reservation, paid, and fought the urge to divulge the surprise to Senator until we were on the trip. The only option was a morning cruise, so we had set the alarm for 5:45am, double-checked it, triple-checked it, and then gone to sleep with visions of marine life dancing in our heads.

As planned, the alarm shrieked at us at a quarter to six. We got ready, improvised a microwaved breakfast, and set out for the docks of Bar Harbor. With slight trouble we made our way to the correct line, but we were still plenty early-- all according to plan. When I reached the ticket counter, I lay my printed paper ticket on the desk and gave my name. Instead of directions of where to board, I was met with an apology. "Oh, I'm sorry. That cruise has been canceled today."

"What?!" I was crestfallen. The extreme fog had won out. Rescheduling was not an option, as we only had one more day in Maine. I knew it was hardly a tragedy, but I had let myself build anticipation toward what was to be the highlight of the summer. There was also the glaring fact that we would *not* have awoken at such a ridiculous hour.

Senator looked tired and unenthusiastic. The mood

was flat, but we agreed that we should still use the day to hike. Our first stop was the Gorham Mountain trail, which looked interesting but had not made the top of the priority list. It was an empty, smooth walk over mainly flat rocks. In some places there were scrambles or narrower squeezes, but nothing too difficult. At least, it should not have been too difficult, but Senator's footwear was not working for hiking. During the past year, some changes to his feet had developed, necessitating careful experimentation.

It had started raining anyway, so we deemed it a good time to drive to a large shoe store we had seen the night before. After trying on several styles of hiking boots, he selected the most comfortable and supportive. They cost just about the same amount as the refunded cruise tickets, so maybe it was for the best. Reshod and laced up, we were back on the trails.

Since we had more hiking time than expected, we drove to another portion of the island, further west. While Flying Mountain trail offered a relatively easy climb to lovely views of an ocean sound, we had entered a much different socioeconomic region. One rude champagne socialist yelled sarcastically at Senator as he drove normally down the main highway. Apparently he was supposed to slam on the brakes and let her enter from the side road. Yard signs attacking anyone with opposing beliefs told the rest of the story.

Our next stop was Bass Head Lighthouse. It was very crowded, but we at least wanted to walk out to the beach to see the light. Though we could not go inside, the real draw was the bell buoy shrouded in fog, somewhere out on the water. Ominously it clang as it rocked back and forth in the waves. I wish we could have recorded it, but we might have only captured other tourists' voices, like the woman who was dismayed and irritated that we had paused for three minutes to take a photograph where she apparently wanted to walk. There were plenty of other spots, but she huffed and called to her husband as he clumsily made his way over some rocks, "I don't know if they're going to leeeaaave...."*

We continued along the highway, stopping at a few more trailheads. One easy path led us into the woods, eventually ending at the shoreline, where tide pools dotted the dark pink, rocky beach. Some day I'm going to sit at the edge of the ocean for a full twelve hours and just watch a complete tidal cycle. In the meantime, I was just interested in getting more water. The unusually high temperatures left us constantly soaked with sweat and thirsty.

We found our necessary water at a camp store a few miles away. Inside, an older hippy woman was contentedly minding the store as Neil Young played from her stereo. I think she may have lived in the back of the outdated shop, and that was fine. She sold the requisite bottled water, and for that we were grateful.

Each of us took a long swig of water and got back into the car. "Want to try one more time?" asked Senator.

I knew he was referring to a drive to the top of Cadillac Mountain. "Why not?" We were already hot and tired. We might as well try to catch a breeze. Given the constant fog, I did not have great hopes of seeing any sweeping vistas, but maybe it would be different this time.

---

*Not to stereotype, but it does seem that everyone rude we encounter in New England has a Massachusetts accent.

Though it was nice to walk at a higher elevation, we still could not see much. After a while of sitting among the boulders, we gave up. Three strikes and we were out. I suppose we might get back to Acadia National Park someday, but we would always have much fonder memories of the drier, wilder, lonelier Nova Scotia Atlantic coast.

It was nearing dinner time, and we knew better than to waste time trying to find any new options. Encore calzones it would be. I then remembered that we had passed a sign for a road that led to a state park, so I suggested we get them to go and take a picnic supper. Senator approved, and we grabbed the grub and drove the eight miles to the park.

It was the peaceful antithesis to the crowded areas we had encountered the rest of the day. Only one other family was taking advantage of the picnic area, and we had the pier to ourselves for a short evening walk. The sun was drooping downward, and fishermen were returning from another day on the job, still cheerful after a laborious day. Once inside the car, we balanced marinara sauce while slicing through hot crust and cheese. On the radio another episode of *The Lion, the Witch, and the Wardrobe* was taking on new meaning among the quiet of nature. I think it was my favorite part of being in Maine.

*   *   *

It was still rainy and foggy when we left the Acadia region the next morning. At least we were not taunted by a perfect dry, sunny day on our way out. Whale cruises were probably canceled that day as well. I did not mind. Jingles and I were getting along better, and I was looking forward to entering New Hampshire. A few hours into the drive, the sun even started to make some rare appearances. So far though, we had not had a day without rain.

Since we were on the east side of the White Mountains by early afternoon, we made a stop at the Gorham Historical Society & Railroad Museum. Like most such places, there was next to no advertisement and no other visitors. Even so, we parked and entered the old train station. Initially we were greeted with a surprised and guarded, "Can I help you?" Thinking maybe we had invaded some sacred space, I asked if the museum was open to the public. The woman behind the counter then relaxed a little and told us that we were free to look around.

Once she noticed us taking interest in the antiques and displays, she gladly volunteered more information. She told us that there were separate waiting rooms for men and women. My guess is that the men did not want to listen to crying babies while they smoked and read their newspapers. She also showed us a unique piece of furniture that distributed tickets when a ball dropped down the appropriate slot. We must have passed her test, because she then invited us to walk down to the converted boxcar to see the train layout.

I have always loved miniatures, and they take on special meaning when they depict actual places. Here, shrouded among the elongated model train layout, stood a jovial mad-scientist type of man. He explained that he was a retired architect and went on to point out the painstaking detail he had personally incorporated into the scale model of the local town. Like everywhere in New Hampshire, a river spilled down from the mountains. Naturally, the logging industry was represented. I could have stared for hours, enjoying the soothing swish of the cars rolling over the tracks, but the small space was getting very warm, and we still had to get to our destination. We thanked the man and continued along the northern edge of the Presidential Range.

It was wonderful driving the familiar and scenic Highway 3, and it was easy to find our accommodations. This time, we skipped the inn and opted for a more convenient cottage to use as our base for the next six nights. In case we forgot where to turn, we could just look for the iconic covered bridge next to it. Upon check-in, we learned that the owner was a Kentucky transplant. *We better move here soon, or everybody's gonna' find out about this place,* I thought.

The downpour had timed itself perfectly to coincide with our arrival. We did our best to dodge it as we loaded in to our temporary home. It was just big enough for two, although I found it funny that there were two televisions. More importantly, there was a little kitchenette to heat up easy meals.

The weather had ruled out the walk I had envisioned. Instead, we explored the small town by car, first stopping for gas at Wayne's and hoping for the homemade maple fudge that they usually sold in the convenience store there. As the tides and everything else change, though, our fondly recalled maple fudge was now a poor chemically-laden substitute churned out in a factory, probably in Boston. The local grocery store did not quite hold the charm for us that it used to, either. Oh well. When it comes down to it, cauliflower is cauliflower, right? At least the bookstore next to the grocery store had not changed; it was still dingy and ill-managed by a guy who could not quite decide what to do with his life. At least that was as we had remembered.

In our little cottage, Senator concocted a microwaved meal while I folded some laundry. Afterward, the night lent itself to sprawling out on the bed with our respective reading material. Senator was quickly getting hooked on one of his new Civil War books. I was perusing my travel notes and a few tourism booklets that were on the table. Then I did something I have never done and will probably never do again. I made breakfast reservations.

*   *   *

The first time we traveled to the White Mountains, in 2012, we entered the region from the northwest corner, through the small town of Sugar Hill. With a name like Sugar Hill, it is no surprise that the dominant feature there is an over-seventy-five-year old pancake house, or pancake parlor, more properly. From what I have read, pancakes are a thing in New Hampshire. No, I do not mean the chain-produced, flavorless puddles of reconstituted Bisquick that some establishments serve. Granite Staters take their pancakes almost as seriously as their politics, which is to say, quite.

The large billboard we saw in 2012 advertised Polly's Pancake Parlor. Senator feigned exaggerated interest when he first saw it, but it did stick in the back of our minds as a potential stop someday. Now, that day had come. As I learned from their website, every day in summer that day comes for many people, so reservations are highly recommended. Okay, done. With a weather forecast that only promised a few rain-free hours in the middle of the day, it fit perfectly into the schedule.

Like many dynastic restaurants, Polly's was decorated with several generations' worth of history sprinkled among agricultural antiques. Our window-side table provided great views of the sloping farmland and mountains. Service began with a friendly server, who explained the unusual menu configurations. Because everything was made to order (by the servers themselves), we got to pick the type of batter and the add-in ingredients. Not that you would have figured otherwise, but fake syrup in any form was strictly banned from the premises. Instead, a triad of pure maple syrup, real maple cream, and an interestingly-textured maple sugar were placed in between us, suitable for use on pancakes, in coffee, or straight.* Sadly, I could not finish my pancake sampler plate, but I had enough to agree with Senator that the whole wheat with blueberries was our favorite.

Each time we come to New Hampshire, I try to find new places for us to explore. We had hit the main guidebook trails and overlooks, so this time I wanted to check out some state parks. These gems are often overlooked because of the spectacular Presidential Range, but they offer their own beautiful solace. At the top of my list was Weeks State Park.

We drove north toward the town of Lancaster. Though Senator had purchased new boots in Maine, he was still looking for something a little different for other terrain. Amid the historic brick buildings of downtown Lancaster,

---

*   I stuck to only indulging on my pancakes, but I could see that others were more adventurous, or perhaps hopeless addicts.

he found a shoe shop with just what he needed. Now we were really ready to tackle some ground, so we drove back south a few miles to the entrance of Weeks.

One cannot get lost in Weeks; there is only one road, and it swirls to the top of one of the smaller mountains. Every so often, the trees open to views of far away peaks, seemingly turning bluer with distance. In a few places, we noted where trails broke off into the woods. When the short drive ended, we were in a parking lot on the mountain top. The most notable sight was the large arts & crafts style home at the top. It was more inviting than the random trails into the woods, so we walked the steep incline to learn more. It was not far, but we were already sweating steadily, wondering again what had happened to our New Hampshire summer.

Circling the home just beyond its lawn was a nature trail. We decided to start with that, since the rain had stopped. There were also interpretive stations that told a little about specific gardens the owner had chosen or designed in the early twentieth century. We tried to read one or two, but stopping for more than a few seconds brought on mosquito attacks. (The signs said nothing about that.) Soon it got too bad to be in the woods at all.

Stepping back out onto the open lawn, we saw a fire tower on the property. It appeared to be both mosquito-free and open to the public, so we began our ascent. Forty-eight spiral steps later, we had 360° views of New Hampshire wilderness, and a breeze that was the best thing we had felt since we left home. "Maybe we can spend the next five days here," I suggested. I smiled at the ridiculous notion of squatting in a fire tower for days. I suppose eventually the good folks at the Department of Natural Resources would be called upon to escort us down.

We did come down, though, without incident. Feeling refreshed, we kept walking down the road to get a little more exercise. There was no way we were going to go back into the buggy woods, but we definitely got a workout on the steep paved road. By the time we came back up to the parking lot, we were soaked. I'm not sure we even felt the difference when it started to rain.

At the car we wiped ourselves off as well as we could. I figured we were done there, but Senator asked if I wanted to go into the home. I had not planned on it, but he was right when he said we might not get back anytime soon. "Yeah, why not?" I said. It was only early afternoon, and nothing else was going to happen outdoors that day.

As we waited on the porch for a guide to let us in, we saw a doe hanging out on the lawn grass. A little further away was her spotted fawn, casually nibbling some long grass. We were the only visitors there, so the girl at the desk seemed happy to have something to do. After waiving off our apologies for our appearance (and likely stench), she started to take us through the first floor of the two-story home. As she pointed out items of note, she educated us on John W. Weeks. The late Victorian gentleman served in both the House of Representatives and the U.S. Senate. Though his career had many noteworthy accomplishments, his greatest legacy may have come in 1911, when he saw the passage of a law he had worked hard to sponsor. It henceforth allowed the federal government to purchase private land, opening the vast potential of national and state parks. Weeks did battle some fairly heavy opposition from another congressman, who, I could not help noticing, was from Illinois. Using clever appeals to both the conservation and business worlds, he wove together seamless arguments that eventually prevailed.

We toured the rest of the downstairs, including all of the bedrooms, the kitchen, the dining room, and a hallway flanked by dozens of stuffed bird species, some of which were now illegal to kill. Then we went upstairs. At the top of the dark wooden staircase, it was immediately obvious why all of the regular necessary rooms of the home were on the first floor. The entire upstairs was an open lodge-style room with high ceilings and magnificent views to match those we had seen from the fire tower. Massive fireplaces and stuffed game heads anchored the two far ends of the room, and built-in leaded glass bookcases lined the corners. *Forget the fire tower. This is where I want to stay!*

Between Senator and the tour guide, they did eventually drag me away from the grand room. Then we thanked her once more and returned to the car. "Now where?" asked Senator, ready to drive anywhere that led to a dry activity. "We're done hiking, right?" he asked/announced.

"Yes, definitely," I assured him. "In fact, I came prepared in case we had bad weather days. I have a list of little museums and historical societies in a bunch of small towns. I can see which ones are open on Thursday afternoons," I answered, rummaging in my purse for my notes.

"Sounds good-- as long as it's indoors." With that, we drove to Jefferson, whose museum would be open just before we reached it.

"Are you sure you have your information right?" asked Senator. We were the only car in the parking lot, which was more of a gravely sprawl of rain-filled potholes. The converted church did have a sign about the museum, but no one was around.

"How about we give it five minutes?" I bargained. With that, a car pulled up, and a mother and daughter popped out and ran up to the door, trying to defend themselves against the downpour as they fumbled with the key. We gave them a minute and then followed them in.

They seemed amazed that anyone would come there, especially from the faraway fabled land of Illinois. "We're so sorry we're late! This is our first day doing this," they explained. Evidently there was some sort of caretaker rotation, and this was their turn. As a result, they did not know much about the exhibits, but they gave us free roam of the large space. For the next hour we absorbed the compact history of Jefferson, from family farms to tourism hot spot. Clothing, furniture, church items, newspaper clippings, obsolete gadgets, and an array of dairy farm items[*] told the story of a proud and hardworking town that represented so many others of nineteenth and twentieth century America.

We were on a roll, and we needed to make our way southward anyway, so we drove to the Bethlehem museum, too. Before going inside, we ran across the street so Senator could acquire some caffeine. As he waited for his triple espresso, I couldn't help but overhear the local conversation. Three people were commenting on how

---

[*] Who knew there were so many ways to separate cream?

wonderful it was that they were finally getting some rain. They had been in a drought for most of the summer. *You can thank us for that,* I thought. *We brought it all the way from home.*

Like the railway museum in Gorham, the requisite host senior citizen greeted us suspiciously upon our entry. Actually, 'greeted' is a stretch. "Can I help you?" she asked quizzically. I think she narrowed her eyes a little.

"Is the museum open?" I asked, knowing full well, that she and we could see the OPEN sign in the window.

"Yes, you can look around," she pronounced. No further discussion was invited, and Senator and I are the type who can take a hint. We shuffled our way to the side of the room to look at the closest display. It was mainly composed of old glass dishes, some of which displayed painted scenes of local towns. They did not interest us too much, so we continued along the wall into the next room.

That is where things started to get interesting. As in Jefferson, the local tourism history was on display, with artifacts from the early ritzy hotels. We glanced at those for a while and then moved on to a section on the White Mountain region's contribution to World Wars I and II. In the center of the room, the best part of the museum caught my eye.

The wooden dollhouse easily drew me in. As I quickly learned, however, this was no ordinary dollhouse. There were the regular three-sided rooms, decorated with small-scaled furniture and people, but that is where the similarities to my dollhouse and all others I have seen ended. The typed paper alongside the display told the story of Frances Glessner Lee, the "Nutshell Detective". In retirement, Ms. Lee turned to the hobby of constructing dollhouses-- nothing unusual there. She did it with a twist, however. Instead of recreating pretty, austere and idyllic scenes, she designed murder scenes, exacting every detail from newspaper clippings and other informants. As a result, weapons, corpses, and clues all made their way into her tiny rooms. She got so good at her bloody craft, in fact, that law enforcement eventually looked to her for new developments in forensics. *Hhmmm...*

It was late afternoon, so we drove back toward the town where we were staying. I wanted to make a traditional run through the White Mountain Visitor Center, just to see if anything was new. I do not think the interpretive display was new, but it did have more of a personal connection than the last time I had walked through it. I now had a new appreciation for the section on Senator Weeks.

Just beyond it, I noticed a small wooden seating area set up like a little theatre. There was a television screen, but it was turned off, and I did not find any button to start it. Since we had some time, I asked the woman at the desk if there was a film to watch. She looked at me suspiciously, as though no one was supposed to inquire about such things. Slowly she nodded her head affirmatively, but she frowned. "It's two and a half hours..." I think she was afraid that we were going to keep her there that long. "It's all about forestry, if you're into that..." she continued, still trying to dissuade us from it, in case we were not thoroughly deterred.

"No, that's okay," I assured her. We'll pass." She looked relieved, especially considering they were supposed to close in half an hour. I wondered why in the world they would have a movie that long in a place where people typically stopped in for fifteen minutes just to grab some pamphlets.

As long as we were keeping traditions alive, we stopped in front of Maps-Books.* For the first time in any of our New Hampshire traveling, we hit it on a day that it was open. Inside it was smaller than it looked, but it was a niche market. This was ground zero for all literature White Mountains, and the owner was the guru behind the counter.

After a few moments, I selected a book on New Hampshire curiosities. I needed another Granite State guide book like New Hampshire needed another waterfall, but why not? It also gave us the in to glean a little knowledge from the knowledgeable. As we paid for the purchases, Senator asked the owner for his professional recommendations on which 4,000-footers would be best for beginners. I was happy when he mentioned Mt. Osceola, which I had planned to tackle on this trip. At least we were on the right track.

As long as he was a friendly sort, we also brought up the subject of the difficulty rating scale. Everywhere else we have hiked in the United States and Canada has been faithful to the established and commonly understood 'easy-moderate-strenuous' rating scale. Once one has researched the level in guide books, one can reasonably assume what to expect. In the White Mountains, however, all of that is out the window. What would be an easy, paved path elsewhere is a rocky forage in the the Whites. The owner's

---

* not actual name

eyes twinkled. "Well, they say if you can hike in the White Mountains, you can hike anywhere..." We had our answer. Then he added, "We don't believe in switchbacks!"

We regrouped back at our room and then headed out for a bite to eat. A local tavern offered veggie burgers and a comfortable atmosphere, so we parked ourselves there. Because it was not a tourist hot-spot, we did not have to deal with crowds, waiting for a table, or Bostonians. Instead, we enjoyed a quiet meal in the schoolhouse-themed dining room. There were a few old desks around, some books, and a globe perched in the corner. I didn't get it, but I liked it.

The last event of our long day was the fireworks show at a nearby resort. As outsiders, we had to park across the street, but it gave us a perfect view of the sky. As we waited, we noticed a bright silver light near the silhouette of the mountain top. We thought it was a flood light somewhere on the resort's property. I hoped it would not interfere with the fireworks. Then the light defined itself into a curved streak. Finally it emerged to become a commanding full moon. It was so beautifully riveting that we almost did not care about the pyrotechnics. (That was good, since they were late anyway.)

*   *   *

Friday morning we were still playing the dodge-the-rain game. It seemed that every day the forecast extended the rain for one more day. "It's supposed to rain today, but that should be it," became our morning greeting for this trip. Senator was sick of it. I wasn't too keen on it myself, but I was trying to make the best of it. Yes, it was also much warmer than we expected, but we were still surrounded by beauty, and who knew when we would return again? I was determined not to waste a trip we had both anticipated. It did challenge the itinerary when the hourly forecast gave no trustworthy break.

"Well, we're definitely not doing any big hike today. Want to try a few shorter, easier ones?" I asked Senator.

"Sure," he answered unenthusiastically.

Off we drove to hit some of the familiar trails where we had first gotten a feel for the White Mountains. The Forest Discovery trail was our first stop, and apparently we were its first visitors. As the trail meandered through different stages of new and old growth forests, open areas, and meadows, we found ourselves blazing a path through the morning's spider webs, (or spider strings, more accurately). Soon we were both brandishing sticks in a criss-cross motion while we trudged on toward the little bridge over the brook. I remembered it as my favorite part of the loop, but even it was lackluster that morning, bearing witness to the (until very recently) dry summer.

At the car, Senator reapplied the bug spray. I gagged a little, as I always do when the strong chemical smell hits me. Then we continued down the Kancamagus Highway, where we could at least depend on gorgeous scenery. Occasionally we parked at the pullovers to take in the views. Sometimes we caught an updraft from a valley, but it was still uncharacteristically muggy.

Beyond the weather, for some reason, the overall mood was just blah. I could not place my finger on it, and it felt sort of silly, but something was certainly off. It surprised me, then, when Senator suggested stopping by Lily Pond for a traditional non-sighting of moose. "Sure, we can do that," I said, knowing that we would see exactly zero moose, but grateful for some interest on his part.

Predictions came true, but we did find ourselves engrossed in watching some unusual birds. The gang of eight flocked around a clump of birch trees, rotating and fluttering around every few seconds. They almost seemed to have worked out a pattern. We had never seen them before. They were shaped like a cardinal, but with deep black markings around their eyes. Their bodies were a light brown, with almost lavender tones, and yellow-tipped tails. Above all, they had personality, and we were hooked on studying them for at least fifteen minutes. For all we knew, a parade of moose could have been right behind us.

Further east on The Kanc we stopped at Sabbaday Falls. Normally this area would be fairly busy in summer, but there were not many people there. *Good*, I thought. I was also glad of the fact that the short, wide open, steep walk would be free of any arachnid paraphernalia. Up we hiked, quickly becoming sweaty again despite being next to a roaring waterfall the entire time. The payoff came at the top, where the sun was positioned perfectly to catch the fall's spray and create a miniature rainbow. On the way down, I was pleased to see the water was as clean and clear as ever, even in the deeper, narrower portions of the carved out rock. Senator did not say much. He was observing the water, deep in thought.

Still in a melancholy mood, we drove to Rocky Gorge. The wide, flat rock ledges there lead to an innocent-looking shallow point of the Swift River, but swirling whirlpools all around the random jutting rocks create dangerous currents. The water then converges in a sizable plunge into a gorge, so swimming and even wading are forbidden. We started with a short walk along the river, but the brush soon obscured the view. We did not really feel like walking anyway, so we scouted out some rocks to sit on while the sun shone.

Neither of us said anything. Both of us were still sort of lost in thoughts. I still could not pinpoint why. At one point, Senator was so deep in thought that he about jumped out of his place when I moved a lock of hair that had blown across his cheek. "Whoa! Sorry-- I didn't mean to startle you!" He was not upset, but he was definitely surprised.

We sat awhile, but the sun quickly warmed up the rocks. More people were arriving, mainly with the goal of violating the swimming ban. I suggested we move on further along the road. Senator was neutral on the matter and still kind of off-kilter, so we left and began the loop back toward our cottage.

I felt badly that he was not enjoying himself, but I also believed things would look up the next day. After all, we were on vacation, away from our jobs, spending time together, in small towns in the mountains. Things felt too murky for the reality of the situation. We knew this, but it was turning out to be a dud.

Still, we kept trying to salvage the week. We turned north onto Bear Notch Road[*] for a variation in the return trip. Bear Notch does not get the publicity that The Kanc receives, but this means that the overlooks are serene and often quieter, provided you don't miss them. When I spotted a turnoff, I asked Senator to stop. He liked the

---
* closed in winter

idea, so we pulled over. On my way out of the car I grabbed a peach. Again we were both silent, but it was a little more pleasant this time. For the moment, my attention was split between the welcome tasks of avoiding the excited bees that were buzzing around some fuzzy pink flowers and gauging the distance to the white steepled church tucked in the valley beyond the trees.

Turning west, we drove past Silver Cascade. The tall waterfall, which is visible from the highway, energetically tumbled down between the evergreens. It was just as active as it had been the last time we saw it, during the spring melt. We walked up to the accessible rocks at its edge, but almost as soon as we did, the afternoon shower began. It was ahead of schedule, but not unexpected.

It continued to pick up all the way back to our cottage. By that time, Senator was spent, and I was ready to retire to laziness for the remainder of the day. We stepped inside the door and he immediately put on a small pot of coffee. That sounded good to me. I handed him the bag of dark roast that already weighed considerably less than it did two nights ago. Despite the caffeine, he was napping soundly shortly afterward.

I was not sleepy, so I watched the rain. Pockets of brilliant sunshine broke through the clouds, magnified by the water droplets. I checked each window in the cottage, but I saw no rainbow. I am sure there must have been one, but I was not dedicated enough to run outside and search. Instead, I read and reworked our plans for the next day, aware that the weather forecast had extended the rain predictions yet again.

The rest did us both well. Maybe we had just been

shedding the day-to-day tensions that creep into a busy life. "Are you hungry?" I asked Senator.

"Yes, what are you thinking?"

"Want to grab some food and drive somewhere?" Even as I said it, I wondered if I was asking for trouble. Hadn't we just spent the day wandering around semi-aimlessly in a blasé fog? Maybe we should order a pizza and put on pajamas.

"That sounds good," he answered, convincingly. Two veggie wraps later, we were in the car and headed back on The Kanc. When we came to an empty area along the woods, we stopped. 6:00pm was not a likely time to see moose in summer, but we probably would have missed seeing them regardless; the car was quickly steamed up from the humidity. As the rain poured down, we listened to another installment of *The Lion, the Witch, and the Wardrobe* as we picked up olive slices and shreds of lettuce that had escaped our dinner.

On the way back to the cottage I saw one of the classic Smokey the Bear signs. His friendly but sober gaze seemed to simultaneously stare at us and his fire danger-o-meter. According to Smokey, the danger was "moderate" in spite of days of rain. I appreciated his concern for us and the woodlands, but the odds of anyone being able to generate an accidental spark in the soppy verdant forests were about as good as me seeing a moose in my Illinois back yard. Thank you, Smokey.

Our weird day concluded in front of the television. The old movie channel was about to run *The African Queen*, with Humphrey Bogart and Katherine Hepburn. Neither of us had seen it before, and it was on our list, so we settled in with a mound of pillows. The day's activities had not been great, and the temperament took a while to improve, but at least we were not hiding from Germans while coaxing a steam boat through crocodile-infested, unnavigable waters. It was important to keep perspective.

* * *

The more I exist around humans, the further north my retirement fantasies propel me. Currently, my preferred county for someday hermitage is the northernmost in New Hampshire-- Coös. This area of the state is commonly referred to as the Great North Woods, and seeing it on a sign as one wanders up the scenic west-side highway is exhilarating for me. Saturday's weather called for rain again. To further make it virtually impossible to plan any sizable hike, it was to be evenly distributed on and off throughout the day. In other words, it was a perfect excuse to make the two hour drive north. The dense pines, birch, and maples beckoned.

In the west we could see Vermont. Up ahead was the first of several small towns, all smaller than our little city at home. This one was celebrating something or other that gives small towns an excuse to pipe music into the streets. When we turned eastward the land opened up into meadows that formed the northern border of the White Mountains foothills. We followed the road along until we reached Dixville State Park, another one I had been wanting visit.

Unfortunately, the main entrance to the park was blocked due to construction, but we found a few other inlets, none of which had another soul around for as far as the eye could see. We were in the right place, but again the humidity was much higher than it should have been. That brought the bugs out, so we only climbed a very short, steep trail to a waterfall. No matter how many New Hampshire waterfalls I see, I am always literally stopped in my tracks by how clear the water is. It was especially crystal with the deep mossy greens on either side of the sharp gorge. We watched for a while and then returned to the car for a snack. I couldn't help throwing one of my cherries in, just to see it ride the current downstream.

I could not tell if Senator thought we had wasted our time driving so far for such a short hike, or if he was just getting sick of the weather, or maybe the whole trip. He was quiet again, but he agreed that we should continue the long loop toward the Maine side of the state. Since it was early and the weather was holding out (for the moment, anyway), I found another state park on the way back. "Want to check out Milan Hill?" I offered.

"Is it on the way?" Senator asked.

"More or less. Just a few miles off the main highway..."

"Okay, let's try it," he decided. Route 16 follows the beautiful Androscoggin River through the Lake Umbagog area. Wildlife abounds on the water, which has me curious to canoe it someday. At times, drivers share the road with A.T.V.s, which actually works out better than you would think. Supposedly drivers also share the road with moose sometimes, but you know better than that by now.

Milan Hill State Park was small, as state parks go. Their main focus was the campground, but they did boast a fire tower that was open to climb, so we made that our focus. Up the single road we curved, finding one spot in which to park. As soon as we exited the car, a swarm of large gnats welcomed us, but thankfully they were not interested in biting us. Perhaps they had already feasted on campers.

The fire tower was a four-sided metal cage that rose several stories into sky. The staircase was open, so the ground rotated 90° every few steps. Altogether, there were fifty stairs, but the payoff was grand. Due to the temporarily clear day and the relatively flat landscape immediately surrounding the park, the 360° view spanned out to Vermont, Quebec, and Maine. To the south, we could see Mt. Washington, the granddaddy of the northeast. The views were beautiful all around, but we both found ourselves drawn to that highest peak.

Once we had our fill of the fire tower, we got back on the highway. It was early afternoon, and the rain was still holding off, playing games with us. It was too late to start any major hikes. On the other hand, we did not want to waste the best weather we had had the entire trip by going inside museums. As part of the loop back toward our cottage, we found ourselves closer to Mt. Washington. Soon there would be a turnoff toward its base. I knew what we were both thinking. "Want to just drive near the base of the mountain? It's something to do, and it's been a while since we've been that close to it..." *Plus, I have no other plan, and I really don't want to just watch you mope around the cottage the rest of the day*, I thought.

Senator agreed, and we soon found ourselves at the base camp. Inside there was a small nature exhibit and a snack shop. Outside we found a porch with rocking chairs facing the mountain. We sat for a while watching the thin parade of cars ascend. We had always planned to someday hike Mt. Washington, but we kicked around the idea of possibly selling out and driving up the mountain. I wondered if our car could even handle it. As we considered it, I was also concerned because Senator was in shorts. After all, July at the base is not July at the summit. We were antsy, so we walked back outside.

Next to the main building was a converted barn. Since we could not make a decision, we wandered around the displays inside. Each was dedicated to some event or milestone in 'taming' Mt. Washington. I was surprised to see some of the earliest vehicles that safely transported people up and down the mountain a century ago. Then we learned that the drive was only eight miles, and some fools had even made the climb in winter and at racing speeds.[*] We were still tempted. When we found a current weather report that categorized the winds as 'low' and the summit temperature in the low 60s, we were sold. Just to be sure, we asked the opinion of the aged and knowledgeable man watching the barn museum.

"So do you think two Midwesterners (one in shorts) can make it up the mountain in a Honda Fit?" I paused, giving him ample opportunity to laugh, but he didn't. To the contrary, he assured us that there would be no problem. "Okay, but you might have to come rescue us if you're wrong!"

---

[*] In 1899, F.O. Stanley made the climb in two hours and ten minutes. The record has subsequently been broken through the following decades. At press time, the record belongs to Travis Pastrana, who drove up the mountain in five minutes and forty-five seconds in 2017.

That was how we ended up in a line of cars and motorcycles waiting to climb Mt. Washington. Suckers that we were, we shelled out forty bucks for the privilege. Along with our pass to traverse the mountain road, we also received two tokens to a hiker's exhibit at the top, (which we forgot to use), a bumper sticker boldly announcing that "THIS CAR CLIMBED MT. WASHINGTON!", (which we will never use), and a narrated cd with useful tips and useless Mt. Washington trivia, (which we used an enjoyed). When you look at it that way, it's actually quite a bargain.

Senator put the car into the instructed gear, and we started up. The guy on the cd talked about the different levels of vegetation. At one point the pine trees looked like a new forest of dwarf trees. Not so, CD Guy explained. In fact, the trees were over a hundred years old, but the harsh conditions limited their growth. A few miles later, the trees disappeared altogether, and pockets of fog and mist took their place. The greens and grays among the alpine setting were eerie and beautiful. It was very hard to believe we were only about 6,000 feet up, but three different converging weather systems create a climate like that of the highest Rocky Mountains.

At the top, there are a few structures. One is called, appropriately enough, the Tip Top House. Its humble rooms have accommodated hikers since the early days of Mt. Washington adventurers. There is also the ginormous weather equipment that looks like something ominous fell from space and has been communicating back to the mother ship ever since. Less intimidating-looking but equally fascinating is the weather station, whose claim to fame is its chains. That's right-- chains. Due to record wind speeds like the 231 mph set back in 1934, it was necessary to secure the entire building via large metal chains that run up one side, over the roof, and down the other, firmly planting it in the ground.

We also took plenty of time to survey the distant world beneath us and suck up the refreshing 58°F weather. Behind the scattered masses of fog were endless summits and valleys of shorter mountains. The gray-green hue set an alpine stage to rival the Colorado Rockies, even though Mt. Washington is not even half as high. I was now even more obsessed with New Hampshire.

As we took it all in, we watched a train slowly chugging up the cog railway. In other directions, we could see two hiking trails converge. When successful climbers reached the top, they were greeted with cheers and applause. If they were feeling patient, they could celebrate their accomplishment by waiting in line to take a photo near the summit signpost. Would we ever make the climb? Who knows, but in the meantime, we both felt uplifted in a literal and mental sense. (Plus, we were pretty proud of ourselves for not accidentally driving over the edge.)

Nothing was going to top that experience, in any sense, so we continued our loop back westward toward our cottage. On the way, we stopped briefly in Carroll. There was not much there, but I had to get a quick picture. Trying not to raise suspicion, we pulled into the parking lot of the local police station. There, Senator got out with the camera to capture the giant plywood moose, who was painted in jailbird black and white stripes. What other police station offers so friendly a greeting?

To our relief, we also noticed it getting considerably

cooler and drier. Maybe we were finally going to have some of the weather we had been craving. We continued south for the final leg of our grand loop. Fifteen minutes later, we reached our cottage... where it was very warm and muggy. *Yuck!* We later learned that a bizarre damp weather system had stubbornly settled in near Franconia Notch, and we were its target. Oh well.

Later on that evening, when we were feeling slightly ambitious and when the brief rain shower quit, we went out for a bite. Before picking up some calzones, we stopped by the town park. On the triangle of grass stood the gazebo, where bands play on Saturday nights in summer. It was where we had once discovered a senior citizen jazz group with a June Cleaver-type drummer. This night it was a baby boomer ensemble belting out Proud Mary. My beloved little town was losing a little of its charm, but no matter. So the band was younger and the fudge was now fake. I could still see us living somewhere near there, or at least coming back many more times.

We returned to our cottage and settled in for the evening. This time our ritual weather check brought different results. There was nothing on the radar to suggest rain, and the temperature would remain in a manageable range. Sunday we could finally attempt a big hike. Thankfully, the overall mood had improved a lot during the past twenty-four hours, too. Hopefully we could make the most of our last two days in the mountains.

*   *   *

The night did not cooperate. Most people do not sleep well away from home, but this night was exceptionally bad. Senator was either awake, or not sleeping soundly when he was asleep. Or maybe that's the wrong terminology, since he was definitely making sounds. Therefore, I was not getting much rest either. By morning, we were both looking rough and dragging.

Physically, it would have been manageable, but Senator's mood was taking a disproportional dive. In fact, he was ready to pack the car and head home. I was not feeling that impulsive, nor did I want to return to Illinois any sooner than necessary. Besides, we were finally facing a clear, somewhat cooler day.

The discussion did not progress well. In fact, it was downright miserable, and it migrated into illogical territory unrelated to hiking. Like a trek up a mountain, however, we reached the climax and the journey out was somewhat easier. Confusing, but easier. An hour and a half later than planned, we were on our way to our first 4,000-footer. Only *we* would begin our most ambitious hike after probably our worst morning on a vacation. Against all odds, though, it was working.*

Before we drove to the trailhead, we stopped to grab a breakfast sandwich at a local shop. As we waited to give our order, Senator circled his arms around me from behind. It was nice. *Why didn't the morning just start this way?* I wondered.

The employer interrupted my thoughts as she quickly stepped up to the counter. "Sawry to keep you waiting! What kin I get for yah?" We made our requests as

---

* Why doesn't somebody write a guidebook with a section on that situation? Appropriate gear-- check. Trail maps-- check. What to do in case of a wild animal attack-- check. How to maneuver through a pre-hike argument-- not so much.

another woman came in the door and got in line behind us. Obviously she knew the worker, because they starting chatting at New England speed as our order was being prepared.

"Oh my gosh," the worker began. "I can't believe it. They left the ayuh on awwwl night!"

"Thayut's ridiculous... and expensive," returned the customer. Then she nodded a friendly greeting to us. "Hello." She turned and again addressed the worker, who, I might add, was doing a lovely job packing Senator's sub with ample veggies. "Hey, I didn't even know you had breakfast heyah."

"Oh, yeah. Fo' a long time," she responded, before turning back to the matter at hand. "Now A'm tryin' ta' leave it wawmaw fo' a little while until it gets too hot in heyah."

"Thayut's a good idea." Then, back to us: "Hey, thayut looks good! I'll tell ya', thayut's a good breakfast right theyuh! Best thing you kin do-- lots of peppuhs," she advised.

We paid, thanked the worker, and said good-bye. They wished us a great day and went on talking to each other. I was glad we had witnessed the exchange. The tourists were all in long lines at restaurants. We were with two locals, eating cheap food while driving to an adventure. *Now* bring on the mountains.

It was an easy drive to the road that led to the trailhead. We hopped down the highway an exit or two and then turned east into the woods. The road was paved for a while, but the last five miles were gravel. It also got a little tricky because vehicles were parked along the roadside for the walk-in campsites.

When we reached the lot, it was full. Evidently everyone had been waiting for the one nice day out of the week. We turned out of the lot and drove a quarter mile away to the first available roadside spot. Then we added the distance to our hike by walking back. As I checked our route against the map on the kiosk, I remembered that we needed to pay a few bucks for a trail pass, so I dug through my bag for the necessary cash. That was not a problem, but it meant that the proof of payment stub would have to be returned to the car. Senator insisted he go, so his hike netted another half mile over mine. After a few minutes, he jogged back, and we were finally ready to set out.

Truth be told, I figured we had about a 40% chance of actually accomplishing the task at hand. It was the longest hike I had ever attempted, and the most strenuous of those we had tried together. Senator also had some debilitation in his knees and feet, but he was wearing his new boots, which helped. We were decently prepared, too, carrying first aid supplies, water, nuts, sunscreen, bug spray, and a moderate amount of cash with which to bribe expert hikers to carry us out if necessary.

Up we started. The first sixty feet were a tease; the trail was level, wide, and graveled. We were no fools, though. Anything rated 'moderate' in the White Mountains would not stay that way for long. As expected, we soon found ourselves climbing over small boulders and up streaming brooks. The hardest part was the slanted section of sheer granite. We could not walk over it because of the sharp angle. Instead, we held onto saplings at the edges to hoist ourselves to each next step. After two hours and forty minutes, we reached the summit.

It was not a private affair-- there were about twenty people and a dog-- but the views were spectacular. It felt much higher than the 4,000+ feet of elevation. Behind us was forest. Before us were blue ridges of mountains that stretched back as far as we could see, each a slightly different tone depending on the sky and the tree carpet. The only interruption was in the southeast, where a few lakes gently lay in a valley. We rested for half an hour. There was a great sense of satisfaction at having hiked Mt. Osceola. We were feeling more optimistic in general. I think there is just something that naturally happens to humans' minds when looking out over an expanse.

The phrase "all downhill from here" should mean something is easy, but it indicates nothing in New Hampshire. We still had to slowly and carefully step to prevent going ass-over-teakettle.[*] As a result, Senator's knees were paining him intensely for the last forty-five minutes, despite wearing elastic bands. We were both sweating majorly, but for most of the hike he actually had sweat running down his hair as if he was in the shower. The worst thing we witnessed on the way down was a stupid German family hiking with three children, one of whom was in a backpack type of carrier. One minor slip could have sent that kid sprawling to horrible injury or worse. I will never understand some of the people we encounter.

Two hours and fifteen minutes after beginning our

---

[*] In her book *Headin' for the Rhubarb!: A New Hampshire Dictionary (Well, Kinda),* New Hampshire raconteur and folklorist Rebecca Rule lists this as a N'Hampsha expression, meaning a full-on tumble.

descent, we were down. We had a snack, did our best to dry off, and climbed into the car. As we drove back, we noticed a noise near the front right car tire. We had actually heard it while driving in, but there had not been any loss of air while we were gone. It was probably a rock stuck in the tread or a little twig scraping underneath. It became very noticeable as we continued, but it did not seem to be a threat. On the highway we heard something clank and thought our pest was gone, but then the sound returned upon slowing down at the exit.

We parked in front of our cottage and each got out to inspect the vehicle. I was on my knees trying to see anything from my side. I was also praying that our grand recovery from a bad start to the day would not involve dealing with a car repair. Senator dropped the hood back down. "Everything's fine there," he declared. Then he got down on his knees to check out the driver side. He didn't explain his finding but just laughed as he extracted a multi-sectioned three foot branch. Problem solved.

Inside the cottage we cleaned up, removing multiple layers of sweat and dirt. Then it was out for some hearty food. Though there were only three other tables in our favorite spot for quiet pub grub, the service was strictly in slow motion. We did not mind. It was not like we were going anywhere fast. *Bring on the forced relaxation.*

It was Sunday night, which, like Thursday night, meant free 9:00pm fireworks at a local resort. Because police still have not chased us out, we staked out a parking spot across the street on their or another resort's property. Nine o'clock came and went, as did five, ten, and fifteen after the hour. At 9:18pm we held an impromptu family meeting and unanimously decided to give them until 9:30pm, in keeping with the local spirit of no one feeling any pressing urge to be on time.

At precisely 9:29pm, the show started by plunging in, full-force, with comical speed. There was no gradual build up, but suddenly there was a one-minute pause. Was it over? Nope, another grand-finale-worthy fervor began. Then, abruptly, there was a two-minute pause. Finally there was a last hurrah, and... it was done.

It was the strangest pacing of any fireworks show I had ever seen. We imagined an underpaid worker taking too long on his break and then realizing he was late. In a panic, perhaps he threw down his cigarette and desperately tried to catch up to the schedule. The only way he could squeeze in the whole fireworks display and be done before the neighbors (who graciously put up with the twice-weekly summer event,) complained was to blow it all out in one massive pyrotechnic frenzy. God bless America!

After the spastic fireworks, we drove the few minutes back to our cottage. Before leaving, I had noticed a big spider in the peak of eaves right over the door.* Frankly, I was proud of myself for not overreacting, but I was using caution nonetheless. Somehow though, by being overly careful, I managed to trip over the threshold on my way in. "Ahhh!" I screamed, not because I fell and banged my shoulder while scuffing my knee. No, that was inconsequential in relation to the horror of imagining that I might have knocked a big spider on one of us. Senator was very concerned about my potential injury. I was just

---

* (This is why I argue for emergency exits, even on ground level floors.)

concerned that he was *absolutely* sure nothing was in my hair. "And you can definitely still see him up in the web?" I demanded, probably with more force than the situation called for.

"It's really dark out," he said, failing to reassure me.

"Look hard!" I commanded. This was not the time for polite requests.

"Yes, he's there."

"Really? You're not just saying that?"

"No, you're good. He didn't even notice you." My heart rate was finally coming down. I then turned my attention to my minor scrapes. "Are you sure you're okay?" Senator asked again.

"Yeah, I'm fine now. That could have been much worse!" Come to think of it, I guess that was the theme of the entire day. It was time to go to bed.

*　　　*　　　*

Senator's knees were not happy with us. After all, with what amounted to not much more than two glorified cloth rubber bands for support, we had climbed up *(ouch!)* and down *(ouch! ouch!)* a mountain. During some of our hiking excursions in the past, we have encountered people using trek poles. These devices look like cross country ski poles, except they collapse and clip together neatly. They also tend to have mud on the bottom tips, rather than snow. We have considered purchasing them before, as they do give the possessing hiker a distinct glow of surefootedness that makes us wonder what we've been missing. Senator now decided that the time had come to invest in a pair. I, on the other hand, still pictured myself coming down a rocky trail and using them to brace my steps only to stumble and vault head-first over them. I determined it was best for me to skip them. One trip to the local Walmart later, we were set.

Bald Mountain, which we had hiked before, was rated by some sources as "easy" and others as "easy/moderate". By now you know that even a 1.5-mile loop in that category in New Hampshire provides a good morning workout. For example, in one part, it is necessary for me to rely on Senator to give me a boost up to where the trail continues, simply because there is nowhere to get my footing without raising my ankle higher than my shoulder. I actually think I can still do this, but the side of a mountain is not the place to test such a belief. You can imagine my satisfaction then, Reader, when a family came through, commenting on how the rating system seemed so much more difficult in the White Mountains. *Further vindication!*

The new trek poles were already paying for themselves. Senator's knees were greatly eased, and all was progressing well. We were sweating as we stepped over the rock piles, but the weather was pleasant. Others were taking advantage of the conditions, too. Along the way we met two ladies who were discussing the trail. They were looking for Artist's Bluff, which supposedly shared a loop with Bald Mountain. I would have described it as more of a T-intersection than a loop, but that was before I knew better.

We completed the Bald Mountain section and then went onto the Artists Bluff[*] part. After a short walk and

---

[*] Depending on the source, it is also listed as Artist Bluff, Artist's Bluff, and my favorite grammatically: Artists' Bluff. Nevertheless, this is what the sign says.

mild gain in elevation, we found the open rock overlook and sat for a while, enjoying the view of the green, snaking ski slopes on a nearby mountain. The bluff was tucked off to the side of the trail, just as we remembered. Like the last time we were there, we had the spot to ourselves.

Just a few moments after we left, we met the same two ladies we had seen earlier on the trail. They said they could not find Artists Bluff. We told them we had just been there, pointing out the direction as we talked. They were sure that that was not it, however. One of the ladies said she had been there years before, and it was much bigger and more open than the place we described. I did not know where else it could be, but the lady was insistent, and, as a result, disappointed.

I shrugged it off until we met a family on the same quest. The dad asked if we knew how to get to Artists Bluff. "We *thought* we did; there now seems to be some debate on the matter..." We recapped the discrepancies, emphasizing that 'our' Artists Bluff was very nice, if they wanted to give it a try. He thanked us, but we could tell he was not satisfied. Apparently ours was but a poor substitute.

Interestingly, we did later accidentally find the real Artists Bluff while hiking a different section of what may or may not have been the same trail. It, too, was tucked away, but it offered a pretty good clue. Senator spotted a rock with the low, red, spray-painted name, along with an arrow pointing the way. Faithful to the fables, it was larger and more open, but the view was not as good as the impostor Artists Bluff. From here we could see less trees and more parking lot. It especially lost its appeal when a flock of well-to-do but ill-equipped teenagers quickly invaded. They were uniformed in their designer shorts and tee shirts and each sported an expensive cell phone. It was sort of cute, though, that they were so impressed with the height and the "beautiful view". I think we have bluffs that are that high in parts of Illinois. Anyway, it was perfect for them, and it was our cue to leave.

We descended to road level and broke off from the trail to the street. This shaved half a mile off the trail that was already double what the sign had claimed. Along the way I found few treasures. Wild blueberry bushes sprouted in random patterns, so I plucked a handful. Senator was still leery. Yes, they were delicious. As long as I was splurging, I also helped myself to a small piece of quartz that I found nestled among the gravel by the road. All in all, it was a productive walk.

"As long as we're heading back that way," I motioned, "do you want to stop for gas?"

"That's fine," answered Senator. We got in the car, rested for a minute, and drove on.

When we reached the gas station, Senator got out to pump. I stepped out too, to toss some garbage. As we were waiting for the tank to fill, a gentleman approached us asking for directions. He was towing a very long trailer, so I suppose he wanted to make sure he got on the right highway the first time. I told him what he wanted to know, and he thanked me, adding, "Are you from around here?"

Senator looked at me to see how I would respond. *That all depends on my state of mind at any given moment*, I thought. "No, I just love it here," I concluded. Someday, though, my answer might be different.

It was time for an easy walk, so we drove up the road to the parking lot that linked up with The Basin. We walked under the parkway overpass to the paved path that meandered gently into sparse pine trees. At intervals there were completely smooth, eroded slabs of rock that had been perfectly curved by the clean rushing waterfalls. The result was a crystal whirlpool in one area and a small, fast-moving cascade through a mini-flume in another. Both were clear and ice cold. It was tempting... but I resisted.

Since we were finally in the area, we also made it a point to stop at Boise Rock. Years earlier, near this landmark boulder, we had found the pipe that brought fresh spring water flowing out of the hill for the world to enjoy. In fact, it was the best tasting water we had ever had. This time, we were prepared, too. Armed with four empty water bottles, we stepped up to the pipe-- which was dry.

This had happened to us last time, but for the good reason that it was winter and everything was frozen. What was the reason now? Had there been that much drought? Hadn't we brought enough rain to replenish the cycle? Further research later that night produced no answers; the mystery continues...

We were getting a little hungry, so as drove, we kept our eyes open for somewhere to grab a sandwich. At the same time, we spotted the sign that read, "NY-Style Deli". We thought it was fun, and decided to give it a try. Plus, there were no other nearby options beyond gas station potato chips.

As Senator ordered a simple veggie sandwich for us to split, I browsed the gift area, ultimately increasing my

"Live Free or Die"-wear by one tee shirt. I took my purchase to where he was waiting. "Nothing yet?" I asked, noticing only one other person in line.

"Nope," he responded. "This wins for slowest service this trip." Neither of us minded, but we did wonder what took so long.

"Perhaps they actually go to New York City for the ingredients?" I suggested. When it was finally ready, I had to admit it was great-- fresh veggies and good cheese on soft homemade bread. It was also overpriced, so I guess that part was authentic.

Our last hike of the vacation was a short one. With the Elephant Head trail, we knew exactly what we were in for. Though the first third of the path was strewn with the assumed rock piles, the overall climb was light, and some parts involved mere skips over level sawed logs. Upon reaching the top, there was a surprisingly ample view of one corner of the Presidential Range, an old train station, a pond, and a wavy ribbon of highway. Positioning ourselves at just the right angle behind a skinny tree worked well to hide the construction, too. At less than a mile round trip, it was a good payoff for a minor investment.

Our New England hiking was done, maybe for the year, maybe for a few years. Back at our cottage I condensed and packed a few items to get ready to leave the next morning. Senator had been ready to leave days ago. I appreciated that he stuck it out, but I still didn't really understand those couple of crummy days. I never like to leave, but I was craving being in our home together.

For supper we picked up some simple food and headed back to the scenic Kancamagus Highway one more time. Neither of us felt like driving far, so we parked at the first overlook we came to. As we ate, we listened to an episode of *Prince Caspian*[*]. Part of the narration described trees slowly starting to walk and move like shadows coming across the land. With a view of endless forests covering the mountains and valleys, the episode took on its own eerie realism. This place was still rugged. This place was still unknown. This place was still alluring.

*   *   *

On the last day of July, we left the White Mountains. We were on the road a little ahead of schedule. Senator was quiet, but he was not in a bad mood. I offered to drive several times, but he had his coffee and he was content.

Southwest we traveled, winding our way through New Hampshire's peaceful and flowered rural community of Haverhill. It's a little outside of mountain country, but I like Haverhill. I can't imagine there ever being much action there, although we did see a few turkeys roaming around. The sight reminded me of the similar gang that wander in our local state park back home.

Then it was over the Connecticut River to Vermont for some interstate driving, but even that was relatively calm. From there, we switched to state highways through more farmland and small towns. Some of the towns were older than the country itself. Let that sink in. Older or newer, they were all so tranquil. How could anyone choose the crime and grime of a city over this?

After a few hours of being on the road, we crossed into New York. This always signals the end of a northeast vacation. The terrain is flatter, the roads are busier, and,

---

[*] second volume of C.S. Lewis' *Chronicles of Narnia* series

frankly, the towns are uglier.* On one two-lane state highway we saw a semi truck flipped over on one side. Half an hour later we stopped for gas and heard the cashier and a customer discussing the accident. They had not seen it, but they had heard that the driver had died. How tragic. I prayed for his/her family, and paused a moment in humble gratitude for our own protection.

All in all, we ended up driving twelve hours that day, all of which were executed by Senator. By the time we reached our night's destination in Ohio, he looked rough-- more than tired. He was also excessively dizzy once we stopped. "You look like you're about to fall over!" I told him.

"That good, huh?" joked Senator. We put on pajamas and lay in bed to relax in the hotel, but Senator was having some anxiousness. It was nothing major, but he was antsy. I attributed it to the long ride and his readiness to go home. Eventually it was time to go to sleep, but he couldn't. He did not have insomnia, but he had become engrossed in extensive internet research about symptoms he had been experiencing.

Later he confessed to me that he started by searching the question, "Why do I hate going on vacation so much?" Yet, he did not hate going on vacation. Logically, he knew that we had fun and got to see many wonderful places, but there had been too many lousy moments that didn't make sense. That question led to, "Why am I so dizzy after driving?" Step by step he narrowed down his descriptions, in turn discovering a lot of writings about people who felt nervous and suffered from migraines, often on road trips.

---

* You know where to direct the hate mail.

They also confirmed his experience that it was actually worse to have someone else drive. Strangely, it made them feel out-of-control and as if they were going to crash into someone or get hit. It was especially bad when vehicles zoomed past on one side or another.

The first major breakthrough came when Senator came across an online test composed of questions and visual items. He took it and scored high for a condition called vertical heterophoria. What's that, Reader? You say you've never heard of it? Don't feel bad; almost no one has. Though it was discovered and documented by the medical field over 100 years ago, it is still a routinely misdiagnosed affliction caused by a slight misalignment in vision between the two eyes. Most people have this to a tiny degree, but just a little too much misalignment sends the brain reeling as it constantly tries to rectify what it's taking in by working extremely hard to marry the two images into one solid picture.

I was asleep this entire time, oblivious to the fact that my boyfriend was on his way to making a revolutionary discovery that would change both of our day-to-day lives. Senator went to bed feeling hopeful and excited. As he would later reflect, "Never have I wanted so badly to be diagnosed with something." The next day he would accept my offer to drive the rest of the way home. He would also test his theory about vertical heterophoria with a clever, self-devised method. Perhaps the most amazing aspect of the night was that he got any significant answers while looking up medical information on the internet. After all, with symptoms like headaches, dizzyness, anxious mood swings, and excessive sweating, it could have determined that he had anything from organ failure to pregnancy.

*   *   *

I slid the seat closer to the steering wheel until I heard the distinct *click* that locked it into position. Next to me, Senator adjusted himself, looking pleased and more relaxed than I had seen him in days. We both fastened our seat belts. "Ready?" I asked.

"Yep," he responded. Then he sat slightly back and placed his hand over one eye.

"Does that help?" I asked, wondering if all of the research he had been telling me about would lead to something beneficial.

"We'll find out..."

I pulled onto the highway for the remaining six hours of the drive home. As I drove, Senator filled me in on more details of his discovery. I was intrigued, wondering if there could really be some answers to questions I did not even know how to form. I was eager to get home and do more research together. The whole idea of the brain fighting itself (and us) just because of visual input seemed weird, but the more he told me about the preliminary test he took, the more I started to think we were on the right track.

We were home a little earlier than expected, which is always a welcome bonus. Though we were calm, I could tell both of our minds were racing with thoughts, ideas, and a drive to learn more. We just wanted to unpack and attack the computer to continue the process. I was already missing the mountains of New Hampshire, but I was more excited about our own mountain that we might be able to overcome.

Before we could even bring the first load of gear into the house, an elderly neighbor lady caught us. I don't think she realized we were just coming back from a long, draining trip. "Hello!" she greeted us. "I just have to ask you about these flowers..." I looked down to where she was pointing. I don't think I was even aware of the flowers, which had popped up while we were gone. Meanwhile, her little fluffy white dog licked my toes. "What do you call these? They're beautiful!" As tired as we were, we had to laugh. It was wonderful to have someone so intently focused on such a seemingly trivial matter.

"I've heard them called resurrection flowers," I responded, trying to draw my thoughts to the yard I had not seen in almost two weeks. "They sprout up very quickly each summer, after their daylily leaves are dead." She appeared pleased with the answer. Her dog appeared pleased with my toes. In a way, the flowers seemed very appropriate.

Chapter 5
Lake Effect,
(or Horizontal):
Late August 2018

Senator's new findings meant plenty of questions and more digging for both of us. How could we find someone who understood this 'vertical heterophoria'? Would he need surgery? Was there a chance that his headaches and dizziness could diminish? Did this explain the less pleasant moments and days of the last trip? Were we even on the right track? Fortunately, a reasonably paced schedule for him and an extended month of summer break for me[*] gave us sufficient time to get to know this mysterious condition.

Learn we did. Through more in-depth research, we were now almost certain that something strange was going on behind Senator's deep, chameleon eyes. The next step was to find a doctor who had real understanding and experience with the condition. The average optometrist

---
[*] Don't worry, Taxpayer; I'm making it up next June.

would not cut it, as evidenced by Senator's many exams with different eye doctors throughout his life. To find someone qualified, Senator started by calling the office of a woman whose research and presentations on the subject clearly defined her as the vertical heterophoria guru. She was located in Michigan, and we were prepared to drive there if it meant answers and relief.

The staff at the office was helpful and efficient. They sent Senator an online questionnaire, which he submitted the same day. His results indicated that, as suspected, he likely suffered from vertical heterophoria. He asked about an appointment, but we both wondered if her international acclaim rendered her schedule too busy. As it turned out, the receptionist was able to give us a list of other highly qualified optometrists whom the expert herself had trained. Their schedules might be more open.

It was a short list, spanning the continental U.S. with only a few far-flung states. We almost could not believe that one of the top names was located less than two hours away. We would not even have to drive into a city. All that lay between us and this top-rated specialist were a few small towns and cornfields. Senator practically scrambled to dial the phone number. I had already made the decision to take off as much time from work as necessary to attend any and all of his appointments. Maybe I would even have to drive. We both hoped and prayed it would not be months of waiting to get in to see the doctor.

In less than two weeks, we found ourselves in the optometrist's waiting room. It had been a somewhat tense drive. Jingles and I had differing opinions on the fastest route, and Senator was annoyed with both of us. Still, he had insisted on driving. He purposely wanted to arrive in a condition or mood that might accurately depict his recent travel experience to the doctor. I sat silently. *Mission accomplished in that respect*, I thought.

We registered and I went to use the restroom. By the time I came out, Senator was already in an examination room. That was encouraging. The nurse continued her list of questions to establish his medical history, symptoms, and general reason for looking for a diagnosis. Together we developed the story of how things had progressed during the past three years, and how they had come to a head a few weeks earlier. The nurse completed her notes, thanked us, and said the doctor would be in momentarily.

"Are you nervous?" I asked Senator.

"More excited," he answered, "but I'm going to be awfully disappointed if this isn't it. Maybe I'm wrong about all of it, and they won't find anything. Then I'll be back to square one..."

"I don't think that will be the case," I answered honestly. I had a good feeling about what we would learn. "Even if you don't have vertical he... whatever it's called... you know more than you did, and we can keep looking into it and learning. I don't think we're wasting our time."

Just then the doctor entered. I liked him right away. He was old enough and professional enough to inspire confidence, yet young enough and absent-minded-professor enough to be real. Immediately he started in as though we had all been chatting for the previous hour. In between physically and mentally taking notes, he mentioned that he had to find time to build a new cabinet for some of his optical supplies, commenting that he really needed to get them organized but probably would not get to it. Had I not seen him work so effectively, I might have thought he had lost focus regarding the matter at hand.

There was no cause for concern. This man's process was more amazing than any doctor I had ever witnessed. In fact, his diagnostic methodology was much more that of a scientist than a doctor. He moved quickly and smoothly, asking unique questions that determined his next move. Instead of just asking which image was more clear, or having Senator read the fourth line on the chart, he deliberately guided him in ways to bring about the most accurate information, even asking him to perform optical tasks that were impossible for him. When Senator struggled and told the doctor so, the doctor promptly and proudly declared that Senator did, indeed, have vertical heterophoria (or 'v.h.' as the cool kids called it).

The doctor then seemed almost excited as he explained that Senator had the added interest of "really unusual eyes". *They always fascinated me*, I thought. In addition to the v.h., we learned that one eye has a vertical astigmatism, and the other eye has a horizontal astigmatism. He used his pen as a pointer on the computer monitor as he confirmed that, otherwise, Senator's eyes were in great shape. I looked over at the super-magnified green orbs with bits of red and yellow and could only think of what a great album cover the image would make.

The good news (besides confirming that there was nothing neurologically wrong) was that v.h. was easily treatable. It did not require surgery or even therapy. We simply had to order a correct pair of glasses that contained a very specific amount of prism within them. It would take about ten business days to receive them, delivered directly to our home. The bad news (though really not bad at all in the grand scheme of things) was that Senator's regular glasses were now rendered useless without the temporary clip-on lenses that the doctor was loaning Senator. Actually, they were worse than useless; they were dangerous. Because the doctor had gradually manipulated Senator's eyes to a place where they could work together correctly when looking through the new lenses, his brain had finally relaxed. Taking those lenses off, even though he had just driven capably for two hours with his old glasses, could and would send him into a fight-or-flight-or-freeze panic attack.

Knowing how powerful the brain's response to the eyes' intake was, we decided that we would not go on any more long car rides without the new glasses. The tricky part was that we were supposed to leave eight days later to visit my parents, who were staying in Ontario. I did not think we could get the glasses by then, but Senator made enough of the right phone calls to expedite the process. On the following Tuesday afternoon, just two hours before leaving for a recording job in Chicago, Senator's glasses arrived. He tried them on, noticing instant improvement. The timing was impeccable, but leaving on a long trip less than twenty-four hours after receiving the new glasses would surely be submitting them, him, me, and us to the acid test.

*   *   *

Wednesday morning I slipped into the driver's seat. Everything was packed, including the large, medium, and small coolers, which were strategically crammed with prepped food for several dinners. We were smiling, but I know we were both nervous. Neither of us had a backup plan if the glasses did not work. I supposed we would have to seriously reconsider any future road trips. As we began, at least, things were looking up.

A few hours into our drive, we noticed a real change. Senator's dizziness was almost nonexistent, There was no sign of tenseness. He was casually joking and genuinely relaxed. Adding to our enjoyment of the drive was the surprising fact that we had entered a magically dry, breezy, pleasant climate. The refreshing wind whipped around as we filled the tank. Inside the gas station, we celebrated our initial success by *not* passing up the enormous cinnamon rolls.

As we washed the decadent frosting down with large swigs of coffee, the mood was downright blissful. An hour later, an eagle soared over the car. We were heading north, and it was starting to feel the way a northern summer vacation should feel. This was what we had been longing for all summer. It was free, and fun.

I had driven the ten hours to International Falls, Minnesota. Our hotel was just a few miles away, on the other side of the international border. When we stopped to gas up, Senator decided he wanted to drive into Canada. That sounded good to me, so we switched seats and rehearsed our answers.

We knew all the basic questions, having crossed the border many times, so we drove up to the booth and presented our identification. Despite this foreknowledge, our minds went blank when the border patrol officer began his quiz. "Where ya' headed?"

"International Falls," Senator answered confidently, completely forgetting that we were driving *away* from International Falls.

"No, Vermilion Bay," I corrected.

"I was about to tell you you were going the wrong way," the man teased. "What's your license plate say?" he continued.

Senator had nothing. "Uh..." he fumbled.

I jumped in but suddenly could not remember which of our two similar black cars we were in. "It's either _____ or _____," I responded lamely, giving him the choice of our two license plates. Why he did not pull us over to search us right then and there, I do not know. We must have looked dumb enough or happy enough or both not to be deemed a threat. Whatever the case, we were on our way to Canadian soil.

We checked into our room, then sought out the vegetarian-traveler's-fast-food-friend, Subway. As the employee started constructing Senator's sandwich, she recited the cheese options, "White, orange, Monterrey, or Swiss." We both stifled laughter in order not to appear rude. Who knew what "white" or "orange" meant? I imagined the nearby factory churning out blocks of cheese simply labeled with a 'W' or an 'O', with no ingredient list available. For the record, we played it safe and went with one of the known options.

The day was pronounced a grand success. Senator had no headache, no dizziness, and no agitation. In fact, he described his state as so relaxed that he almost would have believed someone had slipped him a mood-elevating drug. We could not truly believe that such a difference was merely due to a change of glasses. I think we were both skeptical, but the day had been so great, neither of us would dare admit it.

*   *   *

It was a gorgeous morning. We had slept well, and we were eager to get to the cabin. Senator was also eager for a little breakfast. Though the stale pastries in the hotel were tempting, he chose to partake of that great Canadian ritual and grab some food from the local Tim Horton's. "I'm going to run inside," said Senator, seeing the long line at the drive-through. I was surprised it was so busy on a Thursday morning. Most people would have started work by that time, too. A moment later he was back. "It's just as crazy in there." Now I am convinced: Tim Horton's is some sort of weird, underground Canadian cult. It's probably best for Americans to keep their distance.

The sun shimmered on the lake as we crossed the gateway into the back country. Senator requested that he drive again, and he was confidently and comfortably rolling along the curving ribbons of highway. People were few, but trees were countless. We rolled down the windows to enjoy the slight chill of the breeze. Near the north end of Highway 502, we saw a female black bear run across the road, about a block in front of us. A little later we saw a doe with her fawn, which still had its distinct white spots. It was like a little series of gifts leading up to our destination.

A short while thereafter, we arrived at my parents' cabin. At our first view, it was still the beautiful yet simple fantasy land that lives in my memory. I know it would take away some of the magic if I saw all of the behind-the-scenes work and endless projects my grandparents and parents have done, but it would still be a special place. I was happy and hopeful as we began the assembly line of unloading.

Greetings were shared all around, and we settled in to the familiar cozy rooms. The clear day soon beckoned us outside, where a steady wind roared up the hill to the wooden chairs and swing. Their weather, called "hot and humid" by the local reports, was a mild 78°F with 55% humidity. We had not seen moisture levels that low since winter.

In view of the lake, we caught up and traded stories about our nephews. The boys (my parents' grandsons) were now two, three, and four years old, which gave us all plenty of hilarious material to work with. This included the three-year old's firm belief that he was now sufficiently experienced to run Papa's boat. After all, he had clearly demonstrated the three 'simple' steps. It was nothing short of an insulting affront to his dignity to insist that he might need some assistance!

Eventually it was time to go in and make some cool, sloppy sandwich wraps. We sat in our customary seats, blessed the food, and shared our first meal together in a long time. Veggies galore and strips of cheese leaked out of any available gap, making a fresh, hearty mess. Dinner was good, but we were more grateful for all we had learned the past few weeks.

"Anybody interested in taking a boat ride?" my dad asked, as if anyone would pass up the opportunity. The wind had died down just enough to get the boat out for a short evening ride. As we stepped from the dock to the floating vessel, all at once I thought about Senator's dizziness. Maybe a boat ride was not a good idea. It had not been a problem in the past, but enough symptoms had ramped up over the summer that I was cautious. I looked at him, and he nodded back definitively, as though he had read my thoughts. He did not want to miss out, and he was right; we needed to test everything we would normally do if we wanted to continue to understand vertical heterophoria.

We saw several eagles on our ride. One was what I deemed a teenager. It had just a touch of white on its tail. It reminded me of the students I would soon be meeting for the start of a new school year. They, too, had just a bit of adult to their composition.

We also saw two adult loons with two babies. The urgent call soon went out. In spite of their alarm at seeing us, they refused to dive to safety. They would rather allow risk to themselves than abandon their young at the surface. Instead, the mother quickly gathered the two babies close to her while the father stood guard, rotating to keep us in constant view until we had passed by without incident. I tried to imagine what society would be like if all humans behaved this way. I couldn't.

We puttered back to the dock, and my dad maneuvered the boat into position. The water level was very low, due to a dry winter and spring. As a result, weeds had wound themselves around the motor. As my dad worked on cutting them out, my mom, Senator, and I put life jackets away and disembarked. Walking up to the cabin, we could see the almost-full, pinkish moon rising. It would make a great setting for nibbling dessert and later falling asleep mid-conversation on the porch.

*   *   *

I had trouble getting into my groove the first morning we woke up at the cabin. My well-planned attempt to make fresh smoothies took three times as long as it should have. I forgot ingredients. I dropped berries on the counter. I went to grab things that were not where I expected them to be, mainly because I was not in my own kitchen. Sooner or later I got it together, but I think everyone was waiting on me.

After breakfast and a devotional word of wisdom, Senator and I set out for our first canoe ride since the last time we were at the cabin. Though I was not as incompetent as I had been while preparing breakfast, it still required more finesse to put the canoe into to such shallow water. We used to use a rustic wooden ramp that rose out of the edge of the water. Now even the furthest point of the ramp led only to sand. Somehow we finagled it around to the big dock and pushed it as far as possible without stepping into the muck. Then I stepped in-- the canoe rested nicely on the bottom-- and shifted my weight as far forward as possible, taking advantage of a few inches of water to launch. At the last second, Senator joined me.

It was good to be paddling off into the watery expanse again. We were moving a slower pace, but we did manage to round an island in the distance. The air was hazy, but we could still see plenty. In fact, due to the low water, we could see rocks sticking up that we never knew existed. It was eerily still, with only a few gulls swooping around as we made our way back. All in all, we accomplished ninety minutes of canoeing, and I obtained my annual canoeing blister, in the same spot on the base of my thumb.

I went back in the house to visit with my mom while my dad did dad stuff outside on his well-trodden path between the garage and the boat house. On the porch, Senator halfheartedly made a call on our new and supposedly better cell phone. It was supposed to be better because 1.)it claimed to work in over 200 countries, and 2.)it was not our current phone, which had little coverage outside of cities and suburbs. To our great amazement, it worked! It had not worked in Shenandoah or in most of Acadia, so our expectations were low... which sometimes can be very satisfying. I still have my doubts that it would work on a wilderness road, where we would really need it, but I suppose one can't have everything.

I began to prepare dinner, still learning the subtle differences between cooking with gas and electric stoves. It was taking longer than expected, so Senator lay down for a nap. In between getting stuff together, I skimmed a book my mom had, enjoying the stories of a small-town pastor and his small-town flock drama. In the given setting, it appealed to me more than the political analysis book I was going to bring. In return, we presented my mom with a reference book on North American birds. I figured she would like it, but I did not expect her jubilant reaction.

"Oh, great! I was just thinking I needed one!"

"Oh, really?..."

"Yes, I have a book on plants, mammals, one on stars, fish, weeds..."

"Weeds?"

"Yeah... and..."

"Of course you do!" I laughed. It was time for

dinner, and the smell of garlic and tomato sauce was wafting through the cabin and outside among the trees. We all ate our fill and paused a while to look out at the lake. The weather had looked iffy the past few hours, but now it improved enough to attempt another boat ride.

This time we saw plenty of eagles and cormorants. When we got back to the dock, we also saw a river otter scampering around the rocks. Maybe that was what I had heard the day before. Upon seeing humans, he quickly split to the taller reeds for cover. I suppose it is strange for the animals there; for most of the year, they are masters of the land and water. Then the vacationers show up and think they own the place.

Inside the cabin we claimed our porch plats for the night. The moon (yellow this time) was rising again, and it did not take long for Senator, who was sitting on the floor, to fall asleep against my legs. Next to me my dad was entering the next phase of his sleep cycle, seated in a neck-snapping position that I would not be able to tolerate for two minutes. At the other end of the couch my mom offered her theories on the Midwest climate-land relationship. "I think it's the cornfields that really make a place humid," she proposed.

I built on her idea. "It *was* already dry by the middle of Wisconsin on our drive up..." I reasoned.

"...And that's about where you see the last of the corn," she completed.

My dad sort of rolled his head to the side in a faint attempt to remain aware of the conversation without actually having to submit factual support or alternate theories. Senator also seemed mildly coherent. I took advantage of the moment. "In fact," I added, "central Wisconsin has been so dry that they're growing *dried* cranberries this year!" My mom giggled.* A few tired groans emerged respectively from the floor and the couch. Sorry, I couldn't resist.

With that, my mom declared it dessert time. The 'boys' woke up to join us in eating some key lime pie and watching a travel documentary. On the program, teams of adventurers set out to row around the entire United Kingdom nation "just like our early explorers". It was no small feat, but to claim that they were duplicating the experience of early explorers was a bit of a stretch. For starters, the new crews were in stabilized, partially covered boats, as opposed to being buffeted by every passing wave. They also had ergonomically correct, smoothly sliding seats to make the most of each stroke, which they executed while wearing the best apparel that outdoor outfitters could offer. I'm not saying I could do it; I'm just saying that it is not "just like" their early explorers.

* * *

There is no reason we should not have slept well Friday night, but for some reason, deep rest did not happen. Now the weather was as iffy as my cloudy brain as I tried to focus and get moving. Senator was on the porch with my parents, and they were all watching a line of ducks. I joined them silently, as Senator handed me his cup of coffee to sample.

Slowly, slowly the day was unfolding. I had a little more success with the smoothie creation, and the coffee kept flowing, so there was improvement. I also realized

---

* Thanks, Mom!

Senator had now been relaxed, refreshed, and headache-free for longer than he had been in months. A short devotional led by my dad then led to a very insightful conversation on living out one's faith. By the time we were done, we were fully physically and mentally awake.

The weather was too questionable for canoeing, so I decided I would get some exercise by marching the perimeter of the property. This included uneven surfaces on grass, rocks, hills, and stone steps. It also gave me time to notice little details in the wildflowers. On my third lap around, I started to think about ways to ease the workload for my parents. When I saw my dad, I suggested that he no longer mow a certain section of the side yard.

He laughed, I thought, at my idea. "No, your idea's fine," he explained. "It's just that your mom randomly asked me the exact same thing the other day. So I guess that's settled!"

The sky was clearing up, and we were antsy to move around. I asked my dad's opinion about taking the canoe out. I knew he would give me an honest answer; we don't mess around when it comes to taking on the lake. "It's a little windy, but I think it would be okay now," he said. That was all the confirmation we needed. Senator went in our room to get our sunglasses, I grabbed the sunscreen, and we both gooked up. A few minutes later we stepped outside, ready to begin our clever launching maneuvers. As we got our first glance of the lake, my dad shook his head. Just that fast, the wind had picked up and there were whitecaps on the surface. So much for that idea. Water itself is flexible, and small-craft water-related activities have to be, as well.

We put away the life jackets and picked up our books. The chairs on the hill were making the most of the same stiff wind that drove the waves. I rocked and Senator lounged. Spending an hour catching up on light fiction didn't sound like such a bad idea.

When that time had passed, my parents took a break from their work and joined us. The conversation rolled around to our new discoveries about vertical heterophoria. "No, it's not a psychedelic rock band," Senator joked. My parents were surprised to learn about the intense brain-eye connection, and they were happy that glasses could help so much. I agreed. I could easily get used to it.

Once again the weather teased us toward the water. It had calmed down enough to take out the pontoon, but even then it constantly alternated between strong breezes and motionless sun-bred heat. Small birds that looked like sandpipers floated around in a flock, until our boat almost ran them over. At the last second, they scattered, waiting just long enough for us to pass before reclaiming their piece of the surface. More energetic were the cormorants, who seemed to launch out of the water as if being catapulted from below. At the first sign of dark clouds gathering, we turned the bow and headed back.

Our timing was impeccable. The dark clouds we had been eyeing had now picked up a few allies, and their entire mass was creeping inward. There was no lightning, but the sky was making preparations for something other than a calm, sunny evening. Fortunately, we beat the storm and made it back in time. By the time the first big plops of rain fell, we were shoving the first big plops of pizza into our mouths.

Of course, it can change back just as quickly. Thirty seconds later, the rain was done-- for the whole night. This, however, did not stop the sky's colors from continually morphing. Pink and orange suggested sunset, but once the darker sky followed, a bright mass of cumulus clouds re-lit the heavens. The show went on for a few hours, until a compromise was reached. Darkness overtook the sky, but the moon's light was the centerpiece.

Later that night we ate some dessert while watching a scenic documentary on Saskatchewan. They made it look quite interesting, which made me more than a little suspicious of their editing team. In a previous volume of this series I wrote about driving through Saskatchewan, past miles and kilometers of farmland and prairie. It was boring. That is because Saskatchewan was boring. I guess the filmmakers had to go beyond what one could see while speeding down the good ol' TransCanada Highway to find the real gems. Maybe someday we'll try it.[*]

In total contrast to the previous night, I slept as soundly as a college student in an 8:00am philosophy course. It was beautiful. Senator snuggled in, taking the rhythmic breaths of contentment. I don't know what the problem was the night before, but I woke up refreshed, revitalized, and ready for another day of the outdoors, with a little indoors mixed in for good measure.

*   *   *

Yes, go-to-meetin' Sunday was upon us.[†] My parents issued the standard invitation to the church they attend in the small nearby town: don't come if you don't want to, and

---

[*] probably not
[†] For the record, no one else was calling it that.

don't dress up too much if you do come. It was a good church-- simple, honest, and laid back. They did not take many things too seriously, except their faith in God... and maybe fishing. It was the kind of place where the pastor drives a truck and farms during the week, and puts on his Dockers and buttoned shirt to lead his congregants on Sunday.

Remembering the sensation we had caused as out-of-towners the year before, I prepped my parents. "Do not feel any obligation to introduce us. We're content to lay low."

"Okay," my mom agreed, "but just so you know, we have to sit in the front pew. We originally tried to sit further back, but we were told 'so-and-so' always sits there."

"Then they politely offered us the first pew," my dad added.

Maybe that was to keep an eye on the 'foreigners'. Dutifully we filed into the front row. On her own cue, the barefoot pianist started up Blessed Assurance on the jangly upright piano. A few bars in, she looked back over her shoulder at an older gentleman, who was paying no attention whatsoever to her. She continued, rounding out the first verse and diving into the chorus. Again she checked. Again he ignored. I was intrigued by the situation.

Finally someone poked him and motioned toward the pianist. "Oh, 's that it?" he asked, startled from reading his bulletin. "I missed it! Start over," he directed. The pianist smiled and gracefully brought the familiar chords back to the beginning. Once more she looked back at the man, who was now enraptured in the favorite hymn he had requested.

When the opening song was done, the pastor came to the front and asked if there were any announcements. A few members offered items of church business. Then one more person spoke up. "Well, this isn't really about church, but it's the last day the Co-op is open on Sundays until next year." All nodded a solemn acknowledgment, as if a grave prophecy had been uttered. In a small town with no grocery store, that was a newsworthy piece indeed.

The service continued with prayer requests, a few more hymns and songs, and a brief sermon. Lastly, there was a report on world missions. As the woman leading this segment observed, "Well, the Bible says there will be people from every nation on Earth in the Kingdom, so it might be nice to get to know a few of these folks first." You gotta' love Canadian manners.

The weather cooperated so we could take our second canoe ride. We set out again for Moose Island, the shortest of our usual routes. It was easy to control the canoe in the calm water, so we paddled in closer than we normally do. The low water level meant extra caution when going over rocks, though. I am happy to report that we never scraped.

During our excursion, we noticed a loon crying out. It was a sharp call that I did not recognize. "I think it's in distress," said Senator. He was right. As we watched more closely, we could see that the bird could swim, but it could not fly. There was nothing we could do for it. Hopefully it was resolved in some way, but it was kind of sad to see.

When we got to the cabin, we spent some time hanging out with my parents. They (especially my mom) wanted to see photos from our last trip, so I brought out my baggie of prints and began the narration. We teased my mom mildly, because she kept falling asleep. "Oh, no!" I chided. "We've turned into the couple that bores people with vacation pictures!" Let's face it-- based on where we go and what we like to do, most of our pictures are some version of us, rocks, trees, and maybe water. Rinse and repeat.

After the lackluster photography exhibition, Senator and I went down to the dock to sit by the water for awhile, hoping to soak up enough lake life to last until next year. As we sat, we noticed tiny green frogs in the mud. A few more popped out from the reeds that had been camouflaging them effectively. Some were braver than others, but all were adorable. Is it possible for a frog to look happy? They sure did.

After dinner my dad took us out for a sunset cruise. Even though it was late August and a month later than we normally would have been there, we still had plenty of daylight hours. For an hour and a half or more we roamed around the lake, watching nature transition toward its nighttime mode. At one point, I asked my dad where we were going. "I don't know-- just roaming around aimlessly." It was a perfect answer. Roaming around aimlessly is not a luxury we often have time for, and I cherished it.

We saw small fishing boats of anglers trying for that last walleye of the day. There were also loons, which made Senator and me wonder about the one we had seen from our canoe. We listened to the sounds of nature. Actually, though, we could have listened to music. The boat, we are told, has a digital input for recorded music. Maybe we could make a compilation of seafaring and pirate songs. Of course, if our three-year old nephew got into it, he would no-doubt demand that his papa acquire a parrot and install a plank. Things could get interesting.

Also interesting was another scenic documentary we watched later that night. This one took a round trip tour from Halifax, Nova Scotia. It departed the gray, rugged Atlantic Ocean for points north and west, eventually crossing the tall, jagged Rockies. Dense, over-scaled evergreen forests and plenty of lakes, lakes, lakes were all part of the terrain. The return trip followed the U.S. border at the 49th parallel. As many times as we have crossed the border, I never knew that there is actually a wide, mowed out section all along it to denote the world's longest undefended border. I'll have to watch for it if we ever cross somewhere near a forest.

As we watched other shows, I heard a motor start up in the distance. It was too loud for a boat motor, but I could not imagine what larger vehicle would be within earshot of the cabin. Then I realized it was not a motor. An unpredicted storm was rolling in, and we could already see lightning over the lake. It was a scramble to put the storm windows into the porch window frames, but it was finished in time. Everyone was rewarded for their efforts when the storm passed, leaving us with a wonderfully chilly night.

Senator opened our bedroom window. I arranged an extra blanket on the bed. I relished the cold on my face while my body snuggled into the gradually-warming bed. I do not remember another thing until I smelled coffee brewing many hours later.

*   *   *

Monday morning was dark. It is unusual to have dark, rainy mornings at the cabin in summer. Storms or drizzles usually happen later in the day, which is why I was very surprised to find that it was 8:45am. I thought it was closer to sunrise.

The night's cool temperatures carried over into the morning, settling the August day solidly in the 50s. We all sat down and had some breakfast-- by now I had mastered the blender-- and watched the crows. On that morning, they were the privileged recipients of some stale bagels my mother had tossed them. Though no one was trying to horn in on their bonanza, the pair would alternately sneak up, look around, and then slyly grab a hunk of bread before slipping off to the side of the woods to nibble it. Then they would use one foot to hold down the feast so they could pick it apart. One foolhardy foul tried to fly off with half of a bagel, but finding it much denser than the toast he was used to, soon lost his load.

A boat ride was not possible, so my parents decided to take a car ride deeper into the north country. They invited us along, and we drove on to even further remote areas. There were more lakes; parked float planes were as prominent as cars. Once in a while we passed a junk shop or gas station, which mainly served fishing camps.

About one hundred miles north of the main highway the road ended, and we turned around to return south. Before the long ride back, we made a pit stop at the local hot spot. In this neck of the woods, even a small town would have looked like a booming metropolis. We watched as a few girls, perhaps ten or eleven years old, pulled their

A.T.V.s up to the pumps to gas up. They were laughing because one girl had lost her shoe during the previous fun adventure.

Inside the convenience store, as we waited to use the bathroom, we saw a man browsing the tiny dvd. collection. He made his selection and asked the three employees, who were sitting around and chatting casually, how to rent them. They looked at each other blankly. None of them had any idea. Apparently no one had ever asked before. It did not really seem to upset the man; he just placed the dvds back for the next person to not be able to rent them.

Senator and I both started to doze off on the way back to the cabin. My mom was asking me about my upcoming school year, and I answered her, but mainly I did not want to think about it. Life would get crazy soon enough; I just wanted to tilt my head in the back seat and watch the birch and pine go by. Senator fell deeper into sleep.

It was mid-afternoon when we returned. Though I still held out hope for one last canoe ride, Senator assessed the sky and vetoed my plan. It was a proper decision. Had we been rained on, we would have had to pack wet clothes when we left the next day. That is never a good thing. Trust me, Reader. Instead, we rinsed the canoe and put it back in the garage, maybe for another year, unless someone else decided to use it.

Shortly afterward, I started making dinner. Senator and my mom perused bird books. "Did you know that a loon can dive over 200 feet beneath the water?" one of them asked me.

"I do now," I answered from the kitchen. While

dinner was in the oven, I went back down to the dock to talk to my dad. He was messing around with something on the boat, so I watched the sneaky river otter while we (my dad and I, not the otter and I) talked. He (the otter, not my dad) darted around the reeds busily, eventually departing across the bay, his nose cutting the tell-tale V-path in the water. I looked around for the cute frogs, but none were in sight. Maybe it was too cold for them. More likely the ducks had eaten them.

The house smelled like an Italian restaurant, so I figured dinner was about done. Everyone found their places, and we paused to bless our last dinner together for at least a few months. It was amazing, but not surprising, how fast the time had gone. Even more amazing was that Senator was still completely cool, calm, collected, and having a great time. It was wonderful... even if my frogs were all gone.

After dinner, Senator and I took one last walk down to the dock before going in for the night. The lake was still, and we said a mental good-bye to it. Inside, my mom was already firing up another nature documentary about another beautiful region in Canada. It really is a magnificent, wild, empty country. By the time the program was over, we were already planning how to get to some of western Ontario's wonderful, waterful parks. I think the spice cake may have helped us think, too.

Monday night was the only night we slept with the windows closed. Chilly would have been fine, but it was damp, too. We snuggled in for a comfortable rest, which took effect rather quickly. At 2:30am, however, three high-pitched beeps sounded. At first I thought I had tinnitus, but then I realized tinnitus is a long, constant blast in one's head. It was not loud enough for a carbon monoxide detector, so I knew there was no danger. *It must be Senator's digital watch*, I thought. Then I remembered that Senator does not own a watch.

By that time, my dad had heard it, too. He thought maybe it was the stove timer, but it was not on. His theory triggered my memory of something else I had seen before I went to bed. I remembered that the microwave clock still showed fifteen seconds, probably because someone had removed an item for breakfast before the time had finished. If it sits idle too long with time still on it, it gives off reminder beeps, in case one has forgotten about one's heated rolls. I would, however, assume this normally happens after a minute or two-- not eighteen hours. Talk about delayed reaction... Anyway, I cleared the timer, there were no more beeps, and a good remainder of a night's sleep was had by all.

*   *   *

Packing up went smoothly on that gray, cool Tuesday morning. We sat for a bite with my parents before leaving, and my dad led a final devotion to send us off on the right foot. In Senator's case, it was literally the right foot, as he wanted to drive first. I took that as a good sign.

We said our good-byes and backed out of the driveway, losing our glimpse of the lake. It is always sad to go, but there was a tranquil mood of quiet and serenity. "I feel bad leaving them alone like that," said Senator, half-joking, half-serious. For a moment it felt like we were all kids, each half of whom was losing their playmates.

Before getting too far into our journey, we stopped

for gas. The station was old, and the pumps were not much newer. When the tank was finally full, I went inside to pay. A woman from the local reservation ran the station and convenience store, but her computer was not showing our total. Since she was simultaneously caring for her young boy, she simply asked me if I knew the total. I told her, paid her, and she thanked me, never questioning my honesty. I was so pleased at the contrast to big cities, I gave the change to her son. He beamed, widening his enchanting brown eyes in true appreciation.

    Back on the road, Senator was doing well. He switched on a radio show, which required more concentration. I took that as another good sign. Compared to the last trip, and the past few years of trips, it had become quite obvious that this vertical heterophoria phenomenon had been at the root of the gradually increasing dizziness, headaches, and moments of anxiety. We were both so relieved to see it going in the other direction. It explained so many things, too. As the topic would inevitably find its way into so many of our conversations, it seemed like we gained more revelations by the hour.

    Ever-shifting masses of gray clouds rotated and danced their way over us for most of the day. They kept us shaded and in the 50s. It was marvelous and added to the calm. After about eight hours, we stopped in Wisconsin for the night, satisfied with a successful driving day. We even had fun rummaging the local Walmart's freezer aisle for something to microwave for dinner, when there were no other suitable options.

    Our night concluded with watching the middle part

of a confusing World War II black-and-white movie set in Spain. There were multiple couples involved. Some of them were double-agents. A few seemed to be triple-agents, if such people exist. We were not so complicated. We were just a couple with some salad, some microwaved cheese curds, and a new pair of glasses.

*   *   *

For some reason Senator was up at 5:30am. I think he was just excited to get home. I was up then too, but I fell right back asleep for another two hours. He was content to let me do so-- quite a difference from when he could not sleep the previous spring in Virginia. Early enough, though, I awoke, got ready, and we went down to the hotel's breakfast bar. I was even feeling ambitious enough to attempt to use (with Senator's assistance) the waffle machine. This was significant; I had been too afraid of those contraptions since an ill-fated event a decade before that left gloppy, yellow batter partially burned and stuck to the griddle and partially leaking over the countertop. One lives and learns.

Unlike the previous day, it was sunny. Evidence of heavy rain was all over Wisconsin, though. We saw standing water in farm fields and large fallen branches from very old trees. Between Tomah and the Dells we were sent on an hour-and-a-half detour due to the flooding. I had no idea it had been so bad; we had only encountered some light showers. Senator, however, had used his extra two hours that morning to monitor the weather situation closely. One source he had heard claimed that twelve inches of rain had fallen in twenty-four hours!

As we moved southward, the traffic and the

temperature picked up. Naturally, I-90 was sprinkled with inconvenient construction projects. When we reached the border, our home state greeted us by demanding toll money. Yes, we were back home in Illinois, the 'Deep South'.

This time no one greeted us in the alley. We unloaded the car efficiently, and I started to unpack in the house while Senator attended to business correspondence. The Chicago improvisational jazz scene had had to endure without him for a week, so I loaned him back to them. As I dumped the first load of laundry in the washer, I marveled at how perfectly everything had gone. I also wondered if it would be pushing our luck to squeeze in one more short trip on my extended summer break. Perhaps I would wait a day to bring it up...

Chapter 6
Derailed:
Early September 2018

Cars were usually fine. The boat had been great. What about a train, though? A few years back, I had stumbled on what sounded like a beautiful train ride in Ontario, not far from Lake Superior. The round trip and stopover to hike in a canyon added up to a full ten-hour day of scenic wonder. Plus, everyone knows trains are romantic. The timing and location never quite worked out, but when I learned that my summer break would be extended, I decided it was the perfect year to fit it in.

Before I knew about vertical heterophoria, I thought it would be fun to keep the train trip a secret from Senator. For months he had only known that we had a short three-day trip blocked out on the calendar as a last hurrah before the Illinois public school system once again owned me. Beyond that, he would be surprised. Based on all we had learned the previous few weeks, however, I decided it was best to let him in on my plot.

"I think I should tell you what we're doing next

month," I started. As soon as I said it, I realized that "next month" was actually only a week away.

"Why? Is it something bad?" he asked absently.

"No, I think you'll like it..."

"...But?..."

"I mean *you* would like it, but maybe your eyes wouldn't. Maybe not your brain, either."

"My poor brain," Senator stated self-sympathetically, in what had become our motto since discovering how hard his brain had been working to perform the normal task of uniting visual images.

"Yes, your poor brain is what I don't want to torture," I explained. "We are/were going to go on a train ride-- a long one."

"It should be okay," he said easily.

I was surprised by his unconcerned answer. "No, I mean a long train ride, as in several hours each way. What about the fast images going by the windows on either side?" The more I listened to myself, the more I was convinced it was just about the worst excursion I could have planned, save perhaps bungee jumping.

"No, I think it will be fine," he reaffirmed.

"Okaaaaaay..." It sounded like I had permission to go ahead with our original plans. It would be yet another test that had to be at least attempted. I hoped we would not both regret it, especially since we would be trapped on a train with no way to call it off. I made a mental note to pack extra ibuprofen, in case of a major headache.

The first Wednesday in September, after the Labor Day crowds were heading back to work and school, we entered the local interstate and headed east. It was sunny and windy, and Senator had been enjoying a steady stream of pain-free days. There was still dizziness to contend with, but it was manageable. Overall the v.h. symptoms were much improved, even when we drove through the crazy, congested area around Chicago's south suburbs.

Before we knew it, we were turning north into Michigan's more open, wooded areas. When we were beyond the traffic, we stopped at a quiet, out-of-the-way rest area. While Senator was in the bathroom, I saw a rare Russian black squirrel. He was rooting around between the trees and a garbage can, curious to see what goodies were left behind. Senator came out, and I showed him the squirrel. "You better watch your other side, too," he said. I had my legs dangling out of the open car door, so I quickly switched my eyes to that side. There a chipmunk was venturing closer to the car. I quickly shut the door, lest a furry hitchhiker join us.

We continued northward, turning east at intervals to reach the center of the state. Though a major portion of our route was on U.S. highways, we made the happy discovery that there are several stretches that allow a generous 70mph or 75mph speed limit. As we zipped along, we listened to the fifth book of C.S. Lewis' *Chronicles of Narnia* series. Our day was progressing pleasantly.

Though we have been all over the continent, it was the first time either of us had crossed into the Upper Peninsula of Michigan. We were looking forward to it, especially since the Great Lakes were involved. During the moments one spends straddling Lake Michigan and Lake Huron on the Mackinac bridge, it is a sensory feast. Long, thick, angled cables appear to move as the car's forward motion constantly changes the view. Meanwhile, the wind over the open expanse of the water howls through the gaps in a ghostly whistle. This combines with the deep, rotating drone of the metal grate under the tires. Under the right conditions, it could make for a very nightmarish scenario. Thankfully, it was not wreaking havoc with the vertical heterophoria.

In the U.P. the forests contained more birch, with dense pines filling in the openings. We were also far enough north that some of the trees had started to change to their brilliant fall colors. Given our latitude, and the fact that I can normally never travel in autumn, it was a thrill for me to see the leafy bursts of orange and yellow. The only interruption in the treeline was an open ranch with about a hundred buffalo.

At Sault Ste. Marie we crossed the border into Canada. It was just eight days after we had crossed back into the United States from our last trip. A few miles away, we reached our hotel. I can't say the city was particularly attractive, but it was good enough for a spot to crash for two nights. Overall, it was just gray and dreary. The most noticeable type of businesses were the American chains. It was not pretty, but it was not dumpy.

After checking in and leaving our gear in our room, we looked for some dinner. We tried one restaurant first, but when we stepped inside the vestibule, it looked too formal for us and the casual occasion of grabbing some grub. Next door we found a pizza place/sports bar instead. We were hoping for somewhere a little quieter, but it was close enough. As we waited for our pizza, we noticed the napkins on the table; they were stamped with the logo of the same owners as the fancier restaurant next door. We imagined ourselves asking for a table at the first place, and their host politely showing us to a table-- in the second restaurant. "Yes, um, right this way..." she might have said, as we followed her across the parking lot.

Back at the room we relaxed in anticipation of the big day ahead. Unfortunately, Senator was extremely dizzy, but he was plugging along. It made me seriously second-guess the train ride, but he still wanted to go. Once again I checked to make sure all of our hiking gear and supplies were ready. I triple-checked the alarm, too. Actually, I triple-checked the alarm*s*, (plural). We would be up before the sun, and if Senator was game, there was no way I wanted to miss our adventure after coming all that way.

*   *   *

Because I did not trust the unusual dual alarm clock on the night table, I had also set my portable one. To the best of my knowledge, both were set for 6:00am. Portable German analog alarm clocks being what they are, however, I had actually set it for 5:57am. This was alright, and it performed its duty at the duly appointed hour, minus three minutes. Half a second after it went off, the incessant high piercing beeps scared the heck out of me. I attempted to slap down the snooze button, (which was located in the customary position at the top of the clock,) but it was so lightweight and I was so animated that I sent it flying across the room. Had it not been so dark in the room, I truly would have seen time fly.*

By this time, the noise had woken up Senator. My plan was to let him sleep an extra fifteen minutes, but that

---

*   (insert groan)

was now out of the question. I scrambled to the wall to find the light switch so I could find the alarm and shut it off. On popped the bright light, triggering an instant headache and what I dub 'morning blindness'. When I recovered my sight, I grabbed the clock, smashed down the button to silence it, and apologized to Senator for the chaos.

"It's okay," he mumbled. "I had to get up anyway." We exhaled, gathering our thoughts to start the day. Just then, the room alarm clock started blaring. *Of course.*

It was train day, though, and we were excited. Despite the alarm clock fiasco, everything was going according to plan. The weather was perfect-- sunny and cool, with no chance of rain. Senator's dizziness had vanished during the night. By 6:40am we were eating a good, hot breakfast. Just before 7:00am, we and our gear were in the car, headed for the train station. The camera battery was even fully charged. We were set.

The directions were easy, and we soon found ourselves comfortably parked near the entrance to the train station. Other passengers started to arrive, and we all made our way to the front door, eager for the adventure to begin. I also noticed that no children were around, confirming my brilliant theory that the day and time of year would have them all safely tucked away in their schools and not on our train. Who knew? If we could keep the v.h. under control, it might very well be the highlight of the year.

Of course, in order for a train excursion to be the highlight of anyone's year, it must, in fact, occur. Senator had stepped out of line to go to the bathroom, so he was gone when I heard the first murmurings from the crowd. I strained my ears. Then I asked a random person to confirm what I thought I had heard.

"Yeah, they just canceled the train trip," he nodded in disappointed solidarity. I was stunned. "...but you can reschedule it for tomorrow." Maybe *he* could reschedule it for the next day, but we could not. In fact, we probably could not reschedule it for a few years, and certainly not when there might be a hint of fall colors.

The lady at the desk mentioned that something was blocking the tracks. *I'll move it!* I thought, as she processed my refund. I know there are much worse things that can happen on a trip-- actually, some of them have happened to us-- but I was mildly crushed. I could not believe I had thought about it for years, kept it a secret for months, and dragged Senator eight hours from home, just to be turned away. I had already struck out with the marine life cruise in Maine. By the time Senator came out of the bathroom, he did not have to ask what was going on; he could fully read my Clark W. Griswold moment on my face.[*]

As we had foolishly awoken at 6:00am, we had time to consider other options. Surprisingly, Senator did not want to go back home. That, in itself, was proof that the glasses were working. "Me neither," I affirmed. "So now what?" He suggested we first go back to the hotel to see if our room was refundable, or if that would be our base for the night. As I already knew from booking the reservation, we could not cancel at that point. Anywhere we went should stay within a reasonable radius of Sault Ste. Marie, Ontario.

Now that we knew our limitations, we started on our alternate plans for the day. Though the nice man at the

---

[*] see National Lampoon's *Vacation*

front desk offered us free passes to a few local attractions, none of them interested us. "Did you see that billboard, back by the bridge?" asked Senator me.

"Which bridge? The one into Canada, or the one into the U.P.?" I was pretty sure I knew what he was going to say, but I did not want to influence his idea.

"I don't know, but it said something about a shipwreck museum. Can we do that? Do you know where that was?"

"Yes, I know exactly where it was! It was near Mackinaw City, just on the edge of the Lower Peninsula-- maybe an hour or an hour and a half south. I saw it too, and I thought it would be cool." Coincidentally, it had been the only thing (besides the scenery) that caught my interest since we left home. I liked where this was going after all.

"So we'd have to go back into the U.S.?" Senator pointed out.

"Yes, which might seem a little fishy, considering we have not even been here a day."

"Then we'd come back into Canada for our hotel tonight?"

"Well, yes. That is, if they let us." I did have some doubts about that part.

"Okay," said Senator. He then got on the computer to see what else we could do in the Mackinaw City area. He was excited to learn that there was a lighthouse cruise that departed from the town, but disappointed to find out they were already booked. He should have known better; look at our recent record for entertainment that involved transportation. At least we had not managed to sink my parents' boat.

"They put me on a standby list," Senator informed me, after hanging up the phone. "They'll call if they have an opening." With that, we were on our way to the United States.

"You were here for a train trip, but it got canceled?" asked the border agent, probably noting that no one had used that excuse before.

"Yes." I kept it short.

He looked up at the sky and then at us. "Beautiful day," he stated flatly. It was not meant to be an observation of the pleasant weather. "Kind of strange it would be canceled, eh?"

"They said there was something blocking the tracks." *C'mon, Buddy. Would I really make up something this lame?* This time I did volunteer more information. "I have our original tickets and refund slip here," I offered.

He seemed a little surprised but passed us through with his best wishes for a nice day. "Come back again; it's a great tour, especially in the fall."

In less than an hour, we were staking out our free parking in Mackinaw City's downtown. The sun sparkled on Lake Huron, reflecting and warming us somewhat in the cool air. Since we were by the docks, we checked in to see if there had been any openings on the lighthouse cruise. There had not, but we picked up a ferry schedule for boats to Mackinac Island, just in case.

Around the bustling tourist district we saw several fudge shops. In one block, I think there were four of them. We also drove by the predictable cafés, restaurants, inns, and upscale pubs. Pubs, incidentally, used to be for the common folk. Relatively recently, American trendsetters got a hold of them, redecorated them, gave the drinks crafty names, tripled the prices, and drove out all the public types. I cannot imagine England and Ireland approve of this development.

Jingles successfully guided us to the anticipated shipwreck museum. This was not a huge accomplishment, since it was a whole six or eight blocks away. At her pronouncement of our arrival, we parked the car. There was a lovely view from the northern tip of the peninsula, but we could see nothing that looked like a museum. Senator got out and walked around. I was a little concerned when I lost sight of him, but he was back in a few minutes.

"Did you find it?" I asked, hoping another anticipated plan would not flop.

"Yes, it's actually part of a lighthouse." That sounded interesting. "There's the lighthouse, a shipwreck exhibit, and a gift shop. We can go up in the lighthouse, too." Before he could explain any more, I was out the door with my purse.

The woman in the gift shop made sure we knew everything that was included. We had stumbled onto Old Mackinac Point Lighthouse, which once beamed out toward the strait. In just a few minutes, a guide would lead a handful of us to the top of the lighthouse. Afterward we could learn more about lighthouse operations and lifestyles in the attached part of the building. The shipwreck film and artifacts were in a nearby building across the yard. If we hurried along, we could just make the next climb up to the light.

We joined the tour easily, taking our spot against the

wall in the tiny hallway. The guide gave us and four other people a brief introduction to the role that this particular lighthouse played in Great Lakes history. Then he inspected everyone's footwear to make sure there were no open-toed shoes. We thought he would lead the way up the metal spiral staircase, but he abruptly turned to Senator and directed him to lead the parade. Senator had wanted to go last so he could be extra careful, but everyone was already lining up behind him.

Slowly he started upward. I was right behind him, keeping an eye on my footing and his. At the top we crammed into the partially glassed-in octagon. The view northward toward the water was expansive. From the south, we all tried unsuccessfully to duck the sun, which was creeping around the edges of the covered windows. The guide joined us and spoke for a few more minutes. At one point he made a little joke, which Senator played along with and responded to.

Then the guide finished, and we got ready to descend the four-story tower. Somehow I had ended up closest to the hole in the floor for the stairway. Common sense deemed that I should go first, which I did without hesitation. As soon as I started, Senator was practically clamoring for me to go faster. I knew something was up. As soon as we were both safely down, I was going to ask him what had happened. Before I could inquire, however, he dashed past me, quickly explaining that he would be back. I realized he was sick, so I followed him to make sure he knew where he was going.

When he came out of the bathroom, we both sat outside in the fresh air for a few minutes. "How bad do I look?" he asked.

"You look okay now," I answered. I could tell he had splashed water on his face. "What happened? Did you get dizzy?" Maybe we were getting too confident with the new glasses.

"Worse-- I got nauseous and panicky. It was about to get bad," he explained.

I was shocked. "You're kidding! I couldn't tell anything was wrong. You even joked with the tour guide."

"It was taking everything in me to hold it together."

I was impressed, but complimenting him did not quite seem appropriate. I felt bad for him, but he again reminded me that we were still learning about his condition. "Either way, no more open spiral staircases in tight areas."

"Agreed, and no more medieval bell towers," he added, remembering our miserable time at Koln Cathedral a few years ago.

"That was not even an option," I confirmed.

Having conquered his own small setback, I thought Senator might be ready to head back to the hotel. This was not the case. On the contrary, he was ready to sit through a film on local shipwrecks. Perspective is a good thing. Our problems seemed rather minuscule alongside those of the crew of the Cedarville, which tragically went down in 1965.

In the building next door we continued our education at the shipwreck museum. The first thing we learned was that it was not actually the museum we had seen advertised on the billboard. Ironically, the other one was in a different city, a few hours away, while this one was in the same city as the billboard. This museum was excellent, though. Decade by decade, it pieced together the woeful tales of many wrecks, most of which could have been avoided. The 1880s and 1890s were especially deadly, due to captains going too fast in order to move cargo quicker, or simply waiting too long to order the men to abandon ship. I was intrigued. Senator was hooked. Ten minutes later he was buying two more books for the ever-growing history section of our personal library.

Everyone we met was friendly. One couple was delighted when Senator offered to take their photo against the backdrop of the water. They had been struggling to hold the camera to take their own picture. Other people nodded or said "Hello" as they passed us on the sidewalk along the water. The only challenge was avoiding the goose crap, which was ample along the path.

It was late morning, and there had been no openings on the lighthouse cruise, so we continued with our spontaneous agenda. Just a block away from the shipwreck museum was Colonial Michilimackinac, a reconstruction of a French fur trade-era post and fort. With the exception of the lighthouse staircase, things were falling into place beautifully. As I fished some cash out of my purse for tickets, I had almost forgotten about the train ride.

"Boy, the shipwreck museum was great, and this looks excellent, too," I mentioned to Senator.

"Oh, you went to the old lighthouse, too?" asked the man at the visitor center desk. I nodded and smiled, thinking he was just making conversation. "Then I have to redo your ticket," he said seriously. "You should have gotten four dollars back." This was a man of integrity. He insisted we let him reprocess the ticket. When he was done, he handed us our new tickets and four singles with a satisfied smile. *See what I mean about the nice people?*

In general, the French had better relations with the natives on the American continent than did the British. Michilimackinac was a prime example. Both societies traded to their advantage, and more than a few intermarriages took place. Wine was probably involved, too, keeping everyone a little happier.* Then one day the British took over and the fête du fort was busted up.† They also moved the fort across the water to a nearby island for greater protection, in case those rascally American colonists starting getting any notions about independence.

Michilimackinac was similar to Fortress Louisbourg in Nova Scotia, but maybe one-third of the size. There were storehouses, soldiers' and officers' quarters, gardens, kitchens, and many interpretive exhibits. Good French Catholics that they were, the beautiful centerpiece of the fort was an elaborate chapel. Maybe a few native brides were united with French grooms here.

Our favorite parts were the exposed excavations of archaeological digs. These subterranean windows to the past revealed original foundations, ruins, and artifacts. This, in turn, helped historians accurately design the reconstruction. Bits of daily fort life from weapons to crosses were discovered and meticulously preserved, all for the sake of tourists whose trains were canceled.‡

Outside, the cannon demonstration was about to begin. We found a place to stand in the shade of the

---
* pure conjecture on my part
† more or less
‡ most definitely conjecture

stockade and waited for the reenactor to prepare the artillery. I poked Senator and motioned out into the distance over the water. He acknowledged what I saw and stifled a laugh. Though there was no live ammunition present, the cannon was aimed at a passing freighter ship. It looked like we were ready to attack-- and a civilian vessel no less.

To Senator's disappointment, the lighthouse cruise company never called. I was not really surprised; on such a perfect sailing day, who would want to cancel, unless there was a horrible emergency? Still, we were determined to get out on the water, so we drove back down to the docks and went inside the ferry pavilion. In twenty minutes the next boat would leave for Mackinac Island. Tickets were available and reasonable, so I bought two, plus an espresso for good measure. We did not really care about visiting the famous vacation island, but it was a boat ride nonetheless.

After a short wait we boarded, claiming seats on the open upper deck. As we waited to leave port, a stiff, refreshing breeze flapped the flag and our hair. We nibbled some carrot and celery sticks. Then an announcement came over the speaker, informing everyone about safety procedures and reminding us not to eat while on board. *Oops.* I stowed the veggies.

It only took fifteen minutes to reach the island. Judging by the distance, I would have estimated at least twice that long, but we were clipping along. Soon the famous Grand Hotel came into view with its iconic yellow awnings, made famous in the movie *Somewhere in Time*.* If

---

* My mom liked this movie. Senator's mom loved this movie. We watched it and immediately gave it unanimous thumbs down.

you are a guest there, you may sit on the long front porch. If you are not a guest there, you can 'pay-per-view'. (Even then, you better not be in your jeans and favorite tee shirt.) Somewhere in time years ago, we looked into a reservation there for two nights, for a gift. I knew it wasn't the local Super 8, but I did not expect the rates to start at four hundred bucks a night. Needless to say, the recipients of the gift received a stay back on the mainland instead.

It was 3:00pm when we reached Mackinac Island. The last ferry would leave at 7:00pm. Since we did not want to be stranded overnight on the island, we planned to return on the 6:00pm ferry. That would give us ample time to roam the carless streets, get back to our car on the mainland, and drive to a foreign country to go to sleep for the night.

We disembarked and filtered into the throngs of tourists trailing along both sides of the street. Most looked older and certainly wealthier than us. On the roads bicycles flashed by and horse-drawn carriages clip-clopped along, not much faster than we were moving. We had no real aim, so we window-shopped as we walked, perusing the many shops, restaurants, and confectioneries. Upon careful reflection, I am convinced that a full 50% of the island's economy is based on fudge and popcorn. The other 50% is divided between hotel revenue and the carriage operators.*

We continued along casually, already deciding that a

---

* Why didn't we take a carriage ride, you may be wondering? It was not as romantic as it sounds. Imagine twelve people crammed on a cart with a large plastic covering surrounding the sides, and not enough pooper scoopers following behind to keep up with the demands of said mode of transit.

few hours on the island would be more than enough. Just then Senator yelled out, "Gary!" I looked at him blankly. We did not know anyone from around there, and I doubted he suddenly felt inspired to go to Indiana.

"What are you..." I started. Then I realized he was greeting a familiar face. Among all those people, at that exact time and place, we saw our neighbors from two doors down.

"You could have just walked over into our yard," Gary joked. "You didn't have to drive all the way here to see us!" It was quite a coincidence, but it was not the first time I have had it happen. When I was a kid, we ran into our neighbors while at Disney World. Years later, I met my old high school geometry teacher while Senator and I were walking along a street in Door County, Wisconsin. Is the world really that small, or do we just share some of the same habits and schedules?

We wandered on toward the park. There we read displays about Père Marquette, whose explorations were certainly influential where we lived. There was another iteration of the colonial-era fort, but we did not feel like spending money to see a smaller version of what we had already seen that morning in Mackinaw City. Instead, we ate our contraband veggie sticks and some granola bars at a picnic table. Entertainment was provided by bold but annoyed sea gulls, who netted nothing from our late lunch.

The views of the deep blue water from the island were gorgeous, but we did not have much time remaining. If we had a full day, maybe we would have rented bikes. On the other hand, when we bike, we like to do so on quiet trails, away from people. From what we could see,

Mackinac Island did not offer that possibility, so we started to make our way back to the ferry docks.

"Should we get some fudge or something?" asked Senator.

"I don't know. Why? Do you want some?"

"Maybe, it seems like the thing to do here..."

"True, and we should probably do our part to support the local economy." We stopped in one of the many shops. More tempting than the actual product was the chance to see the giant squishy loaves being made. Neither of us care for chocolate, though, so we were the only people in line with a bag of toffee cashews instead of fudge. The nuts were definitely overpriced, though, so it still counts.

The line for the ferry was already growing. The weather had warmed up considerably, so we were happy to find the last two seats together on the top deck, where we would catch the breeze again. Remembering the earlier instructions, we were sneaky with our cashews. We had really enjoyed our spontaneous day. It had turned out wonderfully, despite being derailed.

Once again we drove across the nightmare bridge into the Upper Peninsula. An hour or so later, we were back at the Canadian border for the third time in twenty-four hours. Thankfully, there had been different border security agents each time. We did not have any hassles, but I can only imagine what now comes up on either the U.S. or Canadian computers when they read our license plate or scan our passports.

As it turned out, our impromptu adventurers were not quite over. Just two blocks past the border station, we turned a corner in a neighborhood and saw a woman standing in the street. In one arm she was holding a baby. In her other hand was a cell phone. It was clear she was calling for help, so we pulled over. Senator quickly scoped the scene and watched for other traffic while I got out to see if she was okay.

It was then that I noticed she was not calling on her own behalf. A little further down the block a man was lying on the ground with blood on his head. He also had a large protruding knot on his head that was the size of my fist. He was incoherent and repeatedly refused help from another man who was standing over him. The man trying to help was also holding the leash of the wounded man's dog, who was visibly anxious about his owner. Somehow the man had fallen and hurt himself, but he was in no shape to be left alone; he probably would have been run over by the next car that came by.

The woman with the phone said that emergency services were on the way. Senator watched for the ambulance and flagged them down from the cross street. I continued to monitor the situation so the woman could take care of her baby and shoo away her other son, who had ridden his bike over to witness the action. Meanwhile, the injured man stood up clumsily, demanded his dog back from the other man, and started to walk down the middle of the street, talking to himself as he left. It would not have been wise or legal to detain him, so we all kept an eye on him. Once the paramedics arrived, we had to guide them to trace him down the lane. As we left the scene, we could see the medics treating the man in the back yard of a house on the next street. Whether he lived there or not, we had no idea. After all, we were just tourists spending the night in the country before leaving again the next day.

We reached our hotel without further incident. The temperature had dropped back down to the mid-50s.[*] Except for the poor man in the street, it had been a good day. Still, it had been a long day, full of walking and fresh air. We were worn out-- too worn out to sit somewhere and eat.

Thinking back to our last night on our last trip, we paid a visit to the local Walmart. Once again the freezer aisle, the hotel room microwave, and a bit of imagination made up our dinner. Round one was a steamable bowl of vegetable curry. The second course was an unfamiliar dish called 'veggie tots'. It sounded like a wholesome, hearty snack. In reality, it was a bunch of greasy, greenish lumps of broccoli mush. I'm not sure we got any nutritional value from it, but it did give us a good laugh. Mostly we were too tired to care. We had just enough energy left to finish off the cashews, clean up, and fall asleep to a double episode of *Last Man Standing*, our go-to mindless comedy series that seems to be on in every hotel we stay in.

* * *

Friday morning we slept in much later. There were no flying alarm clocks or trains to catch. We took our time getting ready and had a quiet bite to eat in the hotel before starting our day. Then we loaded the car and nestled our coffee cups in their holders. Steam was pouring out of their spouts in response to the crisp, biting morning. I wished we could bottle the chill and take it back home to get us through the next month or so.

---
[*]Maybe these were the type of days my mom was thinking of when she claimed September was a fall month.

"Hey, look," I said, pointing to the empty parking space next to our car. The night before, we had parked next to an bright blue Corvette. Apparently the owner was dismayed to find our economy car next to his or her baby. It was now parked at the back corner of the hotel's parking lot, far away from being tainted by us. We thought it was funny.

Our fourth border crossing was a success. We were once more in the homeland. By my calculation, it would be almost a year until we would again be asked to explain our reason for entering Canada. Hopefully we would never have to play hopscotch again at the border.

Instead of continuing south on I-75, we cut west to U.S. Route 2, taking us deeper into the upper peninsula. There were the normal bait and beer stops common to rural areas, as well as several abandoned tourist cabins. They were probably booked solid after the war, as Americans fell in love with their automobiles and took to the highways for leisurely pursuits. Now the old motels and camps fell into disrepair and self-demolition. Somebody must own the property, though. We wondered why no one had bothered to rehab the buildings or construct something new.

The road was empty for the most part. We glided over the pavement, paying attention when the route switched directions at a country intersection. Amish territory was nearby. We slowed down and passed a horse and buggy. I think I would be afraid of cars not paying attention if I was in a carriage on a major highway. I don't know that I would trust my safety to a neon orange triangle.

We crossed into northeast Wisconsin, and I

consulted my travel notes for our preferred route. Jingles could not comprehend why we were ignoring her advice. What Jingles did not understand, however, was that her plan to take us down Lake Michigan, through the north suburbs, downtown, and south suburbs of Chicago on a Friday afternoon, was a disaster in the making. Had we attempted to follow her lead, we would likely still be sitting in traffic, delaying this book's release date considerably.

Strong, dark clouds gathered as we drove through southern Wisconsin. In Illinois it rained steadily. We were so glad we had such perfect weather Thursday and so glad we made a great spur-of-the-moment adventure, in spite of the cancellation. It reminded me of our very first trip together. In fact, it reminded me of us.

Chapter 7
Unconditional Surrender:
Late February 2019

Note: All facts, figures, and quotes in the following chapter are attributed to and verified within the United States National Park Service visitor centers, battlefield sites, and literature at Fort Donelson, Parker's Crossroads, Shiloh, and Corinth Interpretive Center.

    Senator kissed me and I hopped out of the car, feeling like one of the teenagers who were gradually swarming into the main building of the high school where I worked. He dropped me off, and at the precisely determined time, he would pick me up. Then we would evade the buses and crazy drivers, enter the closest interstate that went south, and be off on our adventure. Ever since we had gone to the Civil War battlefields in Virginia, we were hooked. By the time we were driving home last spring, I had the trip halfway outlined. Originally we were going to hit four major battlefields over spring break in April. Then it occurred to me that if I played my cards right, we could break up the battlefields into two smaller extended weekends and save spring break for some hiking. The first weekend, weather permitting, would take advantage of the Presidents' Day holiday. Not that we celebrate or really care about Valentine's Day, but it was a nice touch that we spent the evening of February 14th packing and anticipating our escape. "Is there anything on the list that doesn't make sense?" I asked Senator.

He shrugged and shook his head casually. "No." I hated making a 'to-do' list for him, but usually I was the one to take care of the last-minute house stuff, and I wanted to make sure we would not forget anything important. When he picked me up from work that day, my handwritten list was on the seat, with a neat check-mark next to each item. I smiled, knowing he had it under control.

We had about a five-and-a-half hour drive ahead of us. According to multiple sources, we could expect to encounter some combination of snow, sleet, and freezing rain during the last portion of it. We decided to take it slowly, with the understanding that we would stop if we had to. At 6:30pm, the first flakes flew. By 7:30pm, we had slowed to fifteen miles under the speed limit.

Senator was driving during that time. Thanks to his caution and skill, and the surprisingly well-maintained Kentucky highway, we arrived safely. I actually did not realize how bad it was until we got out of the car. The entire body and side mirrors were encased in ice. Every roof line and sign dripped icicles. Next to the motel's property was a basketball hoop, and every strand of its net sparkled in the streetlight because of the coating of ice.

"Hi there!" the man behind the desk piped up. He greeted us enthusiastically and sincerely expressed his delight that we had successfully arrived. As he delivered his speech relaying the necessary information, I glanced at the plaque above his head. It listed many aspects of life for which we could and should be grateful. It was our first indication that we had, indeed, removed ourselves from the overly bitter and cynical halo of Chicago, to a much more pleasant and peaceful culture. It was also a nice touch when the direction card on the desk in the room ended with "God bless".

For the rest of the night we relaxed in the room. Both Senator and I put far too much effort into trying to decipher the complex t.v. remote control. Then he discovered that the television was unplugged from the box in the back. *Well that could have something to do with it...*

* * *

Sometime during the night the pelting ice and sleet stopped, but the leftover results were stunning in the morning sun. The grass sparkled like it was made of silver shards, and ice and frozen fog coated the rest of the vegetation. It was a nice consolation for a lousy night of sleep. Senator was nursing a headache (probably from the intense concentration while driving), but we were both looking forward to our day at Fort Donelson. As an added bonus, we would be there on the anniversary of the surrender.

We drove south into Tennessee, admiring the frozen fairyland along the way. When we reached Dover, we bypassed the entrance to Fort Donelson National Military Park to drive a mile further to the county visitor center.

There, the national park's visitor center was temporarily housed during a remodeling project. For a moment, I questioned whether they were open; the only vehicle in the parking lot was a park ranger's truck. Inside, though, we were greeted by three people eager to see a tourist or two pop in.

The first man was the park ranger, who immediately greeted us and discerned our purpose. Happy to learn that we were there for 'his' visitor center, he told us about the display room and the events that were scheduled in honor of the anniversary. Another, older woman was present, and she seemed to take a liking to us right away. She represented the county's visitor center, and she cozied up to me in the way one would expect a southern grandmother who volunteered at the local historical society to do. I liked her, too.

The third person was a gentleman sitting off to the side, his hands resting on a cane. "Whereya' from?" he asked, not shyly. When we told him that we lived outside Chicago, his eyes lit up. He wanted to know if we knew certain buildings or businesses that were probably long-since gone. We conversed a bit, but gently explained that much had changed in the city since he had last been there decades ago. He did not care; he was happy with his memories and content to be in Tennessee. It was probably the best of both worlds.

In a room off to the side, we looked around and read panels of information that sketched out the siege and surrender of Fort Donelson. In February of 1862, a Mexican War veteran and brigadier general from the west by the name of Ulysses S. Grant was in the process of executing his plan to take Confederate river forts. His job was made somewhat easier by the lack of consistent command at the Confederate-held earthen Fort Donelson, which was positioned on the Cumberland River. First, the politically-connected General John Floyd bailed as soon as things started heating up. He turned command over to General Gideon Pillow, who, as it turned out, was nowhere near as valiant as the military Gideon of the Bible. Pillow figured that Floyd had had a pretty good idea, and arranged his own safety-bound escape. This left the fort in the loyal and capable hands of General Simon Buckner.

Buckner put up a good fight, even repelling Union Flag Officer Andrew Foote's naval operations. Ultimately, however, enough reinforcements arrived for Grant to successfully counterattack. The fort was lost. When Buckner asked Grant (who, incidentally, was an old classmate and friend) about terms of surrender, Grant's staunch reply came back: "No terms except an unconditional and immediate surrender can be accepted." In case he was not clear, he added his intent to immediately invade. Thus, Fort Donelson was securely placed under Union control.

After reading the narrative, we sat down to view the accompanying film. A moment or so into it, our audience of two realized that we had already watched it on the internet as part of our pre-trip research. It was short, and we had plenty of time, so we watched it again. As soon as it was over, the friendly older lady was ready and waiting to show us a few more artifacts housed in the visitor center. She seemed pleased that I knew what several of the items were, even though they belonged to her era, rather than mine. When we were through browsing, we confirmed the schedule, thanked all three people-- no one else had entered the building-- and departed for the battlefield.

It was drizzly and chilly as we started the driving tour. Our first stop was a large, cold obelisk monument. We did not stay too long, moving on instead toward the site of the fort. Along the way, we pulled over to watch a nesting eagle. No matter how many times I see eagles, I am always mesmerized by their raw, unflinching swoop. They just *look* American.

We got out and took our time walking around the multiple tiers of the fort's main battery, despite the dampness. Several cannon, each on a partially rotating pivot, were preserved. You could almost picture the mounted defense against the approaching Yankee gunboats and their 'iron valentines'. We continued our walk down along the river, sidestepping the deepest mud. I pulled my hood up the side of the head to cover my ears. Senator fingered his pocket in search of any sign of a viable tissue. If we wanted to dive into history, we were not going to do it dryly.

Other stops along the tour brought us to the familiar earthworks we had witnessed the spring before in Virginia. Dead, dried, and rewetted, rematted leaves covered each. How these long chains of mounded earth could have survived over a century and a half is beyond me. It was wonderful that they did, yet sad to think of soldiers hastily working like groundhogs to create some sort of shield against their own countrymen's bullets.

We also stopped at the National Cemetery near the edge of town. At one time, two upright cannon barrels formed the gate posts. They were no longer there, but the rows of humble stones still told of a combat connection. Most were arranged in sections by state. Senator found Illinois, but within the sections, many were still unknown.

We finished our short walk through the cemetery and drove back to the park's entrance. The rain had picked up just in time for the outdoor talk and demonstration of Confederate firearms. Bracing ourselves again, we stepped out of the car. Only one other couple was brave enough to join us, but that did not diminish the presentation by the four dedicated reenactors. Commands were explained, and steps for loading were demonstrated, culminating in the firing of four reproduction rifles. Two were flint models, which, surprisingly, cooperated in the rain. Senator asked the officer if, once commanded to fire, soldiers just kept shooting until they ran out of ammunition. This was basically accurate, but I suppose they sometimes acquired extra rounds beyond their standard-issue forty, if comrades fell.

Our final stop along the driving tour was the famous Dover Hotel, where the surrender took place. The white, balconied, two-storied structure hosted guests as far back as the early 1850s and was eventually rescued for its historical value. Though the mood was not as solemn as that of McLean's parlor at Appomattox Courthouse, it was an interesting foreshadowing of another momentous surrender to General Ulysses S. Grant. In that case, also, Grant allowed the prisoners to keep their personal firearms and horses. He also found immediate provisions for them and forbade any parading or mocking of the losing side. Perhaps it was a little hasty of General Buckner to deem Grant's position as "ungenerous" and "unchivalrous".

As it was the 157th anniversary of the surrender, period reenactors were on hand to interpret several non-combative roles. We first spoke with a quartermaster about the logistics of supplying a nineteenth century army that spanned thousands of miles. Due to the finesse it took, such officers were never involved in combat; their skills were needed behind pens and desks. After all, they had to requisition everything, up to and including the paper for requisitions. I did my best to help. "I hear there's some shoes in a warehouse up in a little town called Gettysburg..."[*]

We next spoke with a surgeon, who confirmed the statistics I had heard during years of studying the Civil War. The ratio of men dying from disease as opposed to being killed directly by combat wounds was about 2:1. Technology was too powerful for the tactics of the time, and a Minié ball was not to be trifled with by mere bones. I also noticed that his wooden medical chest contained square, metal bottles. These were an improvement on the breakable, round, glass ones used previously. Either way, they mainly just contained opiates or crazy, unhelpful concoctions.

We then left the warmth of the hotel for the chill of the front porch. Outside, lower-ranking officers gathered on the porch that overlooked the river. Talking and educating visitors was interspersed with the occasional tobacco spit break. I think it was partly for authenticity and partly because we were in Tennessee. The highlight of the experience was when one of the reenactors read a copy of a

---

[*] Civil War geeks will get this reference, but even they will probably think my joke was dumb.

letter written by his great-great grandfather, who was taken prisoner after the fort's surrender. What a treasure for his family to possess!

We thanked everyone who had braved the crummy weather to share their love of our country's history with us. It had been an even better experience than I had hoped for, filled with a few surprises. I was even more excited to see the other battlefields on our itinerary. Of course, I was also enthusiastic about a heated car as we made our way south.

"Maybe we'll see a place to grab a cup of coffee along the way," I suggested.

"I've already been thinking that for the last hour," said Senator. As we drove and dried out, we nibbled a few granola bars.

We did not find any coffee,* but halfway between Nashville and Memphis, we did stumble on something far better. "Did you just see that sign?" I asked. I had been watching the road, but a flash of a brown sign had grabbed my attention.

"Yeah," said Senator, sitting up from his reclining position. I think it said something about a battlefield. Maybe we had both hallucinated a brown Department of the Interior sign, since the whole trip was essentially planned around them.

"If it did mention a battlefield, it would have to be Civil War-related," I reasoned. There were not too many Revolutionary conflicts in the "far west" of Tennessee.

"There it is again. 'Parker's Crossroads', it says."

"I know nothing about it, but wanna' stop?"

"Of course!" said Senator. I'm not sure how I missed

---

* non-gas station variety, I mean

a Civil War battlefield that was literally on our way. In the thousands of pages of Civil War history we have consumed, I am sure we must have encountered it somewhere, but the name was not ringing a bell.* Either way, I was happy to add it to the itinerary.

Parker's Crossroads, as it turns out, was a battle that took place on December 31, 1862. On the eve of President Lincoln's Emancipation Proclamation taking effect, General John Pemberton was trying to prevent General Ulysses S. Grant and General William T. Sherman from assaulting Vicksburg, the essential hold on the Mississippi River. As such, Pemberton ordered General Earl Van Dorn to lead a raid against Grant's supply lines. Meanwhile, General Nathan Bedford Forrest was sent to sever Grant's rail lines.

During Forrest's brief stopover near Parker's Crossroads, Union General Jeremiah Sullivan moved to capture his cavalry. As he did so, Colonel Cyrus Dunham reached Forrest first, but was repelled with major casualties from Forrest's artillery. Seizing the moment, Forrest then aggressively went on the offensive. Just as it seemed like the battle was over, however, Union reinforcements arrived under the direction of Colonel John Fuller. Upon arrival, they quickly sandwiched in Forrest's men. In true Bedford Forrest manner, he commanded his forces to, "Charge them both ways!" Though the battle was not a victory for the Confederates, Forrest's fast thinking and maneuvering allowed him to successfully escape, yet again.

We perused the visitor center, where Senator upgraded to a better Nathan Bedford Forrest biography. *Good thing we stopped.* There we also saw a horse saddle

---

* I doubt it escaped Mr. Foote's attention.

designed by Union General George McClellan. "What? Did he just finish it?" chided Senator snidely, referring to McClellan's exasperating refusal to move in any timely fashion. I believe Lincoln would have appreciated Senator's joke.

Like most of the battlefields, there was a driving tour, so we hopped in the car to trace more Union and Confederate lines. We continued up to the relatively small battlefield, now silent with only a few deer grazing passively at the edge of the woods. Then we drove back down to the crossroads where Reverend Parker lived. As the story goes, Parker was a staunch unionist until the war came to his farm. He insisted that the cannon be removed from his yard. Unsympathetic to his personal wishes, the Union commander placed the pointed question to the loyal American: "What is more important-- the Union cause or your house?"

Without hesitation, Parker snapped back, "My house!" and lived the rest of his days as a devoted, Yankee-detesting son of the Confederacy.

Our tour then brought us to the local cemetery. There old and new graves overlooked the edge of town and the well where soldiers and horses took water. From there we continued to Red Mound, where some of Dunham's troops were rattled enough by Forrest's attack that they took it into their own hands to try to surrender. Officers soon put a stop to that, and I can only imagine how those conversations with the cowardly few went.

We concluded our driving tour and headed south along Highway 22. Not long after leaving, we saw a coyote running through a field. Had it not been cloudy all day, we might have noticed the sun setting over him. By the time we reached the motel, I had already made a note to find a documentary on Parker's Crossroads. It had been an obscure and fascinating bonus to our day.

As a result of our fun but chilly day, we decided on a hot, probably cheesy dinner somewhere. Nearby was a Mexican restaurant, so we tried that. Senator and I gave our orders, reaching for the chips and salsa as the server left. In between crunches we recapped our day. Before long, my veggie fajitas arrived. Senator's cheese enchilada followed shortly afterward, filled with meat. *Oops*. There is always a mild language barrier with foreign cuisine, but it took several attempts to straighten it out, and none of the food had much flavor anyway. Oh well; at least our friendly server had politely referred to Senator as his "amigo".

Back at our motel we relaxed and flipped through the channels. "Aw, look at this!" I blurted out. Senator had stumbled upon the last half of the star-studded comedy *It's a Mad, Mad, Mad, Mad World*, which we had been trying to see for years. Had I known that was on t.v., we could have skipped the tasteless Mexican food and brought something back to our room. After all, it's not every night you can eat in your bedroom, in front of the television. Once the mystery was solved, the adventure concluded, and Ethel Merman silenced, we fell asleep.[*]

*   *   *

Sunday morning it was pouring. We had to run under the eaves and hop across the impromptu creek that

---

[*] (As our friend Bill pointed out, we technically saw *It's a Mad, Mad World*.)

was spouting out from the gutter in order to reach the motel's breakfast bar. Inside, we made up egg and English muffin sandwiches. It was our day to go to Shiloh, and we were eager to begin.

Less than two months after Grant had taken Fort Donelson, he set his sights on Corinth, Mississippi, home of a major rail intersection in the South. He was not going alone, though; General Don Carlos Buell was on his way from Nashville. Before their forces could join, however, General Albert S. Johnston seized the moment. 44,000 Confederates launched an attack against Grant's 40,000. The fighting was horrific, shocking soldiers and civilians on both sides with its unprecedented numbers of casualties. After "the devil's own day"[*] had concluded, Buell's forces arrived to assist Grant. The next day, bolstered with fresh troops, the Union reversed the battle, sending the Confederates retreating south to Corinth.

Senator and I drove south along the river under a gray sky that showed no signs of changing, except to other shades of gray. I was just fine with that; it added authenticity to a place where thick spring mud played a role in troop movements. It was still raining as we turned down the quiet road into the national battlefield. Before we even reached a parking area or visitor center, we were greeted by large solemn monuments. The somber tone was set.

Inside the visitor center, the expected exhibits told the basic story of the battle at Pittsburg Landing, also known as Shiloh. Displays reiterated the psychological impact of such a large-scale battle, as well as its strategic

---

[*] General William T. Sherman's term

importance. Naturally, the key players were featured. Pictured next to General Grant we found a profile on General William H. L. Wallace, especially interesting to us since he hailed from a town just ten miles from where we live in Illinois.

We had a little time to kill until the film started, so we ducked across the parking lot to the bookstore. It was time to relieve our wallets for the cause. Inside, a Tennesseean with a very thick accent asked us where we were from.[*] We answered with our standard joke, "About an hour and a half from Grant's house." He knew his Yankee geography well, because he did not hesitate to inquire whether we were Cubs fans or Sox fans. It seemed to genuinely baffle him when we told him we were neither. In fact, we do not follow any sports. He was not deterred though. He continued to chat with us as we perused biographies and souvenirs.

When we brought our purchase to the cash register, he took a more serious tone, hinting at rumors he had heard that things were not so great in the Land of Lincoln. "No, it's a mess," I assured him. "It is not what it used to be. Crime in the city is out of control, and we are in the worst financial shape of all fifty states!"[†] I was not alone in painting my dismal picture.

"Yeah," the man nodded. He added his own anecdotal evidence from his friends. According to him,

---

[*] For some reason, I found the western Tennessee accent one of the thickest we have ever encountered. That includes the deeper South, Newfoundland, and even Boston.

[†] I suppose part of me feels a sort of obligation to warn others away from our sinking ship. It's sort of a "it's too late for me, but you can save yourself" sentiment. You know-- like Jacob Marley.

they lived in southern Illinois, and they complained that the high taxes we all pay went to bail out Chicago's problems.

Here Senator jumped in, corroborating the man's friends' story and adding his own example, taken from my job. "I'll give you a for-instance. Her job-- he indicated me with a thumb jutted out to the side-- is grant-funded. That means there is a lot of competition for limited money. Every year there is a conference to bid for those funds. Each school district has to make an appeal to prove their case, hoping to get a piece of the pie. Chicago districts, on the other hand, do not even bother to show up; they already know they are getting theirs, due to a neatly corrupt political patronage system." The man was amazed. I think we scared him from ever coming north of the Mason-Dixon Line, let alone to Chicago.

There was just enough time for a pit stop before viewing the film in the visitor center. It was a very short walk from the bookstore, but the sky had ripped open in a deluge of rain. I tucked our purchases safely in my purse, and we made a run for it. Seconds later we were in the visitor center again, pushing our dripping hair back off of our faces. I'm not saying we will never go camping again, but days like this sure make it sound unappealing.

We found our seats in the dark theatre. It was not hard; there were only three other people in there.[*] Soon the screen lit up, the sound kicked in, and the film began. Within a minute, we recognized the narration. I guess we are getting too good at finding online documentaries, because we had seen this one, too. As Senator rightly pointed out, however, it was too good to leave. We stayed

---
[*] There are definite advantages to traveling in February.

the full forty minutes until it ended. Watching it again as we were about to see the grounds first-hand brought the details and reflections to life.

One of the first stops on the Shiloh driving tour took us to the joint site of Wallace's headquarters (marked by a pyramid of cannon balls) and the beautiful Confederate monument. On one side of the obelisk a draped female figure (perhaps an angel) gracefully took her pen to the stone. There she symbolically recorded the names of the fallen. Her striking pose will not soon be forgotten.

A little further down the drive we found the monument to our local hero, General Wallace. It was not until I came across his name in my Shiloh research that I remembered he had lived in our county. I vaguely recalled someone from the Civil War being connected to Shiloh. Now we stood in front of an undeniable reminder. Sadly and romantically, his last words were uttered to his wife as she held him. "We meet in heaven."

The rain had let up considerably, so we took a short walk along Duncan Field, sight of a great struggle on the first day of the battle. The only creatures we saw struggling were some fat wild turkeys. On the opposite side of the field, a long row of cannon stood as reminders of the field's significance. I have never seen so many in one place, yet it only represented a fraction of those present during the battle.

Our next stop was the Shiloh Methodist Meeting House. We peeked inside the simple log structure to see the single room, with two rows of wooden benches and a crude pulpit. Next to it stood the newer church, where the congregation still meets. A cemetery of graves spanning three centuries lay across the road. Ironically, Shiloh is a Hebrew word meaning 'place of peace'.

Further up the road we reached the corner of Fraley's Field, where it all started. Senator took a quick jog down the mud path to view the expanse of the field. One of my feet already felt wet, so I stayed on the pavement and peered through the opening in the woods. The first shots, but certainly not the last, were fired here.

We followed the driving tour deeper into the heart of the destruction. Near a mass of tangled brush we reached the infamous 'Hornet's Nest'. No stingers buzzed there, but the place was so nicknamed as a description of the constant whizzing sound of nonstop Minié balls flying through the woods. Many of the victims were laid to rest in the nearby Confederate burial trenches. Though five have been discovered in the park, they each contain countless unknown soldiers. Only a cement rectangular outline around a grassy patch remains.

There were several monuments to the men of many different states on both sides. All of the memorials were tasteful and honorable, but one especially caught my attention. The Tennessee monument depicted the almost-sacred role of the flag bearer and the heavy symbolism of the fabric rallying point. Though cast in stone, the emotion and fluidity of movement captured the moment that one bearer was going down, while another was rapidly stepping in to rescue the colors.

The stone was not actually moving, but a herd of deer was. There did not seem to be anything chasing or scaring them, but run they did. They sprinted across another field where the tent hospital had been centralized to offer somewhat more efficient and safer service to the wounded. Senator had a theory about the deer. Years ago we learned that deer typically stay within a few miles of their home. He suggested that these might be the deer descendants* of ones that were there during the battle. "What if they were panicking and fleeing in the chaos, and then they passed that down through the generations? Now maybe they all just run." I started to offer a counter-theory, but he cut me off. I had to admit his was better.

The War Between the States set many records and offers innumerable fascinating statistics. Among those is that the United States (including portions in rebellion) lost its highest-ranking individual to be killed in combat. General Albert Sydney Johnston, whom President Jefferson Davis had appointed over the entire Confederate forces, was shot in the back of the leg. What was believed to be a relatively minor wound, however, hit in such a way to cause him to bleed to death in under twenty minutes. Some sources claim that this ironically occurred while he had a tourniquet in his pocket, but the story is unverified.

We took a few moments at Johnston's memorial before moving on to the Peach Orchard, scene of more savage fighting. Darting near the edge of the woods, something bright caught our eye. We both looked over into the bare trees. With no leaves to obstruct the view, we saw the bright red head and distinct black and white feathers of a pileated woodpecker. We love these elusive birds, and there are a pair of them that haunt the woods near our home. It is always a treat if we catch a glimpse of one of them.

---

*   deerscendants?

Our driving tour circled back around next to the river, where Buell's army arrived in time to turn the battle to the Union's favor. Both victor and vanquished suffered enormous losses. It was appropriate that our last stop at Shiloh was the National Cemetery. It was misting heavily, or maybe raining lightly. Senator took a moment to photograph the site of Grant's headquarters, framed with the river in the distance. I wandered a few rows of humble headstones, all uniform. As we exited the heavy iron and gilded gates, Senator made a proclamation. "When my time on this Earth comes to an end, I want to be able to say more than 'the food was pretty good'." Shelby Foote was right; you have to go to Shiloh.

At some point in the planning process, I discovered that we would be fairly close to another Civil War battlefield at Corinth, Mississippi. When I looked into the events surrounding the battle at Corinth, I learned that it fit in chronologically with our tour. This was convenient, but no accident, as it was really a direct result of the aftermath of Shiloh. I consulted Senator, and it was an easy decision to add it to the list.

It had rained steadily from the time we left Shiloh. Once we crossed into Mississippi, it picked up and was pouring again. Though we were the only vehicle in the lot of the Corinth Interpretive Center, there was nowhere close to the door to park. Instead, a winding road led to a drop-off area, with a long pedestrian ramp leading back to the lot. "There's no point in both of us getting soaked," Senator said. He was already in the driver's seat, so he insisted on dropping me off.

As I waited for him to walk or swim back, I stepped

inside toward the information desk. Another friendly ranger met me. I was glad to learn we had not made the effort to come only to find they were closed. I asked him where we should start our visit. He suggested that we first view the film. (At least I knew we had not seen this one; there had not been time to research the battle or siege of Corinth before we came.) "It's really good," he promised, then added, "I'm in it!" I laughed. "Plenty of seating, too!..." he assured us.

Senator entered, dried his glasses, and joined me. As per the recommendation, we started in the theatre. Like all of these movies we have seen, it did an excellent job of summarizing the necessary events while putting human faces on them. After a costly victory at Shiloh, Union forces pressed south into Mississippi toward Corinth, due to its prized location at a major railroad junction. For the time being, they held it. Then Generals Sterling Price and Earl Van Dorn joined forces to march on the city and hopefully recapture it. Despite General Rosecrans' fortifications, the Confederates were pushing in rather effectively. It was hard fighting on both sides, though. Heat, exhaustion, and the lack of fresh water were especially detrimental.[*] Eventually, greatly assisted by their artillery units, the Union maintained their control, forcing Confederate troops to retreat.

We wandered three other rooms of museum exhibits. One recapped the Shiloh story via seven multimedia panels projected onto a screen that gradually morphed to reflect the progression of the battle. Another focused on the

---

[*] At least one eyewitness claims that his horse refused to drink the dirty, rancid water the men were supposed to use.

successful contraband camp. Since the South declared themselves no longer part of the United States, and since they considered their slaves mere property, the North reasoned that such "property" could be confiscated from a foreign entity during time of war. Thus, former slaves were set up in the model camp at Corinth, behind Union lines. It was set up as a cooperative society, under military protection. Many men and women worked on the farm, while others put their skills to use as well. A church and school were quickly established. Whereas it was a grave crime to teach a slave to read, children now openly learned their A-B-Cs during the day, and the adults were taught at night.[*]

For obvious reasons, we skipped the walking tour. We did step outside for just a few minutes to view the flowing fountain. Arranged horizontally, it used block sculpture to depict the eras of United States history, with particular reference to the major battles of the Civil War. I did not stay out long; I had left my jacket in the car when Senator had dropped me off.

When he rejoined me inside, he could not pass by the last two portions of the visitor center. The research library attracted him like a magnet, and he verified that they did, in fact, possess the full 128-volume set of the Official Records of the Union and Confederate Armies that he had recently purchased on two digital discs. He also could not resist the gift shop. Because we did not have resources on Corinth, he bought a cd of excerpts from diaries and journals belonging to soldiers and civilians. We

---

[*] One teacher wrote about her experience as an educator at the camp, even though she was only nine years old at the time.

looked forward to listening to it on the way home.

It was still raining hard, but it was a cozy sort of afternoon. I looked forward to downing a cup of hot coffee once we got back to our motel. We had no other plans, though, other than continuing to process all we had seen the past two days. That is what drew us in to an unexpected stop.

On the corner of a quiet (but major for the area) intersection, we came across a combination museum and junk shop. "Want to stop?" asked Senator cheerfully. It was the type of place we would normally pass by, but we had free time, and for some reason we both thought it would be fun.

"Sure! Why not?"

Inside, as was the case everywhere we went, we were greeted by a smiling face who asked us where we were from. When we told him, he nodded his head knowingly. "Yep, three of my neighbors are from Illinois," he said. "They love it here... wanted to move out of Illinois." Of course we were not surprised; it was the same story everywhere. After a brief discussion on that topic, we were enthusiastically invited to wander around the shop and peruse his dusty collection.

I had expected the ratio of Confederate flag shot glasses to actual artifacts to be somewhere around 8:1. It was quickly obvious how wrong I was. Larry was nothing short of a local expert on all things Shiloh. He told us how he carefully compiled his collection of every type of ammunition fired during the battle. A few were lodged in tree stumps, and two had even collided mid-air. "That's a one-in-a-million chance!" he proudly observed. Then his humble nature walked it back slightly. "Well, I mean, I don't really know. Maybe not one-in-a-*million*."

It was a large collection, including memorabilia from other wars as well. I noticed his own uniform from Vietnam. It was apparent that he was a solid link in his family's proud, patriotic tradition. They had been on the land near the battlefield since the 1840s. Many were buried at the cemetery we had seen at the Shiloh church. Larry himself gave private tours of the battlefield, along with many of his tales, no doubt. "And guess who got to fire the cannon at the dedication of the Tennessee monument," he hinted, unable to conceal his beaming smile.

"I got a hundred stories," he assured us. I believed him. He kept us entertained with half a dozen of them in the twenty or thirty minutes we spent with him. My favorite was the way he stumbled upon one of the few camp tent tripod devices that are known to exist.

For some reason, Larry genuinely seemed to like us. He showed us his collection of hundreds of books on the Civil War. Every time it felt like the conversation was wrapping up, he would revive it with his standard transition: "Ah'll tell ya' one more..." After talking about the tenderness of the mother depicted in the Illinois monument, he gave us two vintage postcards of it.

The conversation shifted to people's perceptions about the North and the South. "Some people come in here and say 'you're on the wrong side' when they see the souvenirs I sell," he explained, "but I don't get into politics; I just sell stuff." I nodded, thinking he meant people were upset that he carried items with Confederate flags on them. On the contrary, he meant people were questioning his possession of Yankee-related items. It was so great to see another side than the one-dimensional arrogance and misinformed anti-Southern prejudices of Chicago and the metropolitan areas.

We made a modest deposit in his museum donation jar. I wish we had given more. A moment later Larry was handing Senator a plastic bag with four rounds, each of a different caliber that had been fired during the Battle of Shiloh. What an incredible honor! We thanked him profusely, but he waved it off as though it were meaningless. Just in case the mood was about to get too heavy, he sent us off with his rendition of a Johnny Cash medley, played on his electric guitar-- which just happened to be set up next to the Civil War coffee mugs.

It was still raining, and I could still feel that one of my socks was damp. It had been quite a day, and our adventures left us hungry-- for knowledge, insight, and pizza. We pulled into a small parking lot to satiate all three. After placing our order inside, we went back to our car and popped in the cd of journal readings from Corinth. The stories ranged from the predictably sad and miserable to the amazing, and even funny.[*] Our brief immersion in the past and present culture of Tennessee was almost making us think we could add it to the list of potential retirement homes, if it were not for the heat, humidity, bugs, and scary snakes. I guess we would just have to confine our visits to the colder months.

*   *   *

Monday morning was cold and bright. We got ready

---

[*] I had no idea General Pope's cussing aspired to such legendary and thorough depths.

and then went to the motel's breakfast room. No one else was there, so we had the food, coffee, and weather reports on television to ourselves. The next night Senator would be driving to Chicago for a gig, and of course, the forecast was dicey. He had been hired for five out of six Tuesdays, and I think there was significant snow or ice storms for all of them. Two he had canceled; the rest he endured.

Our ride home was easy by comparison. The only minor setback was when we had to carefully squeeze under an overpass, where a large piece of farming equipment was tipped over on its side. The police guided us all through it safely though, and our car managed to avoid the debris that still spotted the road. That was in Kentucky, and before long we crossed the Ohio River back to the home state.

As we drove we listened to more first-hand stories from Corinth. When that was done, we switched over to 1940s radio shows about the Civil War. It is strange to me to think that those shows were as close in time to the Civil War as they are to us. Someday soon they will be closer. We will continue to grow further away. Time is downright odd.

Near the Rend Lake area of southern Illinois, we witnessed another oddity. Thousands and thousands of sea gulls were hovering at the same altitude over inlets of the lake. They did not seem to be flying anywhere or hunting for food-- just hovering. I guess I had spent too much time studying battles; they reminded me of troops waiting for the next spark to set the field ablaze with action. Hopefully theirs never came.

Chapter 8
Be It Ever So Humble: Early March 2019

Note: All facts, figures, and quotes in the following chapter are attributed to and verified within the United States National Park Service visitor centers, battlefield sites, and literature at Stone's River, Chickamauga, and Chattanooga.

Just three weeks after Senator had picked me up for the first round of our winter Civil War battlefield tour, he did so again. Again I bounded down two flights of stairs and out the closest exit of my job. Again he presented me with the fully crossed-out checklist. He was getting pretty good at this. I could see these long weekends getting addictive... at least until I received the credit card bills.

An hour or so into the drive, I took over. Senator had worked late the night before, but he had not been able to nap between dropping me off and picking me up. Hopefully my driving for an extended period would also alleviate some of the strain on his eyes. We were still experimenting and learning about vertical heterophoria, making mental notes every time we found something that helped.

We stopped to pick up some sandwiches to eat on the road. Since I am not nearly adept enough to eat while driving, Senator took this last leg of the drive. He has incredible talent in this area; I have seen the guy alternately eat, drink coffee, steer, shift, adjust the stereo, and hold my hand-- all without even drifting.[*] Competently, he rolled us on toward the same motel we had stayed at last time on our 'escape night'. Meanwhile I tried to doze, but I could not completely sleep. I still heard all of the words to every song, despite somehow missing us crossing the Kentucky state line.

The same friendly man attended the front desk and happily ran through all of the pertinent information, up to and including the items on the breakfast buffet. "That was impressive!" I commented. "How many times a month do you recite that?" He laughed and nodded his head, admitting it was countless.

Once inside our comfortable room, Senator fired up the coffee maker. This, in turn, broke my will to resist the cinnamon apple fritters he had picked up as a surprise. As the coffee brewed, we checked some messages. "Hey, I just realized our phone works," I pointed out. Then I remembered that last time we had come down in an ice storm. Now we had smooth sailing for visits to three more battlefields.

*   *   *

Success! We actually both slept very well, which almost never happens the first night of a vacation. In fact, we were up earlier than planned. This was probably just as

---

[*] Don't try this at home, kids.

well; weather reports were warning of heavy storms in western Kentucky. It was raining steadily, but it looked like we would outrun the worst of it. Still, it was March in the South, so we would keep one set of eyes on the sky while the other was on the road.

We passed through the heavier traffic of Nashville, but it was not bad. Then again, compared to Chicago, most drives are a cake-walk. A little while later we did get rerouted off of I-24. I'm assuming it was related to flooding-- the rivers were all running high due to a very wet month-- but I'm not sure. I do know that it was handled and monitored expertly. Not only were state troopers at the initial point of rerouting, but they were posted every few miles along the detour. I guess that is how states that aren't completely broke work. In our state, you would only see that many cops if somebody (or several somebodies) were killed.

Murfreesboro was in sight, and soon we were parking in front of the visitor center at Stones River National Battlefield. Just a few weeks after the mowing down of Union troops at Fredericksburg, and on the same day that another small portion of the Union army encountered Nathan Bedford Forrest at Parker's Crossroads, General William Rosecrans pressed his forces south out of Nashville toward General Braxton Bragg's position near Murfreesboro. Savage fighting left each side with only two-thirds of the men they had started with. Nevertheless, officially and strategically, it was a Northern victory. Fortress Rosecrans, a massive centralized location of supplies and support, was quickly established, and "Old Rosie" firmly held Murfreesboro.

We entered the visitor center, and Senator peeled off to the restroom. I made a bee-line for the official park map-- absolutely essential for taking in the key sights related to the battle. An employee greeted us and started to tell us about the exhibits, recommending that we start with the film. Senator had rejoined me by this time. "Actually, we thought we'd start outside, in case the weather gets bad later," he explained, confirming our plan to devote the proper amount of time to all aspects of Stones River.

The woman beamed. "Ya'll are so smart!" I didn't think the decision reflected an excess amount of brilliance, but I liked her attitude. She went on to tell us that we could access a recorded narration of the driving tour stops with our cell phones.

We thanked her, but shook our heads. As Senator explained, "We're smart, but our phones aren't." She giggled at this, too. Actually, even if we had this option, we agreed that it was more meaningful to read the interpretive signs ourselves, hearing the voices and the sounds of battle the way we imagine them.

Due to its proximity to cities, including Nashville, Stones River was busier than most of the historical places we visit. Several local residents used the grounds for jogging or biking, which is good, but the element of immersion was a little diluted. On one side of the park local industry is visible, but it was easy enough to turn our backs to it as we studied yet another key Civil War battle.

Winter was holding on at home, but spring had come to middle Tennessee. It was already over 60°F and noticeably humid as we walked along the tallgrass field where Rosecrans' men spent the night before the battle.

Their new year's eve, by contrast, was frigid and overshadowed by the impending fight. I doubt anyone got much sleep.

"Hey look!" I pointed downward at a clump of green along the path to the next stop. The same wild chives that we had seen at so many other Civil War battlefields were abundantly present here as well. The ground was wet and muddy, so every time we stepped on the plants a pleasant oniony smell was released. Something about it was fresh and comforting to me. It was inappropriately ironic, as we were on our way to the Slaughter Pen.

At one end of Stones River there is a section of boulders tumbled along the forest floor. Each stands a few feet tall, reaching the midsection of a standing man. This was both a blessing and a curse. On one hand, the rocks provided effective cover from Confederate fire. When it came time to evacuate the area, however, the impediments created a maze too complicated for a fast retreat. The sad result was a bloodbath, where rivers of red flowed down the slight inclines between the rocks. The Chicago boys, familiar with the meatpacking industry, gave the region its grim name. As we stood quietly for a moment, a few small dead branches dropped from the top of a tall tree. The wind was increasing.

Next we made our way to the cotton field, following the criss-cross wooden railing where the Union artillery met the Confederate attack. Both sides fought hard, and Rosecrans' men were repelled a few miles, but they managed to hold the crucial Nashville Pike. Nearby was the Round Forest, later renamed "Hell's Half-Acre" by the beleaguered Confederates. Each physical segment of the three-days' fighting extended the story.

As with so many aspects of the War Between the States, there were tender components as well. We walked around the short headstones at the Hazen Brigade monument. Some had small stones carefully lined along their tops. Less than one year after the battle at Stones River, forward-thinking citizens recognized the valor here and erected the memorial. No one waited for the government to designate the site to tell them it was special. It now stands as one of the nation's oldest Civil War monuments. Perhaps even more poignant was the headstone just outside the cemetery. It marked the grave of a man who started his life as a slave and ended it as a property-owning American citizen.

Especially touching was the story of a regimental band. On one night of the battle, as soldiers were doing their best to unwind and settle their brains in between the chaos, one side struck up the popular song Home Sweet Home. The men joined in, singing words that took on unprecedented meaning given what they had witnessed. Then it spread to the other side. Soon thousands of Union and Confederate soldiers were unified in their melodic longing for the peaceful homes they had left behind. Be it ever so humble...

As long as we were 'in the neighborhood', we took a short detour to see the site of General Braxton Bragg's[*] headquarters. We ended up in the parking lot of a playground, but a short paved sidewalk led us around to

---

[*] Bragg has the distinction of being the most hated man in the Confederacy and possibly the war. With Jefferson Davis as his loyal friend in a high place, though, he was firmly seated in command.

the marker. Senator, in sympathy with those under Bragg's command, refused to take a picture. I concurred.

Far more fascinating than Bragg's headquarters was the bulging Tennessee River just behind it. A bicycle path ran parallel to the water, and a small sidewalk appeared to lead to the shoreline. With the water level ominously swelled, however, the sidewalk led directly *into* the river. Even the border of trees was growing out of a liquid foundation. I was shocked that there were no barriers or warnings, especially so close to a playground. It was another example of how other regions expect people to take responsibility for themselves.

Further down the river at McFadden's Farm, more trees were growing out of the river. Normally it would have been traversable, which made it another significant stop on the battlefield tour. It was the scene of the final assault of Stones River, yielding almost 2,000 casualties in an hour. Senator and I viewed it from the high ground and started to walk the accompanying artillery trail, but a loud roll of thunder put a stop to that; lightning was sure to follow. Moments later we were in the car, opting instead for a break and a snack as the rain poured down the windshield.

The rain continued as we drove into the national cemetery. On separate plaques we saw lines from a stanza of a military tribute poem. We have seen the same poem represented in other such cemeteries as well.[*] Our walk in the cemetery was short and damp, just around the central monument. Then Senator took a few more photos while I headed for the dry car. On my way back, I noticed that

---

* See Appendix B

several of the headstones had coins placed on top of them. It reminded me of the rocks at the Hazen Brigade monument.

On our way back to the visitor center we made one more stop at a small remnant plot of ground that was once part of Fortress Rosecrans. Along one of the enclosed sides, we could see the mounded earthworks where thousands of men went to work with picks and shovels. On all three of the enclosed sides, we could see at least half a dozen "NO TRESPASSING" and police protection signs. The place was situated along a quiet country road, and I could see nothing of value that could be stolen, but perhaps vandalism had been an issue. We never did figure out why so many warnings were deemed necessary.

Before we dove to the visitor center's displays, I asked a park interpreter about the meaning behind rocks and coins placed on headstones. "Well," she began in a slow, distinct, southern measure, "the different denominations signify different things." I was already learning. "A penny just means that someone has visited or paid their respects. A nickel means the visitor has a connection to the deceased's branch, or perhaps regiment." She was not sure if dimes represented having served in the same regiment or actually having fought in the same battle as the person buried there, but she was certain about quarters. "Quarters mean you were there when that soldier fell... which obviously isn't the case for anyone visiting a Civil War grave." I nodded, recognizing that some unaware visitors had treated it like a wishing well of sorts, or maybe they thought more cents equaled more respect. It is worth noting that the park interpreter did not condone any denominations used in the practice. "The pennies can stain the headstones, and when it gets to be time for mowing, coins can wreak havoc in the mowers." *Good point.*

"And what about the rocks left on graves?" I asked. She shrugged and admitted she had no idea. I guess it was just another random trend or tradition. "Maybe well-meaning people without pocket change thought they were doing something nice?" I suggested. She smiled and shrugged again.

We made our way through the exhibits, refreshing our memories as to details and the order of events. One interactive display caught my eye, or ear, more accurately. A panel of buttons corresponded to ten popular mid-nineteenth century songs. I recognized most of the titles, but I did not know the melodies, so I treated myself to playing each one. To my delight, I learned that a tune I had always enjoyed, often used in documentaries, was that of "The Bonny Blue Flag". It was a name often referenced that made me curious to hear it. Now I could connect the two in my mind.

Another display highlighted women who served in the ranks. Didn't know this was permitted? That's because it wasn't. These hearty ladies somehow disguised themselves convincingly enough to pass the recruiters' requirements. Don't ask me how. I glanced downward. *No chance.* Maybe everyone actually knew what was going on. If the gal could march and shoot, who was going to complain?

Still contemplating the logistics of the unexpected female enrollments, I caught up with Senator, who was perusing the gift shop. There was nothing in his hands.

"No new books?" I asked.

"I'm thinking about everything I have at home. It could be endless." *True, but when has that ever stopped you?* "I'm trying to focus on overall narratives, and then the actual memoirs of people who were involved." It sounded like a sensible plan. I think along the same lines, knowing full well that I probably won't read every page of every book I own, and I will likely forget most of it if I do. I sure hope there are libraries in Heaven.

"I did find this, though," said Senator as we walked to the car.

"What's that? Looks edible."

"It is. It's a piece of chocolate made from an original period recipe." I laughed, amused that the one thing he had purchased at a battlefield was a piece of candy. We don't even really like chocolate. "Want a taste?" he offered.

"No thanks."

"Oh, man!" I looked over. "This is delicious!" he raved. "It keeps changing... and there's cinnamon. You gotta try this." He convinced me to shave off a few flakes with my teeth. He was right; it started as a deep, true, bittersweet cocoa flavor, then morphed into dark coffee before finishing distinctly as cinnamon. I had never tasted such a complex confection. I'm not sure who was making this in the 1860s, but it sure beat hardtack and salt pork.

We had almost a two-hour drive to Chattanooga. I slid behind the wheel, turning on the wipers as soon as we were moving. Half an hour later we slowed to almost a stop, due to a flipped semi trailer in a ditch. The accident was not on our side of the highway, but plenty of onlookers were. It gave me the chance to read bumper stickers, decals, and other words on vehicles. My personal favorite was the donkey trailer lavishly painted with the phrase "Haulin' Ass!".*

The hills were looming on the southeastern horizon. The river bends became more dramatic, and Senator woke from a light snooze just in time to see the landscape change. Billboards began to emerge, imploring us to "See ROCK CITY!" I reached across the stereo, suddenly remembering to change the car's clock to eastern time. "I just did that," he informed me. I looked at the time. *Good*. That was the easiest loss of an hour I had ever experienced. Maybe we should try that every spring.

Before completely crossing into Georgia, I-24 flirts with the state, weaving in and out a few times before returning to Chattanooga. For reasons I will not delve into here, we did not want to go to Georgia just yet. We would be there the next morning, but for the time being, it was best if we stayed in Tennessee. As such, Senator had the idea to see if Jingles could handle a change in mapping parameters. Her usefulness was increased upon the discovery that she possessed an 'avoidance' feature. Off the highway she guided us, up into the hills on a scenic drive along the twisting river. Impromptu waterfalls sprouted from above the rocks. It was very pretty; we just had to be careful of occasional washouts that left narrow pass-throughs and a few rough drop-offs.

Just as we reached our hotel, lightning began. The young woman at the desk said they had recently experienced a total of ten inches of rain in just a few days.

---

* These are the gems routinely missed by people who choose to fly.

Based on the water level we saw near Bragg's headquarters at Stones River, I could believe it. Come to think of it, had that been the case during the battle, Bragg probably would have ordered that the river be shot.

Senator and I checked in and relaxed, already looking forward to the next day of roaming more battlefields. I was thinking it would be cozy to order some carry-out food and have it delivered to our hotel, but Senator found a place online that sounded decent, so we took a ride instead. The "vegetarian-friendly" burrito joint was trendier than expected. Upon entering, it became clear that it was the hot spot for Mexican-food-inclined hipsters. Apparently having a nose ring was a requirement of employment. As we waited in line, I noticed another phenomenon: a disproportionately high number of the people in the restaurant were very tall. I don't mean tall compared to me; I mean tall compared to the general population. This made it even noisier and more suffocating for a short girl.

Thankfully, the line moved along quickly, and we found a separate enclosed patio room in which to eat in relative peace. The seating extension smelled like a locker room, but at least it was tolerable. I will also say that the ingredients were very fresh, if not altogether flavorful. Basically, it was a sandwich in a tortilla. I am still trying to figure out how we struck out twice with Mexican food within a month. Just use a little cumin and melt some cheese over it all-- easy!

Back in our room I devoured the other half of my apple fritter, which had now traveled many hundreds of miles, courtesy of my Essential Other. Once the coffee was made we flopped on the bed and surfed the channels, eventually settling on the last half of an Indiana Jones marathon. In case you have not seen it, just know that Nazis are always evil, and Jesus never drank from a fancy cup. It was entertaining, but most of the plot and special effects seemed downright silly after spending the day studying a real conflict.

We tried to be responsible adults by checking the weather forecast before going to sleep. This yielded absolutely nothing decipherable. Saturday had been worse than predicted. Sunday sounded like it was up for grabs. I concluded that the only consistently correct prediction they could make would be to say that "darkness is expected later this evening". We gave up. I was just happy I remembered to set the clock ahead to daylight savings time, yielding our second lost hour of the day.

* * *

Sunday morning, contrary to all meteorological models, was sunny. Senator and I got ready and headed down to the hotel's breakfast bar. At first there were no available seats, but then two opened up next to a table of four police officers. "This should be safe next to you guys, right?" asked Senator, as he set his coffee down. One of them nodded and grinned. The rest were focused on their business.

"That was silly," I teased Senator, as we walked over to get some eggs and toast.

"What, it was funny!" I just shook my head and grinned.

After breakfast we walked out to our car and performed the stealthy maneuvering required to shift our legally-carried-in-some-states firearms into the locked boxes required by states that do not play nicely with Illinois permits. Frankly, it's a pain, but that is a conversation for a different book. As we completed the transfer and locked the car, our coffee-guarding members of law enforcement drove by. We nodded them a good and safe day. We were now ready to cross into Georgia.

The closest route to Chickamauga did not involve the interstate. This allowed us to drive through a few towns and see the local life. For the most part it was run-down and not a place I would care to visit. As Senator correctly noted, though, it was still nicer than the 'decent' areas we see in Chicago. I agreed; I had been thinking the same thing.

When we crossed the state border and saw a tall Iowa monument at an intersection, we knew we were close. Soon the sprawling fields of Chickamauga came into view. Though we still agree that rainy or foggy days are best for battlefield touring, I had to admit that it was very pretty in the morning sun. Senator parked and we grabbed a quick sip of water before walking into the visitor center.

Chickamauga wins the award for the grandest visitor center entrance, at least among the Civil War sites we have visited. The glass-ceiling entrance is flanked with red, white, and blue cloth bunting that leads down along the walls. One side is devoted to the Union, and the other side honors the Confederacy. Top military commanders of each are represented in strikingly realistic portraits set in oval Victorian-style frames. It was a magnanimous welcome.

The interpretive guide at the desk greeted us and

presented me with a map, as though he had read my mind. As I scanned the unfolded paper for the driving tour, he informed me that Chickamauga was both part of the first national military park and the biggest preserved Civil War battlefield. At over 5,000 acres, we would have some territory to cover. We did not have time to do it all on foot, but we would still get out to experience the land where we could. Before starting, we found two seats in the empty theatre that held about a hundred. Our visit began on the screen, with the reenacted story of the battle of Chickamauga.

In early autumn of 1863, just a few months after the battle of Gettysburg and the siege of Vicksburg, General Rosecrans drove the Confederates out of Chattanooga, believing General Bragg would head back to Atlanta. No one was running away to Atlanta, though. In fact, with reinforcements, Bragg could now make a formidable stand at Chickamauga. Without moving the battle line very far one way or the other, thousands of men from both sides lost their lives, leading some historians to dub the battle unnecessary. In the end, however, it was a decisive victory for Bragg, and one that routed the Union back to the relative safety of Chattanooga, despite General George H. Thomas' valiant stand.[*] In addition to the military loss, President Lincoln mourned the death of his brother-in-law, General Benjamin Helm, who died fighting for the Confederacy.

The first thing we noticed while on the grounds of Chickamauga were the countless monuments. All battlefields have them to an extent, but here they were lined

---

* afterward nicknamed "The Rock of Chickamauga"

up at every stop. Many extended along crude paths back into the woods. Who knew how far? Between artillery, regimental, and infantry markers, you could spend days just reading them. At one stop I spent time examining a stone carved with a soldier lying on his stomach, ready and aiming. As I was studying it, three does ran out from the forest. I thought of Senator's theory about the deerscendants at Shiloh. As I did, the unmistakable scent of damp chives filled my nose. I looked down at the ground. Yep-- they were there.

From the edge of the field we drove back into the woods. It was the spot where Rosecrans ordered his calamitous error. Believing he was rectifying a gap in the line, he actually ordered troops into a position that opened a critical gap. It did not take long before Confederates poured through, slicing the Union line and easily crumbling the smaller segment.

The sun was climbing and the air was warm as we continued to a cabin further down the way. Like most viable shelters of any size, it became a makeshift hospital as the war descended on the family's property. It mattered not that it consisted of only one room and a loft above. The family's men supported the cause offensively as well. One son acted as a highly valued guide, since he "knew every pig trail" through the woods. I pictured him hopping the split rail fence with a rebel shout as he lightly sprinted through the forest, contributing to Bragg's home turf advantage.

Senator and I took some time to walk in Viniard Field, scene of some of the fiercest fighting at Chickamauga. The land straddled the grand prize of LaFayette Road.

During the battle, movements ebbed and flowed, but neither side gained clear control of it, despite massive casualties. It was yet another reminder that, whether in individual combat or the war as a whole, neither side was about to give in easily.

We got back into the car and followed the marked route around a curve to a park-like setting. The centerpiece was a hill with at least a four-story tower. "That must be the Wilder Brigade monument," I reasoned, based on the map. It was huge for a brigade monument; maybe someone wealthy had sponsored it. What really attracted me to the stone pillar was finding out it could be climbed from the inside. Then I remembered Senator's negative experience in the lighthouse in Michigan. I was just about to suggest he forgo it, when he read the sign on the door. We were there less than a week before it opened for the season. It was just as well. "Yeah," added Senator, "I think my roller coaster days are over, too." I was fine with that; nothing could top the first time we went to an amusement park together. I am satisfied with the memory of that day and telling him, as we dangled in harnesses from a stopped ride, "Senator, I really like hanging around with you!"

The winding road took us to the terminus of the tour at Snodgrass Hill. While it is the high point of the terrain, it was the low point for the Union. Once they saw that defeat was imminent, they slipped away in the night. Chattanooga was still a refuge, at least for the time being. History has not been particularly kind to "Old Rosie" for his blunder at Chickamauga. Some attributed it to battle fatigue, others to incompetence. Whatever the case, General Grant would soon step in to change the direction of this facet of the war in the western theatre.

Having seen the important places, we headed back to the visitor center to view the exhibits, which were mainly timelines related to the war. One special exception was the only known surviving artillery wagon of the Chicago Board of Trade unit. As we browsed, we overheard a European couple talking with one of the guides. The man was commenting (in hushed, apologetic tones) that so many Americans do not know their own history. Senator piped up. "You don't have to whisper around us. We know this, and it's terrible!" Sadly, on two continents we have come to learn how embarrassingly limited our fellow countrymen's knowledge of their own heritage is.

Before leaving the visitor center, we took a walk through a unique gallery housed in their building. Though the Fuller Gun Collection was not directly related to the battle, many of the over 2,000 firearms displayed were manufactured during the Civil War. Case after case displayed more guns than I have ever seen. The vast majority were rifles that spanned a period up through World War I. There were also some pistols interspersed among them. (When I say 'pistol', I mean high caliber, extended length guns that would probably still take both of my hands to aim, let alone shoot.)

The collection belonged to one Claude Fuller, a Kansas engineer and inventor, mainly within the brick-making industry. His wife Zenada shared his passion, assisting her husband in the amassing, cataloging, and writing related to the collection. In the early 1950s, they partnered with the National Park System to permanently house their collection at Chickamauga. Appropriately, the dedication was on July 4th, and the casual and serious enthusiast alike have enjoyed viewing it ever since.

It had warmed up quite a bit by the time we left Chickamauga. We had not felt temperatures in the low 70s for at least five months. It was novel to ride with the windows down as we climbed the switchback roads to Tennessee's Lookout Mountain. We watched the continuously expanding view as we drove past expensive homes squeezed onto small plots of rock and dirt. I'm not sure any view would be worth the congestion of narrow roads, roaming tourists, unsure foundations, or the impossibility of navigating steep driveways in icy conditions.

Lookout Mountain was confusing, and I'm not entirely sure it wasn't on purpose. All Senator and I wanted to do was continue our study of the western theatre of the Civil War by visiting the site of the Chattanooga battle and maybe seek out its accompanying visitor center. We did not expect a crowded parking lot with families and junk shops perched among signs and lines for local attractions. Apparently we were sharing the mountain[*] top with people riding the incline train, those who truly wanted to **See ROCK CITY!**, and several others who were just enjoying one of the first warm Sunday afternoons of spring. No one was causing problems; it was just a different atmosphere than the quiet, solemn battlefields we were used to.

There was also confusion as to the actual visitor center. We got in line and paid an admission, (which was

---

* or hill; the debate still rages

fine,) to walk the trail to the edge of the precipice. There were signs for a small museum there, which we took to be the visitor center, as it was, in fact, on Lookout Mountain and in the same location that the related websites described. The museum, though a nice little display, was very hot, not directly related to the Civil War, and took all of three minutes to thoroughly explore. Yes, the 180° view over Moccasin Bend and the squiggly Tennessee River was sweeping, but most of the land below was buried under urban sprawl. It reminded me of Shenandoah, if Shenandoah were in the middle of a city.

We walked back up to the top of the trail and out of the fee area. Honestly, I felt like I had wasted my money, but amid the wandering people and excited children we found the real visitor center, which was free. It was small, and inside it was quiet. There was only one other visitor, and he was finishing up his conversation with the guides behind the desk. When he left, they greeted us. "So this is the actual visitor center? We almost missed you," I said. The man nodded and pointed out the related displays. Frankly, I think the other 'museum' figured out how to profit via miscommunication. Maybe it is run by a Chicago politician.

We read the displays and then moved into the rear room to see the giant painting of the 'battle above the clouds'. It was the size of the entire wall. Hundreds if not thousands of soldiers were represented on it. We looked for a long time as we listened to narration.

After Rosecrans' disastrous defeat at Chickamauga in September, his forces withdrew to Chattanooga. As the boys in gray surrounded the city, holding key geographical points, they laid siege to Chattanooga with the goal of starving the Union out. Then in late October, General Grant's men sneaked past Lookout Mountain with reinforcements, opening up the "cracker line" via a night battle. Bolstered by their new supplies, a few weeks later the Union struck out at Orchard Knob. The next day they attacked the fog-enshrouded Lookout Mountain, earning the battle its moniker.

The real goal, Missionary Ridge, was still staunchly held by Bragg's rebel forces. Determined, Grant decided that attacking rifle pits at the base of the mountain would be a good start. He did not count on the exceptional enthusiasm and bravery of the Army of the Cumberland, who took it into their own heads to charge all the way up the hill. When asked who ordered the charge, General Thomas explained that no one had; there was just no stopping his men. As a result, the Confederates were forced to relinquish Missionary Ridge, retreating all the way back to Georgia.

I had not come across any visitor information about Missionary Ridge, so I figured there was really nothing to see there. Senator was more determined. He had been very taken by the idea that men would order themselves into an assault, and he wanted to see the spot, so he inquired further. "Can we go up on Missionary Ridge?"

"Yes," the man behind the desk began. "There's not much there, but you should at least drive up the ridge and see the site of Bragg's reservation. There's a monument and a parking area there. There's other monuments along the way, but nowhere to park. It's a narrow road, with homes all along it." That was good enough for us. I consulted the map to find the easiest way to access the only road up to the ridge, and we were off.

"Can we make a pit stop first?" I asked Senator on the way to the car.

"Of course."

I was glad to be leaving Point Park. I could not quite figure it out. On one hand, it was good to see families outdoors and people having fun. On the other hand, I did not know what to make of the sign in the bathroom. It strictly warned users against bathing or washing clothes in the sinks. Just in case the message was too vague, it added a reminder that public nudity was forbidden. *Hhmmm...*

Having no contraband laundry and no desire for illicit displays of indecent exposure, we left and drove to Missionary Ridge. As the highway dipped back into Georgia, I suppose we were illegal in another sense, albeit for only a few minutes. Up we climbed on the mostly straight road, past more expensive homes that looked like they might take a plunge at some point in the not-too-distant future. "Some of those driveways are impossible!" exclaimed Senator. He was right. I stared out my window trying to understand why people with money would want to live along a cramped street. A few people stared back, mildly annoyed at the innocent tourist invasion. *Well, what do you expect? Bragg and Grant were here before you were!*

In the middle of one of the residential areas, we found the site of Bragg's line, where the Union broke through via uphill charge. There was a very large monument to soldiers from Illinois, along with a few cannon aimed over the city. A little old white-haired lady spoke to me as I walked around the monument, reading each side. "I sure think this is interesting," she said. I nodded in agreement. "I mean, I guess maybe other people don't..." she trailed off.

I assured her I was in solidarity. "Oh, I'm fascinated by it all! My boyfriend and I both enjoy studying the Civil War, and we've visited quite a few battlefields. They're all amazing. I'm a history teacher, but a lot of people don't recognize how important it is to study this."

The woman brightened up as I told the her the story of the unordered charge. She was my new pal. Then she called over a younger woman, perhaps her daughter, and we chatted for a moment. "Would you please take a picture of us by the monument?" I did my best with the unfamiliar cell phone camera, and they were satisfied.

"Well, it was nice to meet you," I said, turning to walk back to Senator, who was fumbling with his own camera to line up a shot. "I'm headed back to Illinois tomorrow."

"Have a good trip. We live right down in Chickamauga, but we didn't even know this was here," she explained. Sometimes treasures aren't too far away.

We continued up the road to Sherman's reservation, but there was not much there. Senator parked in the only spot, edged out along the side of the road. There was a steep trail up into the woods, so we hiked it for awhile. When it did not seem to really lead to anything, we gave up. "This is too hot anyway," said Senator. I agreed. We were still on the Yankee seasonal schedule.

We left Missionary Ridge, coming out of the northern end into Chattanooga. The sprawling national cemetery was on the way back to the hotel, so we planned to take a short drive through it. "There it is," I directed. Senator turned left into the entrance... only it was not the entrance. It was just a pull off to the side of the road, next to the cemetery's gate. There was no room to turn around completely, so he had to drive over the edge of the curb.

"I wonder if *he* saw us," I said, motioning toward the cop, who was at the traffic light half a block away.

"I hope not, but there was nothing I could do."

"I know. Here's the turn for the real entrance." Senator turned right and drove into the open gate. Naturally, the cop was parked right there. He was not waiting for us, but I was not necessarily hoping to see him again. There was also the matter of the large sign prohibiting any firearms within the cemetery's boundaries. That was a new one for us; I have never heard of graveyard gun restrictions. "We better not stay," I said, giving up on this particular site. Of course, leaving entailed driving right past our friend to do a u-turn out of the cemetery. Fortunately, he was still uninterested in us.

Back at the hotel we relaxed and I updated some notes. We had thoroughly enjoyed our two-part winter Civil War excursion. Being Wendy V, I could not help mulling over ideas for similar future trips. Senator mentioned revisiting Wilson's Creek, in Missouri. "Yes, then we could run down to Pea Ridge. At some point we'll need to get back to Virginia, too," I added, as though I had just remembered to add an item to our grocery list. I sometimes wish I did not have so many ideas.

"Ready to find some dinner?" asked Senator.

"Yep, let's go."

Senator came across a listing for a casual pizza place,

so we decided to give it a try. It ended up being eleven miles away, which was okay. Due to a complicated route, however, it seemed much farther. Jingles stepped up to the task, though, and we were there in plenty of time to order some greasy appetizers and pizza.

I squeezed both of our lemon wedges into my glass of water. As we waited for our food to arrive, we rehashed our latest historical adventures. Another weekend had gone by entirely too quickly. I asked Senator what his favorite battlefield was. Like me, he could not decide; they were all unique in their own ways. We could almost envision the gunboats near Fort Donelson. Shiloh had been extremely profound. Chickamauga had its magnitude. Missionary Ridge still held special magnetism for Senator.

The next day I would do most of the driving home, but I was glad Senator was the one driving back to the hotel that night. As we cruised down the highway against the backdrop of the twinkling lights in the Chattanooga hills, a pack of idiots on motorcycles sped by us at well over a hundred miles an hour. They rode double, weaving past lanes of traffic, oblivious to their or anyone else's safety. One fool did a wheelie right in front of us. It was maddening. I really hoped they would roll over into the median or a guardrail. No such luck.

It felt good to kick shoes off and put our feet up on the bed. Coffee and a little unwinding were in order before going to bed. Nothing-- and I mean nothing-- was on television. Among other amusements, we fixated on a Canadian axe-throwing competition for about twenty minutes. I believe it was the first (and likely the last) time we have ever watched E.S.P.N.. "Hey, look at us all watchin' sports n' such!" I joked.

When the primo axe-tosser was named, we clicked off the television. It took a moment for our eyes to adjust to the dark. I checked the alarm again by feeling for the raised button. Then I leaned over to kiss Senator good night. "Good-night. I love you," he whispered.

"I love you, too," I answered. "And I love watching axe-throwing competitions with you." He murmured a giggle and fell sound asleep.

*   *   *

The breakfast room was crowded again. This time there were no seats, and no law enforcement officers to watch our coffee. As we scanned the area for an open spot, Senator noticed the door to the patio. "Want to eat outside?"

"Yes!" It was cloudy and in the mid-50s-- perfect for a cool, peaceful meal before starting a long drive. As we ate our eggs and English muffins, we chatted about our plans for the near future. January had dragged on, but everything after that was flying by. Part of me was ready to discuss more trips to battlefields, but I knew we had other things to focus on. In the back of my mind, I penciled in another long weekend, perhaps in October.

"Well, we should hit the road," I said, a little reluctantly. Senator agreed, taking another sip of coffee. We threw out our garbage and walked out to the car. As per our strategy to minimize Senator's long-distance driving, I drove first, assuming I would take another shift at the end of the day. I ended up driving the entire way. Surprisingly, it was easy-- just a bit dull once we were in Illinois, but that was nothing new. Maybe it was just my own mental block. Maybe I was just ready for our next adventure.

Afterword

Traveling is always an adventure. Sometimes staying home is, too. Though our journeys during the period covered by this book spanned the eastern half of North America from Mississippi to Newfoundland, some of our most dramatic moments took place right in Illinois, starting with a hunk of metal crashing through our windshield. By all counts, Senator should not even be here. Yet, by the grace of God he is, and better than ever. Revelations about a rare and usually undiagnosed condition literally changed our life. Since then our excursions have been smoother and easier. We have been able to divide our travel time between deeper explorations into Civil War sites, tackling more challenging hikes, and ultimately embarking upon our greatest endeavor yet. While our "to visit" checklist is shrinking, we are beginning to focus our travel more, with the ultimate goal of researching the location of our next home. Who knows where I will be writing from next?

~Wendy V
May 2019

Appendix A: Sesquicelebration Food Awards

The following is the list of food award winners within six key categories. All nominees were submitted, approved, considered, and voted upon by the Jury of Unanimous Selectors of Taste, Uniqueness, and Satisfaction (J.U.S.T.U.S.).

Most Literal Interpretation of a Dish:
Fried Mushrooms
Earl's (Rocky Harbour, Newfoundland)

Most Misleading Name, in Regard to Taste:
Bakeapple Tart
Treasure Box (Rocky Harbour, Newfoundland)

Worst Nutritional Value:
Vending Machine Potato Chips
Marine Atlantic Ferry,
(Canadian waters between Nova Scotia and Newfoundland)

Worst Monetary Value:
Crappy, Overpriced Veggie Subs
Wabo's (Cheticamp, Nova Scotia)

Most Effective Screwing Up of a Simple Entrée:
Crappy, Overpriced Veggie Subs
Wabo's (Cheticamp, Nova Scotia)

Most Effective Improvisation Using Limited Resources:
Microwaved, Doctored-Up Frozen Pizza
Convenience Store & Hotel Room (Louisbourg, Nova Scotia)

Appendix B: Civil War Poem

Excerpt From "Bivouac of the Dead"
by Theodore O'Hara

The muffled drum's sad roll has beat
The soldier's last tattoo;
No more on life's parade shall meet
That brave and fallen few.
On Fame's eternal camping-ground
Their silent tents are spread
And Glory guards, with solemn round,
The bivouac of the dead.

www.ingramcontent.com/pod-product-compliance
Lightning Source LLC
Chambersburg PA
CBHW022100150426
43195CB00008B/208